PROMOTING RISK

SOCIAL PROBLEMS AND SOCIAL ISSUES

An Aldine de Gruyter Series of Texts and Monographs

SERIES EDITOR

Joel Best

Southern Illinois University at Carbondale

Joel Best (*editor*), **Images of Issues: Typifying Contemporary Social Problems**

Joel Best (*editor*), **Troubling Children: Studies of Children and Social Problems**

James A. Holstein, **Court-Ordered Insanity: Interpretive Practice and Involuntary Commitment**

James A. Holstein and Gale Miller (*editors*), **Reconsidering Social Constructionism: Debates in Social Problems Theory**

Gale Miller and James A. Holstein (*editors*), **Constructionist Controversies: Issues in Social Problems Theory**

Philip Jenkins, **Intimate Enemies: Moral Panics in Contemporary Great Britain**

Philip Jenkins, **Using Murder: The Social Construction of Serial Homicide**

Valerie Jenness, **Making It Work: The Prostitutes' Rights Movement in Perspective**

Stuart A. Kirk and Herb Kutchins, **The Selling of *DSM*: The Rhetoric of Science in Psychiatry**

Bruce Luske, **Mirrors of Madness: Patrolling the Psychic Border**

Leslie Margolin, **Goodness Personified: The Emergence of Gifted Children**

Erdwin H. Pfuhl and Stuart Henry, **The Deviance Process** (Third Edition)

William B. Sanders, **Gangbangs and Drivebys: Grounded Culture and Juvenile Gang Violence**

Wilbur J. Scott, **The Politics of Readjustment: Vietnam Veterans since the War**

Wilbur J. Scott and Sandra Carson Stanley (*editors*) **Gays and Lesbians in the Military: Issues, Concerns, and Contrasts**

Malcolm Spector and John I. Kitsuse, **Constructing Social Problems**

Robert A. Stallings, **Promoting Risk: Constructing the Earthquake Threat**

PROMOTING RISK

Constructing the Earthquake Threat

ROBERT A. STALLINGS

ALDINE DE GRUYTER
New York

About the Author

Robert A. Stallings is currently Associate Professor of Public Policy in the School of Public Administration with a joint appointment in the Department of Sociology, University of Southern California. He received his Ph.D. in sociology from The Ohio State University. Dr. Stallings's research deals with "ghost towns" emerging in the aftermath of the Northridge, California earthquake of January 1994, and with the political economy of natural hazards. He is the author of numerous journal articles on risk and hazards.

ALDINE DE GRUYTER
A division of Walter de Gruyter, Inc.
200 Saw Mill River Road
Hawthorne, New York 10532

This publication is printed on acid free paper ∞

Library of Congress Cataloging-in-Publication Data

Stallings, Robert A.
    Promoting risk : constructing the earthquake threat / Robert A. Stallings.
        p. cm. — (Social problems and social issues)
    Includes bibliographical references and index.
    ISBN 0-202-30544-9 (cloth). — ISBN 0-202-30545-7 (paper)
    1. Earthquake hazard analysis—Social aspects. I. Title.
II. Series.
QE539.2.S34S73 1995
363.3'495—dc20   94-35602
                                                                           CIP

Manufactured in the United States of America

10 9 8 7 6 5 4 3 2 1

For R.R.D. and E.L.Q.

Contents

Preface

What follows is something that, as far as I know, has not been tried before. I have attempted a sociological examination of a natural hazard. This may shock some of my colleagues because they know there has been nearly a half-century of sustained interest in disasters and catastrophes in sociology. What I mean is that I treat natural hazards as *social* phenomena and try to identify the *social* origins of them. Most sociologists treat disasters as acts of nature that have social *consequences* but have physical causes. The vast bulk of disaster research uses disaster and the threat of disaster as the setting or context in which individuals and groups respond to "extreme environments" and adjust to "system stress." I think this is sociologically incomplete. It ignores some of the most interesting aspects of the risk of hazards and disasters.

I have attempted to back up one step in the sequence of disaster and response. Rather than asking, What happens after a hazard becomes realized as a disaster? I ask, How does something become a hazard in the first place? What I offer is a prospectus rather than a definitive analysis. I have chosen a single natural hazard, the earthquake threat, to illustrate how one might proceed. A more comprehensive examination remains for some future date.

More than one type of risk is involved here. Beyond the risk of earthquakes as its subject matter, there is a risk that the entire examination may be misunderstood. The risk is that readers may believe at the outset that there is no research problem here. On the one hand, a reader might react to what follows by saying that the facts about the earthquake threat speak for themselves. No sociological analysis is required. Coping with risk is merely doing what is obvious. On the other hand, another reader might conclude that "of course" the earthquake threat is socially constructed like everything else in human experience. No sociological analysis is needed because the process of rendering nature into something socially meaningful is automatic and constant rather than problematic and variable. Hopefully, I can show both types of readers that "facts" about the risk of earthquakes are a function of social structure and historical circumstance.

I hope that Russell and Henry, to whom this work is dedicated, find something worthwhile here.

Robert A. Stallings
Covina, California
May 1994

Acknowledgments

Those of us who work in the research area of risk and hazards frequently remind one another that this is, in the end, a very small field, one in which "everyone knows everyone." What we seldom acknowledge—publicly, at least—is how intelligent and nice the people in this area are. Several of them once again have had a hand in trying to improve the quality of my work. Before I acknowledge them individually, I want to absolve them collectively and publicly of any responsibility for what follows.

Elliott Mittler used up a big chunk of his rare free time to read the entire manuscript and saved me from several errors of both fact and interpretation. His knowledge of the early (pre-1950) history of public policymaking in the natural hazards area and his grasp of both the policy issues and the politics associated with earthquake insurance were especially valuable. Peter May as usual contributed nearly as many words—and definitely more insights—than were contained in the two chapters I asked him to look over. His knowledge of the literature and his ability to connect what I was trying to do to it once again improved my thinking in more ways than show up in this book. Armand Mauss provided several pages of inciteful suggestions despite disappointment with the theoretical paths I have chose. Dennis Mileti offered encouragement and helpful comments on two chapters despite his busy schedule. And Bill Petak was helpful and supportive as always.

Joel Best, sociology editor of this series, was extremely important in identifying the strengths and weaknesses of my application of constructionist theory. As a relative newcomer to the study of social problems, I benefited greatly—and continue to benefit—from his insights on theoretical issues and his recommendations about other works that were relevant to my own. Richard Koffler was more than just a patient and supportive editor. He, too, saw how my work fit into the fields of risk and natural hazards, and his suggestions about related work that I needed to consider were quite helpful.

1

The Problem with the Earthquake "Problem"

> [T]he recognition by a society of its social problems is a highly selective
> process, with many harmful social conditions and arrangements not even
> making a bid for attention and with others falling by the wayside in what
> is frequently a fierce competitive struggle.
> —Herbert Blumer, "Social Problems as Collective Behavior"

There is an old joke about the ultimate California earthquake. Several versions exist, but most go something like this:

Speaker: "I just bought oceanfront property in Nevada."
Friend: "What are you talking about? Nevada isn't on the ocean."
Speaker: "After the Big One, it will be!"

The Big One is most people's idea of a catastrophic earthquake. Like the joke about oceanfront property, the popular image of the Big One is one of widespread destruction. Some people actually believe that parts of California will disappear into the Pacific Ocean. Indeed, earthquakes and California are synonymous. They are part of the image of California along with Hollywood stars, violent crime, theme parks, freeways, and people who dress funny.

Experts who study earthquakes and earthquake safety advocates have a different image of catastrophic earthquakes, however. Rather than what nature may do in the future, they worry about what people are doing in the present. Instead of total destruction, they see scattered pockets of vulnerability associated with structures built on certain types of soil or with design standards that did not take into account the risk of earthquakes. More than just physical destruction, they worry about economic repercussions for the nation as a whole. And rather than seeing earthquakes as simply a threat in California or on the West Coast, they see the risk of earthquakes existing in a majority of states in the United States.

The greatest difference between most people's view of the earthquake threat and the view of experts and safety advocates is how little concern

1

there is in the public at large for doing something about it. The risk of future earthquakes is a low-priority issue for nearly everyone, even in California. Other issues provoke more passionate debate and louder calls for action. In fact, the existence of jokes about the Big One suggests how different the earthquake threat is from other public issues and social problems. Jokes about serial killers, child molesters, wife beaters, the homeless, AIDS sufferers, victims of gang violence, and the unemployed are more likely to be thought of as in bad taste.

The aim of this book is to explain why an event that experts believe is certain to kill thousands of people, ruin countless businesses, and have a serious impact on the nation's economy is not more of a social problem. To understand why there is such a difference between experts' views about the risk of earthquakes and nearly everyone else's will require a point of view that is different from that in previous studies of risk and natural hazards. I will concentrate on the people who create "information" about the earthquake threat rather than on people (like me) who receive such information. Most writers approach questions about hazard information by focusing on the recipients, as if the only important questions were about accurate perception (e.g., Kahneman, Slovic, and Tversky 1982) or producing the "proper" responses to warnings (Perry, Lindell, and Greene 1980; Mileti 1976). I will assume that the risk of earthquakes is not self-evident. In other words, I will take the point of view that whether the risk is primarily a threat to life or a potential economic disaster, whether it is widespread or confined to one area, whether it is more important or less important than other public issues, and so forth, depends on what risk promoters are able to accomplish rather than on self-evident "facts" about the earth.

I will say more about these points shortly. First I will describe some of the ways that people identify what they consider to be our current social problems. Then I will describe what experts expect to happen when the catastrophic earthquake—the Big One—strikes. The difference between people's concern—or lack of concern—and what experts believe to be our future raises the question of whether the earthquake threat is unique and altogether different from other public issues and problems of the day.

EARTHQUAKE RISKS ARE "NO BIG DEAL"

For their victims, earthquakes are serious trouble indeed. They damage homes and ruin businesses. They injure and kill, often in grotesque ways as we saw in 1989 on the collapsed freeway in Oakland, California, and again in 1994 at the Northridge Meadows Apartment complex in

Los Angeles. For most people, however, earthquakes are merely another story in the news. They lose interest long before the injured recover and the damaged buildings are repaired.

Despite the potential for death, destruction, and deprivation, the threat of future earthquakes seems to be "no big deal." At least that is the impression one gets from looking at the ways we keep track of our most pressing concerns. Public opinion polls, for instance, regularly indicate relatively little concern for the earthquake threat. Pollsters frequently ask this question: What do you think is the most important problem facing this country today? (e.g., Gallop 1992:244). Problems mentioned by a large percentage of respondents are then listed in order of frequency. Issues such as the state of the economy, poverty and homelessness, drugs and drug abuse, the federal budget deficit, "ethics and morals," unemployment, and education regularly made the list of current problems in 1991. The threat of earthquakes did not.

Pollsters themselves show no more interest in the topic than the people they survey. During the ten-year period from 1981 through 1990, a total of fifty-seven questions about earthquakes were included in fourteen separate polls. Several of these polls were conducted only in California. Earthquake questions seemed to appear in nationwide surveys only after major disasters. For example, five polls with questions about the earthquake threat were conducted in 1989 after the Loma Prieta earthquake in the San Francisco Bay area; two in 1987 after the Whittier Narrows earthquake in the eastern part of Los Angeles; and two in 1985 after the Mexico City earthquake (*American Public Opinion Index*, various editions, 1981–1990). This contrasts sharply with polling on economic problems. Ninety-eight questions about the economy were used in forty-six separate public opinion polls in 1990 alone. Eighty questions about drugs and drug abuse were included in thirty-six polls that year (*American Public Opinion Index 1990* 1991).

Politicians running for national office do not campaign on the issue of what they would do about the risk of earthquakes. This is another indication that the earthquake threat is not a serious public concern. None of the candidates for president in 1992, for instance, promised to make doing something about earthquakes a priority of his administration. Neither then-president Bush nor then-governor Clinton mentioned this issue in acceptance speeches at his party's nominating convention. Platforms of both the Republican and the Democratic party were silent on the issue as well. H. Ross Perot said nothing about earthquakes during his on-again, off-again campaign. What to do about the economy, "family values," and candidates' fitness for office were presidential campaign issues, not earthquakes.

The opportunity to run on a pledge to increase earthquake safety was certainly present in 1992. For one thing, California's large block of elec-toral votes was up for grabs due to general dissatisfaction with President Bush's domestic and economic policies. For another, the presidential campaign took place less than thirty-six months after the widely tele-vised Loma Prieta earthquake in the San Francisco Bay area. Also, two strong quakes jolted desert and mountain communities east of Los An-geles during the early stages of the campaign. They reminded everyone that the Big One was still a possibility—and scared away millions of dollars in tourism. President Bush's "special handling" of Hurricane Andrew in south Florida contrasts with the absence of attention to Cali-fornia and its potential for future earthquakes during the campaign.

The risk of earthquakes is not the sort of issue to build presidential campaigns around, and neither apparently is it the kind of "cause" that excites those who would change "the system." Getting government to do something about the earthquake threat does not prompt pickets to march in front of the White House nor protesters to hold rallies on the Capitol steps. Letter-writing campaigns, petition drives, candlelight vig-ils, sit-ins, and lobbying by high-priced lawyers are not tactics associated with the promotion of earthquake safety. Neither environmentalists, consumer groups, nor civil rights organizations have adopted earth-quake risk reduction as part of their programs (see the heading "Current Issues" in Foundation for Public Affairs 1992). A case could be made that groups in each of these categories logically might have done so.[1]

Television news both mirrors and reinforces the impression that most people do not consider earthquake safety to be a grave concern. Earth-quakes themselves are often major news stories, of course, but the threat of future earthquakes becomes news only when hooked on other news "pegs." For example, what households can do to prepare for future earthquakes may become a follow-up story in the aftermath of a small earthquake. A prediction that an earthquake will take place at a specific time and place can trigger considerable coverage of the likely conse-quences of a future earthquake. Earthquake drills and simulations some-times give local reporters an opportunity to remind viewers that they live in "earthquake country." In contrast, public policy issues related to the risk of earthquakes rarely receive coverage in television news.

Most sociologists apparently concur with the judgments of pollsters, survey respondents, campaign managers, social change advocates, and television news directors. Textbooks written for social problems courses have no standard chapter on the topic "Earthquakes as Social Problems" or even "Natural Disasters as Social Problems." One widely used text-book several years ago was an exception, and the history of its several editions is instructive. The first edition of Merton and Nisbet's *Contempo-rary Social Problems* (1961) contained a chapter on "Disaster" (Fritz 1961).

This chapter remains one of the works most frequently cited by scholars who write and do research on earthquakes and other disasters. However, the editors dropped it from later editions of their book (Merton and Nisbet 1966, 1971, 1976). Their publisher's market surveys revealed that instructors of social problems courses were not requiring students to read this chapter (Charles E. Fritz, personal communication, 1976).

In short, a variety of indicators that usually give a sense of what the public at large considers to be the most pressing problems of the day all show that the earthquake threat is not of great public concern. Another way of saying the same thing is to say that, by these indicators at least, it is not a social problem. Before considering whether these are the only ways that social problems can be identified and why the earthquake threat does not generate the same level of concern as other conditions that are treated as social problems, I will review some of the things that earthquake safety advocates say about this threat.

THE EARTHQUAKE THREAT RECONSIDERED

The risk of earthquakes certainly seems to have what it takes to be a social problem. Some public officials worry that even rumors of an imminent earthquake will cause panic. Mental health professionals remind parents to avoid frightening children by what they say about earthquakes and by their own reactions to small earthquakes. Many residents of the East and Midwest will not vacation in California for fear that the Big One will strike while they are there.

Earthquake safety advocates cite a potential for loss of life and personal injury that is equal to if not greater than other conditions about which there is more public concern. News accounts of earthquake disasters outside the United States graphically illustrate this potential. Due to different building practices in other countries, death tolls in foreign earthquakes can be staggering. An earthquake in Mexico City in 1985, for example, killed more than 5,000 people and injured another 30,000. In 1976, an estimated 650,000 people died and another 780,000 were injured in Tangshan, China. That same year 22,000 people died in an earthquake in Guatemala, and nearly 1,000 more died in another in Italy. In 1988 at least 25,000 people were killed in an earthquake in then Soviet Armenia, and 40,000 or more were killed in 1990 in northern Iran.

Earthquakes kill fewer people in the United States, but casualties can be numerous here as well. So far, 57 people are dead, 16 in the collapse of one apartment building, as a result of the 1994 Northridge earthquake in the San Fernando Valley region of Los Angeles. Sixty-three people died and another 1,400 were injured in the 1989 Loma Prieta earthquake. One hundred thirty-one people died in the Alaska earthquake in 1964. The 1971 San Fernando earthquake killed 64 people, and the San Francisco earthquake and fire claimed 700 lives in 1906.

Experts estimate that casualty figures in a future earthquake in the United States will be much higher. They expect that as many as 23,000 people could be killed in a single worst-case earthquake in Los Angeles [a Richter magnitude 7.5 earthquake at 4:30 P.M. on a weekday afternoon on a fault running under the city along the Pacific coast (Federal Emergency Management Agency, FEMA 1980:4)]. This number matches the 23,438 homicides reported for the entire country in 1990 (U.S. Department of Justice 1991:8). It is greater than the number of children abducted and killed by strangers in any given year, greater than the average annual death toll from aviation disasters, and dozens of times greater than the number of fatalities in the world's single worst commercial aviation disaster.[2] If the number of people who are likely to be killed were the only thing that mattered, then the threat of future earthquakes should be a social problem.

How about economic loss? Figures produced by earthquake safety advocates match many of those offered by other social problems in their potential for financial devastation. The estimated cost of the Los Angeles riots of 1992 is $775 million in insurable damage alone (Mulligan 1993). The Department of Justice lists direct expenditures for all criminal justice activities in 1988 at $61 billion (U.S. Department of Justice 1991:14). By comparison, the estimated cost of the worst-case Los Angeles earthquake is $70 billion in 1980 dollars (FEMA 1980:4).[3] Such an earthquake is expected to bankrupt many businesses, disrupt the stock market (as insurance companies sell stocks to raise capital), and reduce revenue to cities and towns through a decline in municipal bond markets (same reason). The federal budget would also presumably take a big hit as a result of the cost of providing disaster relief. A member of the House of Representatives from California recently estimated that such a quake would reduce the nation's gross domestic product (GDP) by 5 percent (Rep. George Brown, cited in Palm, Hodgson, Blanchard, and Lyons 1990:7–8).

Maybe earthquakes are a social problem after all. Perhaps I have examined the wrong indicators. A second look at the "politics" of earthquakes, for example, seems to suggest that it is not correct to say that politicians ignore them entirely. We regularly see politicians and political appointees involved in the aftermath of earthquake disasters. Top officials from all levels of government inspect damage, commiserate with victims, and promise to speed up disaster aid. For example, following the Northridge earthquake in 1994, President Clinton and several members of his administration including Vice President Al Gore, Transportation Secretary Frederico Peña, and Housing Secretary Henry Cisneros visited Los Angeles and met with various victims. After a previous California earthquake, *Newsweek* magazine estimated that former San Francisco mayor Art Agnos had "made a name for himself as a formidable leader with state and perhaps national potential" through "his compassion and high-profile performance" (Salholz 1989:37). So it is not true that politicians completely turn their backs on earthquakes. Unfortunately for Mr. Agnos, the *Newsweek* prognostication proved premature. He lost his bid to remain mayor when he was defeated in a run-off election in 1991 by the city's former police chief. The campaign had more to do with potholes and panhandlers than with earthquakes (see also May 1985:119–22; Abney and Hill 1966).

There can also be grass-roots protest in the aftermath of an earthquake. Citizens often do angrily confront public officials, write letters to their congressional representatives, and lobby for change. After the ground has stopped shaking and the emergency itself is over, groups often organize to do something about the condition that they find themselves in (Stallings and Quarantelli 1985; Wolensky 1983). In fact, conflict during the period of rehabilitation is frequent enough that one writer once nicknamed this the "brick bat" phase of disasters (Moore 1958:315). Why is such activity not proof that earthquakes do constitute a social problem?

The question leads us to the central concerns of this book: What exactly is required to call something a social problem? What is it about the threat of earthquakes that makes it different? Earthquakes clearly can have terrible consequences that are real trouble for many people. Nevertheless, the two examples that seem to contradict the impression that the risk of earthquakes is not treated as a social problem (postdisaster morale-building by politicians and the pressing of grievances by disaster victims) actually illustrate how the earthquake threat differs from other conditions that are treated as social problems. Both examples involve action oriented exclusively toward the past rather than the future, for one thing. For another, action deals entirely with a single event—the recent disaster—and is not linked to other similar events.

Social problems involve words and actions intended to make the future better for everyone exposed to some allegedly harmful circumstance (discrimination, financial hardship, disease, etc.). In talking about problems, people express their hopes and fears for the future. They link events in the present or the past (e.g., the latest government report on unemployment) to expectations that the future should be different (e.g., the federal government should do something to stimulate the economy). After a disaster, on the other hand, talk is about restoring what has been destroyed. The aim is to recreate the past—that is, to make things the way they were before disaster struck. Rebuilding, recovery, and "getting back to normal" are the central themes, not making changes intended to provide for a safer future.[4]

Social-problems activity and responses to earthquake disasters differ in another way. Social-problems activists call attention to circumstances that affect people at many locations, but postearthquake complaints are localized and event specific. Grievances typically center on unfair treatment by some federal agency or by a department of local government. Disaster victims' "cause" is a personal one arising out of local circumstances. Their private troubles do not produce a lasting organization dedicated to change in the name of earthquake safety (Mills 1961:8). Their protest does not spread to victims of previous disasters or to potential victims of future earthquakes. The contrast between localized concerns of disaster victims and the growth of Mothers Against Drunk Driving (MADD) illustrates the difference between personal troubles and the widespread activity characteristic of social problems (e.g., Reinarman 1988).

IS THE EARTHQUAKE THREAT UNIQUE?

One reason the risk of earthquakes may differ from other public concerns is that the earthquake threat is somehow unique. It may be that earthquakes threaten only one part of the country (e.g., California) and only a fraction of the nation's total population. "Putative" conditions (Spector and Kitsuse [1977] 1987:75–76) associated with a social problem, in contrast, are found anywhere. In other words, only conditions that are widespread "enough" generate the level of concern necessary to be a social problem.

This argument does not hold up, however. First, it is a mistake to think that conditions by themselves create social problems. Nor are problems and conditions one and the same (Spector and Kitsuse [1977] 1987:46; Ibarra and Kitsuse 1993:25–32). Problems are what people say and do about conditions. Second, what people say about earthquakes— at least, what scientists who study the earth say—is that earthquakes are a threat not limited to California. Physical conditions that can cause earthquakes are present in all fifty states. Residents of the Pacific Northwest have been told for a long time that they too are at risk, as have those in the Salt Lake City area. South Carolina's history includes a major earthquake in 1886 that killed 60 people, damaged 90 percent of the structures in Charleston, and shook such faraway cities as Boston,

Chicago, and St. Louis. The Midwest has its own history of record-shattering earthquakes including three in the winter of 1811–1812 centered in Missouri that destroyed an entire town, changed the course of the Mississippi River, and toppled chimneys in Cincinnati and Richmond. Bostonians who did not know that they too live in "earthquake country" must have been surprised by a front-page article in the *Wall Street Journal* whose headline asked if the Big One there would tumble that city into the harbor (Pereira 1989).

The earthquake threat may be unique in another respect. It may be that earthquakes are acts of nature beyond human control. They are not like unemployment to which people contribute by their decisions (e.g., to lay off employees). They are not like violent crimes caused by people who "decide" to use force. They are also not like the risk of disease, which people can control by taking medication or changing their behavior. The putative conditions associated with social problems involve some degree of human choice. Earthquakes seem to be different. People do not cause the forces of nature that threaten them. We cannot pass laws that will "deter" earthquakes.

This argument does not hold up either. Scientists may work in a world where earthquakes are viewed as nothing more than the release of energy, but for others earthquakes are the shaking of a house, the sound of breaking glass, cracked fireplaces, toppled utility poles, and collapsed bridges. It may be impossible to legislate the laws of nature, but it is possible to pass laws against locating buildings on top of "active" earthquake faults or for requiring specific construction designs and materials. People may think of earthquakes as acts of nature in some respects, but they are also capable of linking the consequences of earthquakes to prior human decisions and actions. There is no reason why these decisions and actions cannot become targets for groups mobilized to "do something" just as conditions produced by decisions and actions that underlie "real" social problems have become.

EXPLAINING SOCIAL PROBLEMS AND NONPROBLEMS

The uniqueness of the earthquake threat, it seems to me, does not lie in the conditions that produce earthquakes. No matter how long we study the earth and its physical properties, we will never be able to explain why the earthquake threat is different from others that I would classify as social problems. Earth movements do not tell us whether the risk of earthquakes should have high or low priority, whether the hazard is more of a threat to our well-being than the risk of AIDS, whether relying on market forces or on government intervention is the better way to handle old buildings that collapse more frequently than newer ones when the ground shakes, or even whether there is so little we can do to make ourselves safe that doing nothing is a good idea. How people treat the earthquake threat is not the inevitable result of the objective reality of the earth and its dynamics.

My conclusion that the question cannot be answered by studying the earth is at odds with conventional wisdom about both earthquakes and social problems. Oversimplified, conventional wisdom holds that social problems arise when people recognize intrinsically undesirable conditions. This undesirable quality is part of the conditions themselves. Problems are "out there" in the world around us even if we are not aware of them. Sooner or later, problems get "discovered," and experts propose solutions for them. [Some writers argue that the reverse also frequently occurs, that people with "solutions" find problems that fit them (Ross and Staines 1972; Cohen, March, and Olsen 1972; Kingdon 1984)]. According to conventional wisdom, people who are unaware of a problem after it has been discovered are ignorant or at least uninformed. Those who dispute the seriousness of a problem are irrational. Obviously, many academics—including many sociologists—accept the conventional wisdom when it comes to identifying social problems.

Conventional wisdom explains the risk of earthquakes in much the same way. Scientists have identified faults in the earth along which earthquakes occur. Safety experts have discovered ways to "solve" the problem or least reduce the harmful consequences of sudden earth movements. Such consequences are inherently undesirable. Nobody could be in favor of death, destruction, and deprivation. If people do not recognize the seriousness of the hazard, it is because they are ignorant or uninformed, or because they are acting irrationally by "choosing" to downplay the threat.

Conventional wisdom, in other words, posits a rational view of the world in which the existence of the earthquake problem as objective reality—as fact—is taken for granted. Rational solutions to the problem are undermined by various "villains" and "fools" [as these terms are used by Klapp (1954)] who, intentionally or unintentionally, let self-interest get in the way of "doing the right thing." An apathetic public at large, for example, is unwilling to bear the costs of earthquake hazard reduction. Developers and business property owners are more concerned with profits than safety. Local politicians are too dependent upon business interests to take the necessary steps to minimize risk. National politicians are more concerned with other issues that have larger constituencies—and greater numbers of votes.

One hint that there are serious flaws in conventional wisdom as an explanation for the risk of earthquakes is that it turns out to be a thinly disguised form of name-calling. It contains "good guys" and "bad guys," right and wrong, enlightened thinking and ignorance. The trouble is that in the everyday world it is hard to tell the good guys from the bad guys. Historically, what looks like enlightened thinking at one time looks like ignorance and superstition at another. In our time, home owners have many concerns besides the possibility of earthquakes. Given costly premiums and large deductibles that exceed the average amount of damage, a home owner's decision not to purchase earthquake insurance is not necessarily "irrational." "Greedy" developers who ignore public safety for the sake of profits may wear the villain's hat for some, but for others they are heroes who create jobs, generate tax revenues, and provide places for people to live. Politicians who seem more concerned with things other than earthquakes may be representing their constituents very effectively on matters of more immediate interest to them.

The reason it is hard to tell the good guys from the bad guys, the ignorant from the well-informed, is that conventional wisdom about the risk of earthquakes contains a fundamental flaw. By taking for granted that risk is part of nature, it assumes that there is only one way to view risk, that there is one accurate view that correctly describes "the way things really are," that all other views are incorrect descriptions of the "true" risk that is "out there." In other words, since the risk of earthquakes is objectively real, it is a "thing" that can be perceived only correctly or incorrectly.

The problem with risk as objective reality and the one-correct-view assumption is that it is hard to explain how the "correct" view can change without nature itself changing.[5] The early tribes of central Europe undoubtedly thought that their view of the causes of earthquakes was the one correct view (Fried 1973:24). They believed that earthquakes occurred when a water buffalo carrying the earth on its back paused to shift its enormous load from one foot to another. The Algonquins of North America also must have believed that theirs was the correct view. They thought that a gigantic tortoise rather than a water buffalo supported the weight of the world (ibid.). The ancient Greeks were certain enough in their belief that Poseidon, god of the sea, produced earthquakes whenever he was seriously displeased that they erected sanctuaries in his honor all around the Mediterranean Sea in an attempt to prevent disaster (ibid.). In ancient Japan people had little reason to doubt that earthquakes occurred when giant catfish thrashed about inside the earth (Bolt 1978:2–3). Today we are equally certain that our scientific description of the objective reality of earthquakes is the only accurate one. As Iacopi put it: "Early Indians *thought* that a tortoise supported the earth; when the beast took a step, the earth trembled.

Today we *know* that earthquakes are only part of a great geologic process" (1964:10, emphasis added). In other words, they were ignorant;
ours is the one correct view.

What if scientists themselves disagree on the correct description of the
objective reality of the earth? What if proponents of each competing
description think that theirs is the only correct one? If reality is only one
thing, you and I might not have an accurate picture of it, but how can the
experts—those who really know about these things—disagree? In fact,
scientists have disagreed about the structure of the earth and the causes
of earthquakes. Proposed by a German scientist early in this century, the
idea of continental drift was ridiculed by most earth scientists before the
Second World War. Even as late as 1960, this theory of the structure and
dynamics of the earth had few proponents. By 1970, however, the theory of plate tectonics that is a direct descendent of continental drift theory
was the dominant paradigm in the earth sciences (Stewart 1990). The
emergence of this currently correct view of earthquakes is not simply the
triumph of truth over ignorance.

Earthquake faults, stresses and strains in rocks, p-waves and s-waves,
plate tectonics, and continental drift do not tell us how important the
risk of earthquakes is. They do not tell us how much money to spend on
this threat compared to other issues such as health care, crime, infrastructure development, pollution control, job stimulation, or education.
It is the ability of advocates to convince others that determines whether
an issue such as earthquake safety is more important than some other
issue. Not science but the *use* of science is key to understanding why one
issue has higher priority than another.

In short, it is some people's ability to promote risk that determines
why one threat is treated as a social problem and another is not. In order
to explain what is seen as threatening and how the threat is responded
to, we need to examine what people say and do. It is not nature itself we
need to study but people's views of nature. In other words, we need to
ask questions about the social universe, not the physical universe. We
need to adopt a point of view that does not require us to figure out who
the good guys are or to correctly distinguish between the informed and
the uninformed. We can accomplish this by assuming that, whatever the
"true" nature of objective reality, people's ideas about that reality is the
only reality that counts. The reality of the risk of earthquakes is what
people think, say, and do about that risk.

There are significant advantages to treating risk as people's views of
earthquakes rather than as somehow a part of the earth itself. For one
thing, it solves a fundamental problem noted earlier, namely, how the
nature of the earth and its dynamics could presumably remain unchanged for thousands of years while the way we think about earth-

quakes changed so much and so often. It is not only a question of causes, whether by tortoises, catfish, angry gods, or moving tectonic plates. It is also a question of changing priorities, of the consequences of earthquake disasters, of who is at risk and what that risk consists of, and of what should be done. People, not nature, account for variations in the answers to questions like these. Whether the risk is localized (as in, "That's California's problem") or nationwide, whether the "real" problem is physical destruction in one area or its economic consequences everywhere, whether earthquakes are the responsibility of local or national government, whether they should be dealt with by being prepared to act quickly after they strike or by changing where and how we build beforehand—all depend upon some people convincing other people.

Putting people at the center of the process of promoting risk allows us to see that "doing something about the risk of earthquakes" means advancing claims in public "arenas" or settings such as government hearings, news reports, and meetings of civic groups. Whatever is or is not done about the earthquake threat must be due to the success or failure of the people making these claims. Who the claims-makers are, what kind of message they carry, how persuasively they argue their case, and what resources they have to carry on their fight all should make a difference in how successful or unsuccessful they are in promoting risk. If the earthquake threat is not a social problem, then the reason it is not must have something to do with the people who are promoting it, they way they go about it, and so forth.

The tools needed for explaining the current status of the earthquake threat are those that will help assess the strengths and weaknesses of earthquake risk claims-makers, how they match up with their opponents, the advantages and disadvantages presented by the "playing fields" on which they compete, etc. Two bodies of literature provide most of the tools required.

Resource mobilization theory is one way of explaining people's efforts to promote change (Zald and McCarthy 1977; McCarthy and Zald 1973). It focuses on the resources that groups generate in order to bring about change and how they use those resources. The support base of change promoters, the networks of communication facilitating their efforts, and the credentials of their leaders are examples of resources (McAdam, McCarthy, and Zald 1988). Writers in this tradition deem such practical matters more important for the ultimate success of organized change efforts than either the "just-ness" of a group's cause or the reasons for its discontent. Resource mobilization theory provides tools for examining the organizational base of risk promoters.

A *constructionist theory of social problems* explains problems and policy issues by focusing on people's actions rather than on the putative conditions that are the object of those actions. The adjective *putative* always modifies the noun *conditions* as a reminder that these conditions are alleged to exist and to have harmful qualities by issue advocates and claims-makers, but explaining why conditions exist and explaining why social problems exist are two different things:

> Thus, we define social problems as *the activities of individuals or groups making assertions of grievances and claims with respect to some putative conditions*. The emergence of a social problem is contingent upon the organization of activities asserting the need for eradicating, ameliorating, or otherwise changing some condition. *The central problem for a theory of social problems is to account for the emergence, nature, and maintenance of claims-making and responding activities*. Such a theory should address the activities of any group making claims on others for ameliorative action, material remuneration, or alleviation of social, political, legal, or economic disadvantage. (Spector and Kitsuse [1977] 1987:75–76, emphasis in the original)

More recently, the term *condition-category* has been introduced to emphasize the commitment to understanding the genesis of claims about physical conditions rather than the causes of the conditions themselves (Ibarra and Kitsuse 1993:30–31).

I want to examine who makes claims about the risk of earthquakes and what kinds of claims they make. Using a theory of social problems to do this does not mean that I have decided in advance that the earthquake threat is a social problem, however. Whether it is or not will ultimately be determined by examining how well advocates have been able to "sell" the earthquake threat.

I will call the people promoting the earthquake threat "claims-makers." These are not people who want more and bigger earthquakes. On the contrary, they want to see more done to reduce what they identify as the potentially catastrophic consequences of future earthquakes. Like participants in other forms of social movements, they participate in a network of relationships in an attempt to increase public awareness of the threat, change the behavior of businesses and individuals, and influence the public-policy process. I will call this network the "earthquake establishment." Its characteristics and how well it serves in promoting the earthquake threat are prime topics in my inquiry.

SO WHAT?: THE SIGNIFICANCE OF THIS EXAMINATION

What is gained by trying to answer these questions about the risk of earthquakes? Consider first what these questions are really all about. When I ask why the earthquake threat differs from other conditions that are treated as social problems, I am asking how a society decides that there is more harm in one thing than in another. When I ask how something becomes a problem, I am curious about the circumstances under which anything could attain a certain level of attention, concern, and action. If I am able to answer such questions, it will be because I have begun to understand the barriers and the opportunities that determine the fate of public issues.

There should be both practical and theoretical benefits from what I am about to do. On the practical side, a better understanding of the career of the earthquake threat should identify things its promoters might try if they would like to change the priority this threat has on the public-policy agenda. Comparing the promotion of the earthquake threat with claims-making on behalf of other putative conditions will expose the things that would have to change (or would have to be different) if this issue were to generate a different response. Discovering how and why the earthquake threat is treated differently from social problems also should provide a better understanding of social problems in general. By explaining the failure of the earthquake threat to achieve a level of concern equal to that of social problems, I will be explaining at the same time why claims-making efforts on behalf of other putative conditions have been more successful.

Improved understanding of social problems and public issues has more than just practical benefits. There are theoretical benefits as well. One is that the constructionist theory of social problems will be put to the test in explaining why something is *not* a problem. Following the logic of the *method of difference* described by John Stuart Mill ([1843] 1919:253–66), support for this theory will increase if it can be shown that the things that characterize a social problem are also the things that are absent in the case of a nonproblem. Most constructionist studies of social problems deal with issues that are controversial. Claims-making is a useful concept for studying issues in which opposing groups of claims-makers promote quite different views of reality, including whether or not a problem even exists. More challenging is using constructionist theory to examine an issue in which all the "facts" seem both obvious and independent of one's point of view. For example, there is little disagreement that earthquakes are bad things. Apart from very cynical entrepreneurs who see profits in chaos, no one publicly favors more and bigger earthquakes. Constructionist theory will benefit if it proves capable of explaining something as seemingly straightforward and "obvious" as the peril of catastrophic earthquakes.

Before we begin, a word about terminology. I use the term *putative condition* to refer to risk, risk objects, and the threat of future earthquakes. While some readers might not think of these as exactly synonymous, I prefer what I regard as the more general term because it ties the present examination to social problems theory.[6] For the same reason I prefer the general term "claims-makers" to such alternatives as risk promoters or earthquake safety advocates.

AN OVERVIEW OF THE BOOK

The next chapter examines the content of claims made in promoting the risk of earthquakes. After discussing the importance of images of risk and their consequences, the chapter examines claims advanced to describe the nature of the earthquake threat, the solutions proposed for dealing with it, and the justifications presented for acting. A final section identifies what is different about claims used to promote the risk of earthquakes by contrasting them with claims made in promoting other public issues. Because I initially assume that social problems are societal (that is, societywide) problems, my focus here is on claims-making at the national level.

The third chapter examines the claims-makers themselves, the people who promote the risk of earthquakes. Two different types of claims-makers are identified. One type is the technocrat. These are the experts who provide most of the technical descriptions of the earthquake threat and its potential consequences. Most technocrats are scientists, engineers, and policy analysts. The other type is the bureaucrat who carries out the day-to-day programs related to earthquake safety. Bureaucratic claims-makers generally fall into one of two categories: those who are involved in planning and preparations for future earthquake disasters and those involved in efforts to reduce the harmful effects of earthquakes before they strike.

The fourth chapter examines the several public arenas or settings in which claims about the risk of earthquakes are formulated, presented, and distributed. Some of these are elements of the federal government. Because local and state concerns differ from federal ones, the content of claims in local and state arenas differs from that of claims at the federal level. Two other arenas are the general-audience media, including news reports as well as documentaries and news specials, and popular culture, in particular, feature films.

Chapter 5 examines changes in the typification of earthquakes over the years. Historically, fundamental shifts in typification are visible as the explanation for earthquakes changed from the mystical to the religious to the scientific. Within the present century, domain elaboration has occurred wherein new elements have been added to the description of the threat. Domain expansion—the discovery of new segments of the population especially vulnerable to the effects of earthquakes—has also occurred. Most recently, the threat has acquired new meaning as an economic threat and, to a lesser extent, as a psychological threat.

Chapter 6 looks at the social organization of claims-making. Here, the claims-making process is treated as a social movement. The structure of the "earthquake establishment" is described first. Then challenges facing claims-makers in promoting risk are examined. These include the acquisition and allocation of resources and the choice of strategy and tactics. Both opponents and supporters of the movement, visible as well as "invisible," are examined. Finally, how the movement handles a special kind of threat from the outside—predictions of future earthquakes made by people outside the earthquake establishment—is described.

Chapter 7 takes up the question of why the risk of earthquakes rose to such an unusual level (albeit a relatively modest one) on the national policy agenda in the early 1970s. Two explanations are considered and rejected: one, that nature provided a "wake-up call" in 1964 and repeated it in 1971, so that the seriousness of the threat became "obvious"; the other, that the state of the art in the earth sciences and engineering had finally reached a point where an attack on the threat was feasible. Neither provides as satisfactory an explanation as a third, which holds that the period 1964–1977 saw the convergence of several *social* changes increasing the probability that the earthquake threat as a national problem would be "discovered." The remainder of the chapter identifies some of the changes that occurred during the second third of the twentieth century and concludes with a section reviewing social science theories in search of those that are consistent with the career of the earthquake threat.

Chapter 8, the final chapter, revisits the questions of whether the earthquake threat is a social problem, how and why it differs from fully constructed social problems, and exactly what kind of problem it is. Alternative future developments in the career of the threat are discussed, including the benefits and costs associated with changes in claims-making that would likely be necessary to alter the way the threat is defined.

Two shorter sections wrap up this examination. One is a postscript addressing two issues. The first issue is an explanation for the handling of material on the Northridge, California, earthquake of 1994. The second issue is the normative question of whether or not the earthquake threat *should be* a social problem. The final section is an appendix describing how materials used in the examination were selected and the author's relationship with some of the documents, people, and events included in the book.

NOTES

1.   One exception to this empirical generalization was the emergent citizens group, CASCADE (Citizens and Scientists Concerned About Dangers in the

Environment), founded in the State of Washington in 1973. For a description of the six-year history of this short-lived group, see Drabek, Mushkatel, and Kilijanek (1983:127–28).

2.   I will deal later on with the issue of how I can accept certain "facts" such as data on homicides, kidnappings, and aviation fatalities, while denying the power of other "facts." Here I am only pointing out that, in terms of the "data" currently available from official sources and commonly used within the public at large in discussing such things, the life-loss potential in a major earthquake looks roughly comparable to other risks and threats.

3.   Estimated damages in the moderate (seismically speaking) Northridge earthquake in Los Angeles are set at $30 billion in 1994 dollars—and counting—at this writing.

4.   Government relief policies have historically been based on the ideal of "making people whole again." Implicit here is the belief that victims should not benefit from either their victimization or from public policy (see Stallings 1988).

5.   That the nature of nature has remained unchanged for several thousand years is an assumption that I make. The assumption seems consistent with observations in the earth sciences. I will address later the theoretical issue here, labeled "ontological gerrymandering" by Woolgar and Pawluch (1985).

6.   I find the term *putative condition* preferable to the more recently proposed *condition-category* (Ibarra and Kitsuse 1993) *because* it calls attention to the condition whose objective qualities are to be taken as given (that is, ignored) in the ensuing examination.

CHAPTER

2

Claims About the Earthquake Threat

Jokes like the one about Nevada having ocean-front property after a catastrophic California earthquake contain an image of the future. One component of this image is a picture of total destruction. The earth separates, presumably along the famous San Andreas fault, and an entire section of land mass disappears under the Pacific Ocean. This is the image captured in a novel about the Big One, *The Last Days of the Late, Great State of California* (Gentry 1968). A second component is that the risk of earthquakes is a localized threat; it is California that is at risk. The image of California disappearing into the ocean (an image that must delight many non-Californians) is surprisingly widely believed, even in southern California (Turner, Nigg, and Paz 1986:140–41). Kate Hutton, a scientist at the California Institute of Technology who frequently briefs the press after earthquakes, recently noted that she was making progress in educating southern California's news reporters about this image: "[O]nce prevalent 'stupid questions' such as 'So when are we going to fall into the ocean?' are now rare," she observed (Weinstein 1992).

The subtle differences between "correct" and "incorrect" images of risk are evident when one contrasts the disappearance of California in humor and in fiction with the following description of the seismic future of the state. The description was written by one of the world's best-known earth scientists:

> The displacement occurring between the Pacific and North American plates along the San Andreas fault enables us to make a graphic—if long-range—forecast. The City of Los Angeles, which sits on the Pacific side of the San Andreas fault, is grinding northwards relative to San Francisco at the rate of 2 centimeters or so per year. This means that in thirty million years it will become a new suburb of San Francisco. But, for the consolation of the residents of both cities, in a further thirty million years Los Angeles will have moved another 600 kilometers northwards to enjoy the rainy pleasures of northernmost California! (Bolt 1978:59)

The image of California breaking away from the rest of North America may be inaccurate, but the scientifically correct description of the earth's dynamics is not very different—give or take 60 million years.

IMAGES OF RISK AND THEIR SIGNIFICANCE

Imagery is important in the promotion of risk. Defining risk is really a process of creating a description of the future. For example, saying that there is a certain probability of developing lung cancer associated with smoking three packs of cigarettes a day creates an image of what is likely to happen in the future and links that image with current behavior. Much of the focus of risk analysis is on the creation of numerical descriptions of the probability of future consequences, as in this example of cigarette smoking. Probabilities are not the only elements in images of future consequences used in constructing risk, however. Pictures of what that future may be like are also aspects of risk promotion. For example, high school students are shown gruesome films of highway carnage to illustrate potential consequences that await them if they drink and drive. Some law enforcement specialists recommend that executions be televised to show what can happen to lawbreakers. The Los Angeles County Coroner's Office recently received funding to begin a program requiring gang members to witness the autopsies of other gang members who died violently (Meyer 1993).

Images of the future have a very specific purpose in the process of promoting risk. They are created especially to cause changes in current behavior patterns in order to reduce the likelihood of future harm. Safety education films attempt to discourage drivers from drinking, public executions to deter potential law-breakers, and witnessing autopsies to divert young people from gangs. Similarly, claims-makers use images of a future catastrophic earthquake in an effort to change both individual behavior and public policies. The significance of images in the promotion of the earthquake threat is illustrated in the following two examples.

Universal Studios in Los Angeles opened a new attraction in the spring of 1989 called "Earthquake—The Big One":

> Record-breaking crowds are bombarding Universal Studios to experience this newest attraction of Universal's tram tour. In it, a fake California subway station shakes, quakes and sinks as everything surrounding it collapses. Thousands die. Onlookers are thrilled. The RTD [Southern California Rapid Transit District] is not.
>
> "It is a spooky ride, impressive but not real. It's okay as long as people understand it's *not* real," says William Rhine, RTD Assistant General Manager for Transit Systems. Rhine is building the Metro [subway] system for

Los Angeles . . . which will run substantially underground, through several earthquake faults.

The Universal Studios ride has seemed real enough to have caused concern among the Los Angeles residents calling the RTD to ask: What will happen to the Metro system when the actual Big One hits?

"The Universal thing is quite wrong," concludes [Dr. George] Housner [Emeritus Professor of Engineering at the California Institute of Technology].

"The subway system will not collapse," concurs Eric Lindvall of earthquake engineering consultants Lindvall, Richter & Associates.

"Riding the Metro will be safer than riding in your car on the freeway," says Ed McSpedon, director of design and construction for the light rail. (Austin 1989)

The remainder of the article contains additional reasons provided by these and other transit officials and earthquake safety experts for why the subway system will perform differently than the image portrayed in the attraction. It also cites the excellent safety record of subway systems in San Francisco and Tokyo during actual earthquakes. Earthquake safety advocates took this fictionalized image seriously enough to deny its authenticity publicly.

Similarly, California's college admissions officers frequently worry that the threat of earthquakes keeps many out-of-state students from applying to the state's universities. Addressing these fears is an important part of maintaining enrollment levels of high-quality students. The University of California at Santa Cruz mailed posters to high school guidance counselors all over the country immediately after the 1989 Loma Prieta earthquake struck the San Francisco Bay area. These posters featured two virtually identical photographs of a campus building in before-and-after fashion. The captions were "October 17, 1989, 5:00 P.M." and "October 17, 1989, 5:15 P.M.," respectively; the earthquake struck at 5:04 P.M. Titled "UC Santa Cruz: A Safe Place (Open for Business)," the posters were part of a campaign to head off an anticipated 20 percent decline in applications to the Santa Cruz campus from out-of-state students.

These two examples illustrate some of the competitive aspects of promoting risk. They also show that so-called experts are not the only source for images of future earthquakes. Images emerge in many arenas and change as they move from one arena to another. Television news reports of earthquakes, public television documentaries, and motion pictures such as *Earthquake* and *Miracle on the I-880* contain different images of risk. Small earthquakes also provide an image that is different from what experts expect the Big One to be like. With the exception of the 1994 Northridge temblor, recent earthquakes in the United States have produced relatively little damage, either because of their moderate intensity or their location away from major population centers. Even the Northridge quake is a poor model for what is expected to occur in the Big One due to its moderate seismic intensity, its location, and the time it struck (4:31 A.M.). Foreign disasters produce more damage than is expected in this country due to different construction practices and building materials. Thus, using actual events to create an image of a future catastrophic earthquake requires downplaying some types of consequences (e.g., widespread fires), calling attention to others (the collapse of unreinforced buildings), and even "inventing" consequences that have not happened (waist-deep piles of broken glass on the sidewalks surrounding high-rise office buildings). Furthermore, there is a fine line between creating images of risk that are effective enough to produce change but not so extreme that they trigger a backlash. Giving critics an opportunity to label safety advocates extremists or alarmists creates the danger that the intended target of the images will ignore them altogether.

Images of the risk of earthquakes do not create themselves. They are created by people. Nature may supply some of the raw material, but people construct images of risk to serve specific purposes. As these purposes change, images of risk should change as well. Since different risk promoters have different concerns, the aspect of risk that each stresses should also differ. Whether the risk has high or low priority, whether it is primarily a threat to life or a threat to the nation's economic viability, whether it is a threat only in California and the West or nationwide, each element reflects people's purposes. The image that people create about the risk of earthquakes explains a great deal about the career of the earthquake threat.

CLAIMS ABOUT FUTURE EARTHQUAKES

Claims are what people say about risk in an attempt to increase awareness of a putative condition seen as harmful and to promote action to change that condition in some way. Claims contain descriptions of one or more of the following: (1) an image of the nature and cause of the condition; (2) proposals for what should be done about it; and (3) justifications for why those proposals are warranted (Best 1990:24–40).[1]

It should not be surprising to find that statements containing specific claims reflect the social location (occupation, education, organizational membership, etc.) of the people who make them. It should also not be a surprise to find that the way individual claims-makers see the causes of a putative condition like the earthquake threat follow rather than precede what they believe to be the appropriate "solution" (Ross and Staines 1972; Cohen, March, and Olsen 1972; March and Olsen 1976;

Edelman 1988:21–23). For example, research scientists should see the threat as greater than necessary due to lack of knowledge and argue for increased spending on research as a solution. Federal officials, who have funded research on various aspects of earthquakes for a long time, should see at least part of the solution as making better use of the knowledge that already exists. Local government officials, besieged by citizens to address a multitude of concerns and believing that local revenue is insufficient to accomplish everything, should see the threat as one requiring increased federal funding for local programs.

We are interested here in claims that are representative of earthquake risk promotion as a whole rather than in idiosyncratic claims statements by particular individuals or groups. Unfortunately, claims are not products of a single bureaucratic organization with a unified chain of command, clearly defined lines of communication, and centralized decision-making. Risk promotion occurs in a loose network of individuals, professional associations, and subunits of public agencies. Therefore, there is no single claim representing an official view analogous, say, to the platform of a political party. However, there are documents whose *use* identifies them as key components of the collective claims-making effort. "Use" is exemplified by claims-makers citing a document in an effort to produce action by others. Use also refers to the fact that some documents become the basis for the production of other documents. Documents-in-use serve as norms or definitions of the situation. Fortunately, there is enough overlap in the content of most documents so that it is feasible to concentrate on a few without undue concern that they are unrepresentative of all such documents. (Questions of "sampling" and "data collection," implicit in this paragraph, are addressed along with other aspects of "methods" in the Appendix.)

The following examination focuses on published statements most frequently cited in reports and most often referred to in various public arenas. The publications include the National Academy of Sciences' report on the 1964 Alaska earthquake (e.g., Committee on the Alaska Earthquake 1970); testimony given at several congressional hearings on federal earthquake hazard reduction policy between 1964 and passage of the Earthquake Hazards Reduction Act of 1977; a report prepared by the National Security Council estimating losses that could occur following a major urban earthquake in California (FEMA 1980); and public comments by claims-makers cited in newspaper articles.

Images of the Causes of the Earthquake Threat

Two causes of the risk of future earthquakes are identified in nearly all claims-making statements. One is the natural forces that produce earth movements. These are treated as necessary but not sufficient for the existence of the threat. The other is the social trends accounting for the location, size, and density of human settlements and the type of structures associated with them. The interaction of these two factors produces the earthquake threat.

Natural Forces.   The image of the causes of the earthquake threat is created using the language of science. Forces of nature such as the movement of plates that make up the earth's surface, the build-up of strain as friction retards normal plate movement, and the sudden release of energy when resistance is overcome dominate descriptions of risk. The narrative from a brochure prepared for the public at large by the Southern California Earthquake Preparedness Project (SCEPP) is typical:

> Earth scientists unanimously agree on the inevitability of major earthquakes in California. The gradual movement of the Pacific Plate relative to the North American Plate leads to the inexorable concentration of strain along the San Andreas and related fault systems. . . . [T]he vast bulk of the strain is released through the occurrence of major earthquakes—that is, earthquakes of Richter magnitude 7.0 and larger. . . . [G]eologists estimate that the probability for the recurrence of [such an] earthquake is greater than 50 percent in the next 25 years. (SCEPP n.d.:1)

Natural forces also explain the destruction caused by these releases of strain:

> Strong ground shaking, which is the primary cause of damage during earthquakes, often extends over vast areas. . . . Casualties and property damage occur principally because of the failure of man-made structures. (SCEPP n.d.:2)

Note especially the causal language in the second quotation. Damage results from building "failures," and ground shaking is the reason buildings "fail." A different sentence could be constructed around the noun "failure" such as: "Damage results from the failure of human beings to locate, design, and construct buildings differently." The point is not that one sentence is more correct than the other. The alternative sentence merely highlights the consistent reference to natural forces in claims-makers' descriptions of one of the causes of the earthquake threat.

Social Trends.   Accumulation of strain and the sudden release of energy may cause earthquakes but not the earthquake threat. Claims-makers frequently note that a major earthquake in the middle of the desert might terrify some animals but in a populated area could kill thousands of people. Put differently, energy release is necessary but not sufficient in the construction of the earthquake threat. Human settlements must be located where the effects of sudden plate movement, energy release, and ground shaking will occur. Claims-makers describe this with language that denotes impersonal social processes and trends: "Given the large concentration of population and industry in southern California, the impacts of a major earthquake would surpass those of any natural disaster thus far experienced by the nation" (SCEPP n.d.:2). Or, in the words of one of California's former senators:

> Indeed, the United States today faces the greatest potential danger from earthquakes that we have ever faced before. It is only in the last decade or so that our population has become concentrated in major cities and along our coastal regions, and major construction has occurred on land-fill and other unstable soils. (U.S. Senate 1977:53)

Use of the passive rather than active voice in these texts depersonalizes the cause of this situation. The passive voice calls attention to impersonal social trends but not the individuals whose actions in the aggregate *are* these trends (Gusfield 1981:88–91, 1976). These impersonal processes (population concentration, demand for housing and other structures, construction on seismically unsuitable sites, etc.) are treated as the sufficient cause of the earthquake threat.

The preference for statements emphasizing impersonal social processes rather than human agents is even more evident in policy recommendations from the panel on human ecology which studied the 1964 Alaska earthquake:

> [W]e need not tolerate the erection of buildings subject to earthquake-induced collapse and on sites that are clearly unstable. The success of most buildings in Alaska in withstanding major damage despite prolonged shaking indicates that we possess the technology to design such buildings. Conversely, the failure of structures in slides or through dramatic collapse, as in the case of the Four Seasons apartment building, gives some evidence (although still debatable) of the types of design or sites to avoid. (Committee on the Alaska Earthquake 1970:27)

The verb *tolerate* in the first sentence suggests that people's actions will no longer be tolerated. However, the language that follows returns immediately to a narrative based on natural (or physical) forces—the "success of most buildings" and the "failure of structures." Apparently we know how to increase the chances of the former and reduce the odds of the latter. The fact that this knowledge is not always used must mean that people chose not to use it. Yet who such people might be and what might be done to prevent them from doing so is not mentioned.

Justifications for Doing Something
About the Earthquake Threat

Claims also contain justifications for why action to address a putative condition is warranted. Best (1990:31–37), borrowing from Toulmin's (1958:98) elements of argument, calls this component of claims "warrants."

The most consistently used justification is that the catastrophic earthquake is a certainty. From the federal perspective, such an earthquake is inevitable; it is just a matter of time. The odds, of course, decline in proportion to the geographic size of political jurisdictions. Thus small cities see the risk of earthquakes as less than do large cities; large cities see it as less certain than states; etc. Smaller units are therefore more willing to play the odds that the catastrophic earthquake will occur somewhere else than is the federal government.

A second justification or warrant is the "We've been lucky so far" argument. Action is necessary now because future earthquakes will be more devastating than anything experienced to date. Social trends (increasing population density, greater demand for useable space, greater pressure for affordable housing, etc.) account for the difference between past and future consequences. Typically this argument is made by suggesting how much more destructive some past earthquake (e.g., San Francisco 1906 or San Fernando 1971) would be if it were to occur today. Often the "We've been lucky" argument is used immediately after an earthquake to underscore how much more devastation there would have been if the temblor had struck at a different time of day, or on a different fault, or with greater intensity. That the Northridge earthquake in 1994 would have claimed many more lives had it not struck at 4:31 A.M. on a holiday continues to be mentioned frequently. The "We've been lucky" warrant justifies action by implying that to do anything less would ensure that the future will be more dangerous than it should be.

Claims-making about the earthquake threat increasingly emphasizes an economic rationale for taking action. This dollars-and-cents approach speaks to people's reluctance to undertake actions that have known present costs but unknown future benefits:

> If the San Andreas Fault were to give us an encore of the 1906 San Francisco earthquake, . . . property damage could exceed $20 billion [in 1977 dollars].
>
> On top of this, we must consider the incalculable losses resulting from the loss of economic and social functioning. Such an earthquake would have enormous repercussions on our national economy and our national psyche.
>
> In the Los Angeles area alone, . . . if the so-called Palmdale Bulge [a suspected increase in elevation of land in the desert north of Los Angeles

in 1976] is a warning that a major earthquake is forthcoming . . . such a catastrophe would certainly have national economic repercussions. (U.S. Senate 1977:54)

Of course, this argument looks different to federal officials who foresee the inevitable budgetary consequences of a catastrophic earthquake than it does to home owners and businesses to whom the economic consequences appear more uncertain.

Another justification for action is that it is an obligation. For government officials, this obligation is a matter of acting in the public interest. Former California senator Cranston testified:

[I]t is still in the public interest to establish a well-funded earthquake program so that we can be better prepared for the earthquakes that are inevitably in our future. . . . It is irresponsible, in the fact [*sic*] of new advances in the sciences of earthquakes and engineering, not to take preventive action now. (U.S. Senate 1977:53)

For scientists, the obligation exists because the knowledge to do more exists, as in the "need not tolerate" quote above. The appeal here is to the American ethic of activism, where the existence of an ability to prevent something harmful justifies using that capability.

Warrants link causes to solutions and solutions to causes. In the case of the earthquake threat the argument justifying action goes like this. A catastrophic earthquake is certain to occur; it is not a question of "if" but rather one of where and when. Due to recent social trends, devastation will be greater than has ever been experienced before unless action is taken now. Economic loss in particular will be great but could be lessened. Because knowledge exists that can be used to reduce these costs (as well as loss of life), taking no action would be wrong.

Proposed Courses of Action

Actually, "action" is inaccurate. A variety of actions, reflecting the different perspectives of various claims-makers within the earthquake establishment, are offered in claims advanced to promote the earthquake threat. Some of these are not at all surprising. Scientists—people in the knowledge business—typically see the threat as one requiring more knowledge than presently exists. Hence, their recommended solutions include calls for more government-sponsored research in specific disciplines (e.g., seismology, earthquake engineering) and on certain topics (e.g., unusual occurrences before earthquakes). This increased-funding solution is advanced by both physical and social scientists.

A major segment of the earthquake establishment stresses the need for planning and preparedness. Both activities address the aftermath of earthquakes without attempting to lessen their impacts. At the federal level, the segment responsible for these activities is a descendant of the civil defense organizations created during the Cold War (see May 1985: 49–56). The Federal Emergency Management Agency (FEMA) is the heir to these programs. The targets of federal preparedness efforts are other governmental entities, especially cities and counties. The Earthquake Program, a combination of northern and southern California regional preparedness efforts, is an example of a federally sponsored program that encourages localities to engage in earthquake planning. At the local level, responsibility for earthquake preparedness is mainly in the hands of emergency response organizations such as police and fire departments. Local earthquake planners target citizens with public education programs aimed at increasing self-reliance both at home and at work— and to decrease potential demand for emergency services immediately following a catastrophic earthquake. Households are urged to be self-sufficient for the first seventy-two hours following impact, and employees are encouraged to have enough extra clothing and toiletries at work for at least one overnight stay.

Another segment of the federal earthquake establishment is responsible for the administration of postdisaster aid. This cluster of organizational subunits targets different elements of local government and stresses the need for "earthquake hazard mitigation" at the local level. Mitigation means using local zoning and other land use control instruments to prevent the siting of buildings in "unsafe" locations. It also includes using building codes to require earthquake-resistant construction practices. The targets of federal mitigation "solutions" are local elected officials and, to a lesser extent, local planning and building departments. Since the Constitution gives local government authority over these instruments of mitigation, the federal government can influence them only indirectly (May and Williams 1986:6–11). Federal mitigation proponents see local government as overwhelmed at best by development interests in attempting to reduce potential losses. At worst, they see local government as an irresponsible co-conspirator for allowing unsafe development while counting on federal aid to pay the bills should disaster strike.

Other earthquake claims-makers—academics mostly, but even a number of federal officials—see changes in federal policy as one necessary component of the solution to the earthquake threat. Their view is that federal disaster aid policy encourages whatever irresponsible risk-taking exists at the local level. The existence of a permanent federal fund, released by the president following a disaster or major emergency declaration, plus the likelihood that additional aid money would be appropriated by Congress in the aftermath of a catastrophic event, provide incentives for cities and counties to "pass the bill to Uncle" [Sam], as federal bureaucrats like to put it. In the cautious words of the National Research Council, "fragmentary and ad hoc policy-making [at the federal level] may unwittingly contribute to an increase in that potential [for greater losses]" (Committee on the Alaska Earthquake 1970:28).

Developing the capability to predict future earthquakes has been a major part of the proposed solution to the earthquake threat since the mid-1960s. A "real" earthquake prediction must

> specify the expected magnitude range, the geographical area within which it will occur, and the time interval within which it will happen with sufficient precision so that the ultimate success or failure of the prediction can readily be judged. (Panel on Earthquake Prediction 1976:7)

Of course, real predictions can only come from real scientists. Federal bureaucrats and scientists see the ability to predict earthquakes as a solution, but many local politicians and business owners see it as a threat in its own right. The latter fear that a prediction would drive away more revenue from a city or county than an actual earthquake, especially since the availability of federal aid to compensate for economic losses following a prediction is uncertain. Federal bureaucrats see the ability to make specific predictions as a weapon to force local government to take action in the face of a certain rather than an uncertain future. In military terms, a prediction would shift defensive forces from having to maintain "constant readiness" to making specific plans for "repulsing an imminent attack."

In sum, a fairly short list of solutions to the threat of earthquakes has dominated claims-making for the past three decades. Variations in emphasis exist as one moves from segment to segment within the earthquake establishment. Disagreements over the relative priority of solutions are evident. Nevertheless, the main solutions proposed have been more support for research in the earth sciences and engineering as well as on societal responses and public policy issues; better planning and preparedness by local governments, employers, and households; greater utilization by local governments of land use and building codes for hazard mitigation; changes in federal disaster aid policy to reduce incentives for risk-taking at local and state levels; and development of the ability to predict earthquakes, the "Great White Hope" of an influential segment of the earthquake establishment.

CONCLUSION

Claims about the risk of earthquakes have one outstanding feature: they depersonalize the threat. Both causes and consequences of future earthquakes are made impersonal. Neither potential "perpetrators" nor "victims" as individuals are identified.

There are no villains in claims about the earthquake threat. Natural forces and faceless social processes combine to cause earthquakes, not specific individuals or even specific types of individuals. Claims contain no hated symbol of injustice, no image of evil personified. There is no terrifying menace like the irresponsible "killer drunk" behind the wheel (Gusfield 1981:112–13) or the stranger who preys on innocent children (Best 1990:22–31). There are no callous and greedy corporate executives who disregard safety for the sake of profits (e.g., Nader [1965] 1972). No one points a finger at the System for placing people at risk (cf. Ross and Staines 1972).

Villains are absent because claims have been constructed without them, not because candidates do not exist. The list of potential villains grew in the early 1990s as conventional wisdom identified some of the sins—and sinners—of the 1980s. Many of these could easily rival the images of "bottom-line" corporate executives and large, impersonal corporations that abound in other controversies involving insolvent savings and loan institutions, the tobacco industry and its advertising, General Motors and its rear-engine Corvairs, or Ford and its exploding Pinto coupes. Parallel images in the earthquake threat could include "yuppie" home buyers craving ever-larger homes with nice views on treacherous hillsides; "greedy" developers devouring pastoral landscapes to feed the seemingly insatiable appetite for suburban property far from the central city; "crooked" politicians all too eager to make the development of suburban housing tracts possible; and a political economy that "stacks the deck" against both the environment and "the little guy" in favor of profits. In short, our cultural tool kit (Swidler 1986) contains many potential villains who could be blamed for causing the earthquake threat, but claims-makers have not used them in constructing an image of risk.

Even though there are no villains, there are heroes in claims about the earthquake threat. The heroes are scientists in dogged pursuit of knowledge with which the world may be spared the worst consequences of the coming catastrophic earthquake. Scientists-as-heroes are portrayed by the press and their fellow claims-makers alike as people unraveling the secrets of nature at the frontiers of knowledge. Their weapons include seismographs that record rumblings beneath the earth's surface, laboratories where building designs are tested for their ability to withstand the effects of severe shaking, and cameras that document the damage caused by actual earthquakes. Heroic skirmishes with city councils over building codes, with zoning commissions over development of land on top of scientifically designated earthquake faults, and with real estate agents over disclosures of seismic risk to potential home buyers are not part of the imagery of heroism in these claims. Nature, not other human beings, is the hero's opponent.

Because of this, some real-life heroes are absent in images of the earthquake threat. Their absence is probably a function of the lack of public reverence for the jobs they hold and the organizations they work for. These missing heroes are the federal civil servants who seem sincerely committed to saving lives, property, and dollars; the people who volunteer their time in public service on commissions and advisory committees; the state and local officials who daily make disaster preparedness a real thing rather than a promise; the building officials who check plans and inspect buildings; and the handful of courageous politicians who sponsor earthquake hazard reduction legislation, sometimes in the face of serious opposition from influential constituents. Because documentaries and motion pictures are not made about such people, because we find the bureaucrat an unlikely hero, and because these people rarely engage in the kind of self-promotion that would attract extensive news coverage means that they are unsung heroes. Because they are invisible, so too are the real-life opponents with whom they wrestle daily.

The emphasis by claims-makers on impersonal forces, both physical and social, makes it unlikely that the public at large will identify human agents as a cause of the earthquake threat. Hilgartner uses the term *risk object* in much the same way that I use *putative condition* here. He describes risk promotion as a process of creating cause-effect links between people (as either producers or recipients of harm) and risk objects. Impersonal forces such as acts of nature usually become "chain terminating objects" (1992:42, footnote 6) because they bring the causal chain-building process to a halt. Such forces are end points because people have difficulty visualizing human agents causing them. Similarly, Stone (1989; also 1988: 147–65) identifies four types of "causal stories" used to advance the careers of public policy issues. The extremes are events whose causes are portrayed as accidental and those whose causes are intentional. She classifies earthquakes among those "unguided" conditions that have unintended consequences and that have thus far escaped being attributed to human agency.

A handful of exceptions demonstrates how unlikely the identification of human beings as causal agents in the earthquake threat is. Some southern Californians believe that testing nuclear weapons in the Nevada desert triggered the Landers earthquake east of Los Angeles in 1992 (Warren 1992). Earlier, leftists in Guatemala charged that such tests, perhaps under the sponsorship of the U.S. Central Intelligence Agency, caused the earthquake that devastated Guatemala City in 1976. Scientists refute such possibilities yet talk about controlling earthquakes by setting off explosions deep in the earth to reduce strain. They also recall how earthquakes were triggered in the 1960s by oil drilling in Colorado.

Not only the causes but also the consequences of the earthquake threat are depersonalized. Claims portray the risk of future earthquakes as an egalitarian threat. The probability of becoming a victim of disaster is shared equally by everyone within officially designated seismic risk zones. In other words, earthquakes do not discriminate. They are a "democratic" threat.[2] Like other natural disasters, they victimize anyone who has the misfortune to be in the way, whether rich or poor, minority or majority, English-speaking or non-English-speaking.[3] A depersonalized threat makes everyone a little exposed to harm. If someone becomes a victim in an earthquake, that person's victim status can be accounted for by one of the stock explanations from the cultural repertoire. The difference between victims and nonvictims can be attributed to luck, to fate, or to God's will.

An alternative image of the risk of earthquakes is that it is unequally distributed rather than universally shared. Exposure to potential harm is socially patterned. In other words, disasters, including earthquakes, do discriminate. Some people (the very poor, in particular) are at greater risk because of who they are, where they live, and where they work. Others (e.g., the middle class and the wealthy) are less exposed because of who they are, where they live, and what they do. Claims-making clearly attempts to establish casual links between the likelihood of damage and the location and design of structures. However, claims-makers rarely go on to link location and type of structure to the social identities of real people who inhabit those structures.

Marske's (1986) study of the risk of air travel in college athletics illustrates the difference between universal and unequally shared risks. At first glance, the risks of an air crash look to be about the same for everyone who flies. Air disasters appear to be an egalitarian threat. However, Marske shows that risk is correlated with the stratification patterns of college athletic programs. Teams representing nationally prominent programs in the major revenue-generating sport, football, most often fly chartered or regularly scheduled commercial airlines. The worst college athletic air disasters have occurred when less prestigious programs, attempting to move into the "big time" in college athletics but still lacking big-time resources, chose some of the riskiest forms of air travel such as air charter services with questionable safety records. Interestingly, even in these cases the chain-building process stops at the accident site. Pilot error, weather conditions, and mechanical failure terminate the cause-effect links before the process extends to the interorganizational stratification patterns in college athletics. Without these links, it becomes unlikely that the alumni and "friends" who pressure college presidents and athletic directors for excellence on the playing field will be identified as a "cause" of athletic transportation accidents.

To sum up, claims about the risk of earthquakes depersonalize the threat. Both the causes of a catastrophic earthquake and its victims are anonymous. Its causes are impersonal processes, both physical and social. Its potential victims are everyone within the reach of those forces. Chance, fate, and luck will determine who is killed and who survives. No claims are made about how social structure allocates risk to some more than to others.

The public statements of claims-makers are the basis for this characterization of claims about the earthquake threat. The documents, testimony, speeches, and news interviews that are the content of claims-making are on the record, so to speak. Off the record, scientists and earthquake safety advocates can describe precisely what kinds of people live in the riskiest of dwellings and which specific individuals have worked hard to block their earthquake hazard reduction efforts. But it is their public statements, not their private comments, that promote risk. The statements they make for the record are the only ones of consequence for promoting risk. Why these public claims take the form they do is explained partly by who these claims-makers are and partly by the nature of the arenas in which they make them. Chapters 3 and 4 examine these two topics in turn.

NOTES

1. My use of the terms *causes, justifications,* and *solutions,* though patterned loosely after Toulmin (1958), is not equivalent to his terms *grounds, warrants,* and *conclusions* (Toulmin 1958:97–107).

2. Fumento (1990:145–59) describes claims-making by what he calls the democratizers who tried to advance the argument that everyone was at risk of contracting AIDS in an effort to broaden the base of support for doing something about the disease.

3. Clarke (1992:704) suggests that "arguments about safety in general typically mask risk inequalities."

3

Claims-Makers: The "Earthquake Establishment"

Who are the claims-makers engaged in promoting the risk of earth-quakes? What difference do the social standing they enjoy, the skills they possess, and the jobs they hold make for the success or failure of the earthquake threat as a social problem? Claims-makers are people who demand that "something be done about some putative condition" (Spector and Kitsuse [1977] 1987:78). Identifying claims-makers in fully constructed social problems is simplified by the fact that they are usually affiliated with groups and organizations active in a controver-sial public issue. Troyer and Markle (1983:65–88), for example, identify claims-makers in the antismoking movement by tracking the efforts of organizations such as the American Cancer Society, the Department of Health, Education, and Welfare (HEW), and ASH (Action on Smoking and Health).

The task here is not quite so simple. There are no voluntary associa-tions or social movement organizations fighting for increased earth-quake safety. There are, however, individuals and organizations who deal with the earthquake threat in other ways and in so doing engage in a form of claims-making. It is not hard to find a few examples because some of these people appear in one public arena or another every so often. It is more difficult to construct a representative sample of claims-makers so that their general characteristics can be described.

Both the general description of claims-makers in Spector and Kitsuse and examples in monographs such as the one on cigarette smoking by Troyer and Markle point to three elements of a working definition. In combination they identify people who contribute to promoting the earthquake threat. A claims-maker is *someone who, (1) in a public setting, (2) describes either a cause, a rationale, or a solution related to a putative condi-tion (3) in a process aimed at doing something about that condition.* "Putative condition" in this case refers to the threat of future, catastrophic earth-quakes. The definition does not imply that claims-makers offer identical or even similar descriptions of causes, rationales, or solutions. In fact, claims-makers frequently disagree, especially about solutions. Disagreements about causes, rationales, and solutions in the earthquake threat are discussed in Chapter 4.

I assume at the outset that social problems involve activity that is nationwide in scope rather than local. That is, social problems are societal concerns. This means that the people who are actively engaged in promoting risk should appear in national settings or arenas (Hilgartner and Bosk 1988). There are three such national arenas in which claims-makers promoting the earthquake threat have appeared over the years. One is the committee or panel of the nation's leading experts assembled to consider the nature of the threat, what should be done about it, and why. Members of these committees and panels usually are selected by officials in the federal government, and their work is typically sponsored by a federal agency. A second arena is the congressional hearing where experts testify about some aspect of the threat. A third is the national news, including both the most prestigious newspapers and the major television and radio news networks.

Not everyone appearing in these arenas, particularly at congressional hearings and in the national news, is participating in claims-making. That is, many people who appear are not describing a cause, rationale, or solution for the earthquake threat. Disaster victims and local politicians, for example, appear frequently at congressional hearings, but each is usually there to appeal for a remedy to some past oversight by a federal agency. Victims, politicians (especially top elected officials), eyewitnesses, emergency personnel, and relief workers make up the overwhelming majority of people in news coverage of earthquake disasters, but they nearly always recall their personal experiences or comment on past events. What they do is not intended to define the risk of future threats as a putative condition.[1]

In the sections to follow, I will identify the people who engage in claims-making in these three arenas and describe some of the things they have to say about the earthquake threat. I will then summarize the composition of what I call the *earthquake establishment* in the United States. The chapter concludes with a discussion of some consequences of the composition of the earthquake establishment for the success of claims-making.

CLAIMS-MAKERS AS PARTICIPANTS
ON EXPERT PANELS AND COMMITTEES

One national arena in which claims-making on behalf of the earthquake threat occurs is the specially appointed committee of experts. The federal government organizes or sponsors a variety of ad hoc and standing committees, commissions, panels, conferences, seminars, workshops, and field teams addressing the risk of earthquakes. Invited participants constitute the elite of the earthquake establishment. Committees and panels usually produce a report identifying the causes of the earthquake threat and recommending courses of action for reducing it. Several such reports have had a significant impact on the career of the earthquake threat over the past quarter-century. I have selected the following to describe here briefly:[2] the public policy recommendations from one of the National Academy of Sciences–National Research Council report on the Alaska earthquake of 1964 (Committee on the Alaska Earthquake 1970); a report to Congress on disaster preparedness by the Office of Emergency Preparedness (1972); two National Academy of Sciences reports dealing with earthquake prediction (Panel on the Public Policy Implications of Earthquake Prediction 1975; Panel on Earthquake Prediction 1976); the National Science Foundation–sponsored assessment of research needs on earthquakes and other natural hazards (White and Haas 1975; also Ayre 1975); a study by the National Security Council estimating the effects of a catastrophic earthquake in California (FEMA 1980); and a recent National Academy of Sciences-National Research Council document prepared as part of the International Decade for Natural Disaster Reduction (U.S. National Committee for the Decade of Natural Disaster Reduction 1991). In each case, I am interested in identifying the people participating on the committees that prepared these reports.

The seven panels of the Committee on the Alaska Earthquake produced a massive eight-volume report published over a period of six years (1968–1973) by the National Academy of Sciences. Earth scientists and engineers, most of whom were from either universities in California or federal agencies, dominated the fifteen-member committee. The committee's panels included experts who examined seven facets of the 1964 earthquake in Alaska and its impact: geology, seismology, hydrology, biology, oceanography, engineering, and human ecology. The Panel on Geography produced a general set of public policy recommendations in its report on human ecology that were frequently cited after publication of the report (Committee on the Alaska Earthquake 1970). A handful of non–physical scientists including a geographer, a sociologist, an anthropologist, an economist, a lawyer, and an architect made up this panel, whose report was the seventh volume of the series. Despite its composition, this panel, like the others, emphasized physical science and engineering problems and solutions.

The staff of the Office of Emergency Preparedness in 1972 produced a three-volume report to Congress as required by a bill passed two years earlier (P.L. 91-606). Though *Disaster Preparedness* (Office of Emergency

Preparedness 1972) might be considered an "in-house" document, in fact the two-dozen or so members of the Office of Emergency Preparedness's Disaster Study Group relied on input from "more than a hundred Federal agencies, State and local governments, professional and trade associations, and volunteer disaster relief organizations" (Office of Emergency Preparedness 1972:v). Among the outside contributors (pp. v–vi) were people representing the U.S. Geological Survey, the American Geophysical Union, the Structural Engineers Association of Southern California, and numerous associations from the insurance industry. A veteran earthquake safety advocate from California, the engineer Karl Steinbrugge, plus two sociologists who had been involved in studies of the Alaska earthquake (one was chair of the Panel of Geography) also served as consultants to the study group.

Volumes 1 and 3 of the Office of Emergency Preparedness report provide a picture of the federal perspective on earthquakes and nine other hazards at the beginning of the 1970s. The report overall emphasizes disaster protection measures (planning and preparedness, stockpiling, warning and evacuation, emergency coordination and control, and public information). However, the examination of the earthquake threat breaks away from this cold war orientation, emphasizing instead mitigation strategies. The study group's first finding about earthquakes is: *"The greatest potential for reducing the loss of life and property from earthquakes lies in restricting the use of land in high-risk areas and in imposing appropriate structural-engineering standards upon both new and existing buildings"* (Office of Emergency Preparedness 1972:84, emphasis in the original). The report describes the potential for far greater losses in the future from a catastrophic earthquake, stresses the responsibility (and irresponsibility) of local government for reducing this risk, gives considerable attention to earthquake prediction and to programs that would be necessary to make it a reality, raises the possibility that earthquakes someday may be controlled, notes the inadequacy of existing urban search-and-rescue capabilities, and even provides a reminder that earthquakes have harmful consequences for the natural environment as well as for the human environment. Neither of the two chapters on the earthquake threat mentions earthquake insurance as a potential "solution." Both chapters reinforce a scientific definition of the threat with tables describing damage and injury, maps showing areas of the country at high seismic risk, pictures and diagrams of seismographs and seismometers, and photographs of earthquake damage to buildings and lifelines (e.g., electrical transmission stations, bridges, highways).

Predicting future earthquakes was the subject of many reports produced between 1965 and 1977. Two of these were prepared by committees of the National Academy of Sciences. The Panel on Earthquake

Prediction, consisting mostly of seismologists and geophysicists, produced a report on the scientific aspects of prediction (Panel on Earthquake Prediction 1976). The Panel on the Public Policy Implications of Earthquake Prediction, made up of social scientists for the most part, prepared a report on the social, legal, political, and economic aspects of prediction (Panel on the Public Policy Implications of Earthquake Prediction 1975). The chairs of the two panels, sociologist Ralph Turner of the policy implications panel and seismologist Clarence Allen of the scientific panel, served as ex officio members of the other group.

The panel of earth scientists formally defined the term *earthquake prediction* [it must specify expected magnitude, location, and time window so that success or failure may be judged (Panel on Earthquake Prediction 1976:7)], evaluated existing methods for predicting future occurrences of earthquakes, examined existing funding levels for research, and recommended that the federal government "make a national commitment to a long-term program aimed at developing a reliable and effective operational earthquake-prediction capability" (p. 3). It estimated that a credible scientific prediction "will probably be made within the next five years [that is, by 1980] for an earthquake of magnitude 5 or greater in California" and, with appropriate "commitment," that "routine announcement of reliable predictions may be possible within 10 years [i.e., by 1985] in well instrumented areas" (p. 2). Commitment was defined as a ten-year effort with "a large increase to several times the current annual Federal expenditures" (p. 2). The panel emphasized that "a realistic attack on the earthquake-hazard problem" would require both the development of prediction and the "upgrading of earthquake-engineering design and construction" (p. 2).

The policy implications panel had input from earth scientists from the Geological Survey, members of the Office of Emergency Preparedness Disaster Study Group who helped write the 1972 report to Congress, sociologists who had been involved in studies of the Alaska earthquake, an earthquake engineer, an economist specializing in risk and insurance issues (Howard Kunreuther of the Wharton School at the University of Pennsylvania), and Karl Steinbrugge, among others. This panel was a little less optimistic about the imminent development of an operational earthquake prediction capability than its scientific counterpart. Nevertheless, it assumed—and its report legitimizes—the inevitability of the ability to predict the time, magnitude, and location of earthquakes. Its report identified topics for sociological, economic, and legal research where results would be needed to reduce the potential for negative side effects of predictions.

An interdisciplinary team consisting mostly of social scientists and geographers was being assembled at about the same time to assess needed social science research on adjustments to earthquakes and fourteen other natural hazards. The National Science Foundation provided funding through its Research Applied to National Needs (RANN) program.[3] Led by a geographer long active in federal flood plain management policy (Gilbert White) and a sociologist involved in all three previously described projects (Eugene Haas), the team's report (White and Haas 1975) reinforced the definition of earthquakes as not merely a California hazard, focused on "social and economic disruption" as the ultimate consequence of earthquakes (death-injury and property loss are treated as two of seventeen antecedent rather than dependent variables in an elaborate conceptual model; see Figure 11.12), and singled out five earthquake hazard reduction strategies for increased research attention: land use management, earthquake-proof construction practices and code requirements, earthquake prediction and warning, earthquake reduction (i.e., the premeditated release of energy to prevent earthquakes), community preparedness and disaster relief, and earthquake insurance. Among the experts who provided advice to the project were George Housner, an earthquake engineering professor from the California Institute of Technology, and Howard Kunreuther, the Wharton School economist. An annual workshop that grew out of this project has become a major integrative mechanism for the earthquake establishment (see Chapter 5).

In May 1980, President Jimmy Carter traveled to the State of Washington to inspect damage caused by the eruption of the volcano known as Mount St. Helens. The amount of energy released impressed everyone in the presidential party. Destruction was widespread, but because the area was sparsely populated the loss of life and damage to dwellings was comparatively light. Aboard Air Force One on the return flight to Maryland, the president worried aloud about what a geologic event with similar energy might do to a heavily populated area. He directed the National Security Council to estimate the likely consequences of a catastrophic earthquake in southern California and evaluate how well the federal government was prepared to deal with it. The evaluation was carried out by an ad hoc group of experts called the Committee on Assessment of Consequences and Preparation for a Major California Earthquake. The committee's report was published by the Federal Emergency Management Agency (FEMA 1980). This report has been one of the most influential documents in defining the Big One although there have been several updates of the estimates it contains in the decade since its release (e.g., Working Group on California Earthquake Probabilities 1990). The committee concluded that preparations in 1980 for a catastrophic earthquake by all levels of government were "woefully inadequate":

Because of the large concentration of population and industry [in California], the impacts of such an earthquake would surpass those of any natural disaster thus far experienced by the Nation. Indeed, the United States has not suffered any disaster of this magnitude on its own territory since the Civil War. (FEMA 1980:2)

Key portions of the scenario created by the committee include:

[G]eologists estimate that the probability for the recurrence of a similar earthquake [of Richter magnitude of 8.0 or larger along the southern San Andreas fault, some 50 miles from downtown Los Angeles] is currently as large as 2 to 5 percent per year and greater than 50 percent in the next 30 years. . . . [E]stimates of fatalities range from about 3,000, if the earthquake were to occur at 2:30 A.M. when the population is relatively safe at home, to more than 13,000, if the earthquake were to occur at 4:30 P.M. on a weekday, when much of the population is either in office buildings or on the streets. Injuries serious enough to require hospitalization under normal circumstances are estimated to be about four times as great as fatalities [i.e., from 12,000 to 52,000]. For the less likely prospect of a Richter magnitude 7.5 earthquake on the Newport-Inglewood fault in the immediate Los Angeles area, fatalities are estimated to be about 4,000 to 23,000, at the same respective times. Such an earthquake, despite its smaller magnitude, would be more destructive because of its relative proximity to the most heavily developed regions; however, the probability of this event is estimated to be only about 0.1 percent per year. . . . Property losses are expected to be higher than in any past earthquake in the United States. . . . Estimates of property damage for the most probable earthquake on the southern San Andreas (Richter magnitude 8+) and the less probable but more damaging one (Richter magnitude 7.5) on the Newport-Inglewood fault, are about $15 billion and $70 billion [in 1980 dollars] respectively. (FEMA 1980:3–4)

The assessment committee was chaired by Frank Press, President Carter's science advisor and an earth scientist who earlier had championed earthquake prediction at several congressional hearings. Contributors to the committee included numerous earth scientists from the Geological Survey (among them Robert Wallace), former members of the Office of Emergency Preparedness Disaster Study Group, representatives of FEMA, sociologists, several officials from the State of California's disaster preparedness agency, and long-time earthquake safety advocates from California such as Lloyd Cluff and Karl Steinbrugge. The committee itself consisted primarily of presidential appointees including two members of the cabinet, members of the president's staff, and the director of FEMA. Between the full committee and the independent contributors stood a working group of staff members from executive-branch units such as the National Security Council, the Office of Management and Budget, FEMA, and the Office of Science and Technology Policy.

Finally, the U.S. National Committee for the Decade for Natural Disaster Reduction was created in 1989 in conjunction with the United Nations designation of the 1990s as the International Decade for Natural Disaster Reduction. The U.S. committee was assembled under auspices of the National Academy of Sciences, whose current president, Frank Press, was one of the leaders in bringing about international attention to hazard reduction. Among the members of the committee in 1989 were long-time earthquake safety advocates (the private-sector earth scientist Lloyd Cluff, California Institute of Technology engineer George Housner, the mayor of Los Angeles and that city's earthquake preparedness coordinator, the head of the Tennessee emergency preparedness agency), one of the nation's most well-known researchers of human behavior in disasters (sociologist E. L. Quarantelli), and a long-time earthquake safety advocate from southern California with a background in both engineering and the policy sciences (William Petak). University of California earth scientist Bruce Bolt was one of the contributors to the committee as were representatives from the Geological Survey (including Robert Hamilton) and several familiar federal agencies [National Oceanic and Atmospheric Administration, the Forest Service, National Aeronautics and Space Administration, the National Institute of Standards and Technology (formerly the National Bureau of Standards), and FEMA].

The committee's report (U.S. National Committee for the Decade for Natural Disaster Reduction 1991), though it deals with a variety of natural hazards both singly and taken as a whole, largely recreates the image of the risk of earthquakes that has existed since the mid-1960s. For example, solutions remain in the hands of experts (earth scientists, engineers, social scientists, policymakers) with ordinary citizens assigned the task of being prepared (pp. 8–11, 17). Earthquake prediction remains in the nation's plans (p. 40). Some new developments in the imagery of risk found their way into the report, most importantly a repeated use of a benefit-cost rationale for encouraging action to address the threat of earthquakes and other natural hazards. Noting in several places (pp. 3, 14, 21) that localities resist hazard mitigation for economic and political reasons, the committee argues: "Postdisaster studies continue to confirm the fundamental fact that community investment in mitigation pays direct dividends when a disaster occurs" (p. 21).

CLAIMS-MAKERS AS PARTICIPANTS
AT CONGRESSIONAL HEARINGS

Service on panels, commissions, and committees is not the only way to identify claims-makers. A second arena in which they appear—and one in which they have the opportunity to shape and reshape public images of the risk of earthquakes—is the congressional hearing. Congress held more than 150 hearings on earthquakes and the earthquake threat during the twenty-eight-year period from 1964 through 1992.[4] This is obviously less than the number of hearings over the same span on other public issues such as foreign policy, economic conditions, and the environment. It is, however, a surprisingly large number in light of the low level of interest in this topic among voters (who elect the members of Congress). I have examined eighty of these earthquake-related hearings in some detail.[5] More than three hundred expert witnesses testified at these hearings. This number does *not* include perhaps half again as many private citizens and business owners who appeared as disaster victims.

Witnesses at "Lessons-Learned" Hearings

There are undoubtedly as many different ways of classifying hearings held by the various congressional committees and subcommittees as there are hearings themselves. However, hearings whose subject is earthquakes or the threat of earthquakes generally take one of two forms. One type is the "lessons-learned" hearing. This type of hearing usually takes place shortly after a damaging earthquake. Its focus is on implications of the recent events for government policies or procedures. The second type I call the "premarkup" hearing. This type is concerned with soliciting comments on some bill (or on a series of related bills) pending in Congress. There is considerable overlap between the two types of hearings because images of some past earthquake or other disaster are clearly on the minds of participants in premarkup hearings, and lessons-learned hearings focus on proposed legislative changes. However, the different orientation of each type of hearing influences claims-making by affecting the types of witnesses invited to testify and the topics they are asked to address.

I will briefly describe three postearthquake or lessons-learned hearings from among several held between 1964 and 1992. Each took place in a different decade and had a slightly different configuration. The first, from the 1960s, is the more extensive of two hearings held less than a month after the Good Friday earthquake in Alaska. The second is a 1971 hearing after the San Fernando earthquake in Los Angeles. The 1980s hearing is one of several held in the wake of the Loma Prieta earthquake in the San Francisco Bay area, this one taking place eleven months after the quake. Four other lessons-learned hearings will be mentioned in passing, two held after the 1985 earthquake in Mexico City, one following the Whittier Narrows (Los Angeles County) earthquake in 1987, and one dealing with a 1988 earthquake in Soviet Armenia.

The 1964 Alaska Earthquake.   The Good Friday earthquake of March 27, 1964—named after the religious holiday on which it occurred, Good Friday, the anniversary of the crucifixion celebrated by Christians—marks the beginning of an increase in claims-making activity on behalf of the earthquake threat. It also is one of the events that bounds the time period of the present study. This strong earthquake (some earth scientists estimate its Richter magnitude as high as 9.6) shook not only the city of Anchorage and several coastal villages; it also shook the federal government (Dacy and Kunreuther 1969:52–57) and the scientific community, though in different ways.

The Senate Committee on Interior and Insular Affairs held three days of hearings less than a month after the earthquake (U.S. Senate 1964a). Its focus was on ways of providing federal disaster aid to the state and to some of its local governments. Witnesses included both of Alaska's senators, the state's governor, a member of its House delegation, the mayors of Anchorage, Kodiak, and Seward, two members of the California congressional delegation, the senior senator from the State of Washington, representatives of the International Longshoreman's Union, a representative of the National Board of Fire Underwriters, the general counsel from the Housing and Home Finance Agency, the executive director of the American Municipal Association, and a representative of the National Association of Insurance Brokers.

What is most striking about this hearing is who was absent. There were no earth scientists among the witnesses. No civil engineers testified. [The same was true of the other two hearings dealing with this earthquake (U.S. Senate 1964b, 1964c).] Nor did anyone testify from the principal federal disaster relief agency at the time, the Office of Emergency Planning. The arena belonged to politicians and to representatives of the insurance industry. They debated mechanisms for financing repairs and reconstruction following major disasters. The hearing treated earthquakes as *economic* threats for which a permanent federal solution was needed.

The 1971 Los Angeles Earthquake.   Not so seven years later. In the aftermath of a moderate (6.1 Richter magnitude) earthquake in the San Fernando Valley section of Los Angeles, earth scientists and engineers were prominent in the next wave of lessons-learned hearings. Three of the half-dozen or so hearings related to this earthquake were major arenas for these "technocratic" claims-makers. One hearing dealt with the collapse and resulting loss of life at a Veterans Administration Hospital (U.S. House of Representatives 1971a) while the other two dealt with the earthquake's implications for federal disaster relief policy (U.S. House of Representatives 1971b; U.S. Senate 1971). The three-day Senate hearing, held in the San Fernando Valley, was the most important opportunity for claims-makers.

Organized by John Tunney (Democrat of California) and his staff and chaired by Birch Bayh (Democrat of Indiana), the primary author of the prevailing federal disaster legislation in effect at the time of the Los Angeles earthquake (the Disaster Relief Act of 1970, P.L. 91-606), these hearings reflected a definition of the earthquake threat that still exists more than twenty years later. Claims-makers identified causes of the threat, suggested alternatives for reducing it, and in some cases provided justifications for giving it high priority. The hearing also produced its share of partisan exchanges between witnesses and members of the committee as well as among committee members. The 985-page transcript remains the best single example of claims-making in this type of arena.

There was an angry tone to much of the hearing. Most of the witnesses representing local governments (the County of Los Angeles, the City of Los Angeles, and the City of San Fernando) complained about "excessive paperwork" and delays in receiving the disaster funds from the Office of Emergency Preparedness[6] to which they were legally entitled. Home owners, owners of businesses, and spokespersons for low-income disaster victims complained about the slowness of the Small Business Administration in processing disaster loan applications. A Democratic member of the California state senate complained that the state's Republican governor had long been indifferent if not actually hostile to earthquake safety. A Republican member of the county's Board of Supervisors complained that the Democratically controlled Congress, including Senators Tunney and Bayh, had shirked its responsibility by not helping to pay for local welfare programs, a failing that he contended would make it more difficult for the county to cope with the fiscal impact of the earthquake. Senator Bayh complained that the Nixon administration had changed one of his earlier disaster relief bills and was thus to blame for some of the problems home owners were having; Democrat Tunney and Republican Bob Dole clashed over the performance of the Small Business Administration in this disaster; and Tunney engaged in a sharp exchange with the Nixon administration's federal insurance administrator over the adequacy of the private sector in providing earthquake insurance.

Earth scientists and engineers were in the spotlight during most of the second day of the hearings and were able to make several points about the earthquake threat: that more money was needed for basic research to understand the dynamics of earthquakes; that future earthquakes in urban areas would produce even worse damage; that "we were lucky" in the 1971 event; that failure to use existing knowledge in local development, especially knowledge of the location of active earthquake faults, continued to be a cause of unacceptably high risk; and that the federal government should impose design standards on all public and private property built or purchased with federal funds.

The experts who testified about the adequacy of private insurance achieved a standoff with Democratic senators over whether or not the federal government should provide earthquake insurance or reinsurance. During the debate over this issue, two different views emerged about whether earthquake victims were at fault for their condition. Witnesses from executive-branch agencies argued that victims were to blame either because they "chose to be reckless" by not purchasing private insurance (U.S. Senate 1971:326) or because they had allowed local government to operate without "self-control" in permitting unsafe development (pp. 322–24). Disaster victims, and local elected officials who testified on their behalf, saw themselves as "innocent victims" who had been made to suffer at the hands of nature "through no fault of their own" (pp. 3, 557, 564). The hearings ended without resolving this contentious issue.

The Loma Prieta Earthquake of 1989.   The lessons-learned hearings held during the 1980s contained many of the same debates carried on at earlier hearings by similar types of witnesses. There were at least a dozen hearings on the Loma Prieta earthquake of October 17, 1989. (Several simultaneously addressed the federal response to Hurricane Hugo, which had struck one month previously.) The list of witnesses at the Loma Prieta hearings varies in accordance with the purpose of the hearings. Most hearings were rather narrowly focused on a single aspect of the earthquake threat. For instance, the earliest hearing, held six days after the earthquake, dealt with the safety of the nation's bridges and with legislation that would make money from the Federal Highway Trust Fund available for repairs to both the collapsed double-decked freeway in Oakland (I-880) and the Bay Bridge between Oakland and San Francisco (U.S. Senate 1990). Those testifying on matters before this subcommittee, in addition to the governor of California, were officials from the Federal Highway Administration, the Army Corps of Engineers, and the National Center for Earthquake Engineering Research; faculty from university engineering departments; and representatives of federal disaster relief agencies. Similarly, a two-day hearing on postearthquake housing needs, held in Watsonville (a small town with a large low-income Hispanic population) and in San Francisco, featured local politicians and housing administrators; state and federal housing officials; representatives of the Legal Aid Society, United Farm Workers, and the Rural Legal Assistance Foundation; advocates for the homeless; disaster victims; and two representatives of FEMA attempting to defend the agency and explain the laws that govern its operation (U.S. House of Representatives 1990). Only one earth scientist, a geophysicist from the Geological Survey, testified about the probability of future earthquakes, although he did supply nearly three hundred pages of documents for the record.

The key hearing as far as claims-making goes was held eleven months after the earthquake. The House Banking Committee's Subcommittee on Policy Research and Insurance held two days of hearings in September 1990 focusing on "solutions" to the earthquake threat in the form of federal policy options (U.S. House of Representatives 1991). Options presented by witnesses included: National Science Foundation (NSF) support for research on earthquake-resistant design and construction techniques, technical and financial assistance by FEMA to state and local governments for mitigation programs, and new Bush administration policies requiring seismic design elements in the construction of federal buildings; further development of seismic provisions in local building codes, getting local governments to enforce seismic safety standards in new construction, and rehabilitating existing structures; and devising and marketing an earthquake insurance plan. Witnesses included structural engineers, the director of the Earthquake Engineering Research Institute, national building code officials, social scientists who previously had conducted research on home owners' decisions to purchase earthquake insurance, specialists in earthquake insurance issues from both industry and from the California Department of Insurance, and representatives of lead agencies designated in the Earthquake Hazards Reduction Act.

Other Postearthquake Hearings during the 1980s. Lessons-learned hearings following both the Mexico City earthquake of September 19, 1985, and the Whittier Narrows earthquake, centered just east of downtown Los Angeles on October 1, 1987, had the same basic format. The two post–Mexico City hearings (U.S. Senate 1986; U.S. House of Representatives 1986a), held one month apart, had virtually the same witnesses testifying on nearly identical matters as in the Loma Prieta hearing. The director of the Geological Survey, the director of the engineering laboratory of the National Bureau of Standards, and the assistant director for engineering research at the National Science Foundation described geological and engineering implications of the Mexico earthquake. Several university-based earth scientists and engineers, earthquake preparedness specialists from California and Tennessee, the director of state and local programs from FEMA, and the federal insurance administrator (by this time housed within FEMA) described implications for earthquake hazard mitigation and disaster planning.

The Whittier Narrows hearing (U.S. House of Representatives 1988a) was nearly identical to the Mexico City earthquake hearings. The director of the Geological Survey and officials from the National Science Foundation, the National Bureau of Standards, and FEMA described implications of the earthquake for the national earthquake hazards reduction program. Disaster preparedness and planning specialists discussed the public response to both the earthquake itself and to public information issued afterward about the earthquake threat in southern California. The chief actuary from the California Department of Insurance and a representative of the insurance industry reviewed policy issues related to earthquake insurance.

The lessons-learned hearing following the December 7, 1988, earthquake in Soviet Armenia showed the shadow cast by events in Mexico City four years earlier. Both earthquakes caused the collapse of high-rise buildings in which many people were trapped. News reports of the massive efforts to find victims and extricate them from debris drew international attention. The possibility that similar situations could arise in a catastrophic U.S. earthquake, despite differences in building practices, led to a growing concern over urban search-and-rescue among earthquake safety advocates. Teams of U.S. experts visited Armenia in late December 1988 to take a close-up look at Soviet search-and-rescue efforts, emergency medical care, and building practices. Consequently, the Armenian earthquake hearing had representatives of these site visit teams testifying about each of these topics (U.S. House of Representatives 1989). Witnesses included an academic researcher with a special interest in urban search-and-rescue, engineers from both for-profit engineering firms and nonprofit research institutes who compared building practices in the Soviet Union and the United States, and physicians and firefighters who discussed the need for improvements in emergency medical services in the United States.

Witnesses at "Premarkup" Hearings

I chose two examples of premarkup hearings to illustrate the types of witnesses appearing at these hearings. Both are from the mid-1970s. This was the period during which various bills emerged and reemerged in Congress before one finally became the Earthquake Hazards Reduction Act of 1977 (P.L. 95-125). The first hearing (U.S. House of Representatives 1976) took place in the summer of 1976 and was the last of several to deal with unsuccessful earthquake hazard bills during the administrations of Presidents Richard Nixon and Gerald Ford. The second was the final hearing on S. 126, the bill that became P.L. 95-124 (U.S. Senate

1977). It was one of two hearings on earthquake hazards reduction held soon after the inauguration of President Jimmy Carter.

The California congressional delegation, and Democratic Senator Alan Cranston in particular, led an effort to establish a national earthquake hazard policy following the 1971 quake in the San Fernando Valley. Claims-making activity during this period produced a more elaborate definition of the earthquake threat than had existed previously. The image of the threat that emerged reflected the unique interests of claims-makers and other stakeholders who participated in hearings at that time.

On the political side, part of the congressional maneuvering was dictated by the Democrats' need for as many votes—including as many Republican votes—as they could acquire in order to get around a Republican administration opposed to these earthquake bills for a variety of reasons. A key to this effort was to line up supporting votes from members of Congress *outside* California. One important consequence of this was the reworking of the image of the risk of earthquakes from only a "local" (i.e., California) threat to one in which the nation as a whole was described as being at risk.

Recent developments in the earth sciences skewed the debate about the earthquake threat to the issue of earthquake prediction. Many earth scientists were becoming convinced that a routine prediction capability was just a matter of time—and dollars—away. Some members of Congress believed that knowing exactly where and when an earthquake would occur would finally force local governments to take the actions to reduce injuries and property damage that otherwise they seemed unwilling to take. The emphasis on prediction as one solution for reducing risk was given an unintentional boost by international diplomatic events. An early consequence of President Nixon's pursuit of *détente* with the Soviet Union and the Peoples' Republic of China was the initiation of scientific exchanges between these countries and the United States (e.g., American Earthquake Study Delegation 1975). Among the first visiting delegations were scientists and engineers interested in advancing the state of the art of earthquake prediction (e.g., Haicheng Earthquake Study Delegation 1977).

Seven different hearings were held from May 1972 through April 1977 on the various bills that finally became the Earthquake Hazards Reduction Act. The most extensive hearing was held during the last summer of the Ford administration (U.S. House of Representatives 1976). Back-to-back hearings were held three months after the inauguration of President Carter (U.S. Senate 1977; U.S. House of Representatives 1977); both of the latter were virtually identical and covered the same points that had been made ten months earlier.

There were two principal foci of the 1976 hearing even though the three-day proceedings dealt with five separate bills. One was the appropriate relationships among federal agencies and their responsibilities regarding the earthquake threat. The other was the prospects for an earthquake prediction capability. As a result, two clusters of witnesses gave testimony, one consisting of Republican-appointed heads of the agencies affected by the bills such as the Geological Survey, the National Science Foundation, and the Federal Disaster Assistance Administration (formerly the Office of Emergency Preparedness, as FEMA was known in those days)[7] and the other consisting primarily of earth scientists. Written statements submitted separately for inclusion in the record came exclusively from professional associations representing geologists, engineers, and the insurance industry.

Scientific hypotheses linking precursors to earthquakes rested on the theory of plate tectonics. By the early 1970s this theory, depicting the earth as having a liquid center with a number of plates floating on its surface, had won general acceptance in American geophysics (Stewart 1990:95–110). Frank Press, professor of geophysics at the Massachusetts Institute of Technology and soon-to-be science adviser in the Carter administration, was a key witness:

> [Arizona Senator Barry] GOLDWATER. "Is the theory of plate tectonics fairly widely accepted by the community of geologists or experts, people who study earthquakes?"
> Dr. PRESS. "I don't think we have taken a vote but I would be amazed if less than 90 percent of the geologists and geophysicists in this country did not accept it as the most important geological hypothesis of the century."
> (U.S. House of Representatives 1976:136)

The subcommittee heard from the chair of the National Academy of Sciences' Panel on Earthquake Prediction, which had just issued its report on the status of earthquake prediction (Panel on Earthquake Prediction 1976). The witness was Clarence Allen, a seismologist from the California Institute of Technology:

> Dr. ALLEN. "Although I will be speaking today primarily about earthquake prediction, I recognize that prediction represents only one facet of the total earthquake-hazard reduction effort, and I recognize that the various bills under consideration by your subcommittee are concerned with the larger problem, including that of societal response."
> "Nevertheless, I am fully convinced that earthquake prediction can and should play a leading and vitally important role in the hazard-reduction effort, and it represents one area where exciting and significant scientific advances are being made right now, and will almost certainly continue to

be made in the next few years if we are able to obtain continuing encouragement and support." (U.S. House of Representatives 1976:143–45)

The subcommittee invited a research scientist from the California Institute of Technology to testify about his experience in actually issuing an earthquake prediction. James Whitcomb had surprised his colleagues by holding a press conference in April 1976 at which he announced his "earthquake prediction hypothesis test." He had disclosed that he expected an earthquake between Richter magnitude 5.5 and 6.5 to strike the Los Angeles area within twelve months. (For a description of Whitcomb's "hypothesis test" and related events, see Turner et al. 1986:25–60.) Whitcomb evidently had been stung by criticism he had received from scientists and citizens alike, and his testimony to the subcommittee two months later was rather self-serving. Nevertheless, he added to the optimism about an emerging prediction capability, implying that only inadequate federal funding for research would prevent the achievement of this goal (U.S. House of Representatives 1976:258–59).

The back-to-back hearings in April 1977 were an "instant replay" of this 1976 hearing. The only difference was that a Democratic administration had won control of the White House in the November 1976 elections. Frank Press testified once again at the Senate hearing (U.S. Senate 1977), this time as the director-designate of the Office of Science and Technology Policy, that is, as the new president's chief science adviser. The Geological Survey director this time testified in favor of a synthesized version of the bills he had opposed ten months earlier as a member of the previous administration. The types of witnesses to appear at this and the companion House hearing (U.S. House of Representatives 1977) were virtually identical.

The change of administration was one of two differences between the hearings of 1976 and 1977. The other was the inclusion of two sociologists, Ralph Turner (U.C.L.A.), who testified at the Senate hearing, and Eugene Haas (University of Colorado), who was a witness at the House hearing. Both were there to address the growing concern among earthquake safety advocates about the possibility of negative social, economic, and political consequences of earthquake predictions. Turner testified as the former chair of the National Academy of Sciences' Panel on the Public Policy Implications of Earthquake Predictions. Haas, codirector of the earlier hazards assessment (White and Haas 1975), appeared as a result of his role as director of a survey of households and businesses in California aimed at anticipating what they were likely to do when various kinds of earthquake predictions were issued (Haas and Mileti 1976).

CLAIMS-MAKERS AS PARTICIPANTS
IN THE NATIONAL NEWS

A third arena in which earthquake risk claims-making takes place is in news about the earthquake threat. However, identifying claims-makers through their participation in the national news presents special difficulties. National news is not a single "arena" but dozens of organizations producing separate national news products each day. Even the general audience media (Gamson and Modigliani 1989) are quite different. Among the print media are daily newspapers with national circulations (*Wall Street Journal, Christian Science Monitor, USA Today, New York Times*, etc.); weekly newsmagazines such as *Newsweek, Time*, and *U.S. News and World Report*; and a variety of magazines with different editorial missions but containing news of national interest as well as news analysis (e.g., *New Yorker, New Republic, National Review*, and *Atlantic Monthly*). Electronic news media include television (four national networks with daily news broadcasts, the Cable News Network and CNN Headline News, Public Broadcasting's "McNeil-Lehrer News Hour," etc.) and radio with local stations served by a variety of radio news networks. In addition, the advent of satellite dishes and cable systems makes local news programs, such as those from New York, Chicago, and Los Angeles stations, available to audiences around the country.

There is no single media arena with an easily accessible written record of its proceedings. Electronic media, radio in particular, are especially difficult to study. What is needed is a representative picture of the *types* of claims-makers who have had access to these media and thereby have either shaped or reinforced the public image of the risk of earthquakes. It is not necessary that every claims-maker who was ever quoted in the national news between 1964 and 1992 be identified. It is not likely that this could be done in any case. What I propose instead is to take a "snapshot" of the national news arena that is likely to capture the kinds of individuals who get the opportunity to speak about the risk of future earthquakes. This snapshot is drawn from published abstracts of the three major television networks' evening news broadcasts.

The *Television News Index and Abstracts* provided the names of individuals interviewed on camera by reporters and news anchors.[8] There were 1,269 news reports of earthquakes and earthquake threats in the evening news between 1968 and 1990, an average of just under 57 per year. Table 3.1 contains the names of the fourteen most frequently interviewed claims-makers for the period. All but one are earth scientists. The other person is an earthquake engineer. These fourteen technical experts made a total of seventy-five appearances, an average of five per person.

Table 3.1. Most Frequently Interviewed Claims-Makers, 1968–1990 (Three or More Network TV Appearances)

Name	Occupation	Appearances
Allen, Clarence A.	Earth scientist	11
Hutton, Kate	Earth scientist	11
Bolt, Bruce A.	Earth scientist	8
Raleigh, C. Barry	Earth scientist	6
Heaton, Thomas	Earth scientist	5
Sieh, Kerry	Earth scientist	5
Wesson, Robert L.	Earth scientist	5
Person, Waverly	Earth scientist	4
Stewart, David	Earth scientist	4
Wallace, Robert	Earth scientist	4
Hamilton, Robert M.	Earth scientist	3
Housner, George	Earthquake engineer	3
Jones, Lucile	Earth scientist	3
Simpson, David	Earth scientist	3

Another perspective on the appearance of claims-makers in network television news comes from examining the people who were interviewed on camera during coverage of the Loma Prieta earthquake and its aftermath. Table 3.2 contains subtotals of all such persons from October 17, the day of the earthquake, through December 31, 1989. A total of 560 people were identified by name or status (e.g., relative of victim) on network television news during this period. By far the most frequent

Table 3.2. People Appearing on Network Television News Reports of the Loma Prieta Earthquake, October 17, 1989–December 31, 1989

Type	Number	Percent
Residents, victims, relatives of victims, eyewitnesses, etc.	204	36.4
Elected officials	75	13.4
Emergency service personnel	65	11.6
Scientists, engineers, etc.	62	11.1
World Series related	51	9.1
Representatives of government agencies	27	4.8
All others	76	13.6
Total	560	100.0

were "ordinary" people, including residents of the various impacted cities, victims, survivors, and relatives of victims. These people made up more than one-third (36 percent) of those appearing on camera. Next most frequent were elected officials including President Bush, members of Congress, and mayors of several damaged cities. These officials represented 13 percent of those appearing in stories of the earthquake. Emergency services personnel, especially rescue workers and physicians, made up nearly 12 percent of the total. Scientists and engineers, including scientists from the Geological Survey and universities, comprised only 11 percent of the total number of people featured in the news. Because the earthquake occurred at the start of baseball's World Series between teams from San Francisco and Oakland, baseball officials, players, and sportswriters made up nearly 10 percent of the people appearing on camera. Representatives of government agencies such as the California Department of Transportation and FEMA were a relatively small percentage of the total (5 percent).

In general, stories about earthquakes and the threat of earthquakes make up a very small portion of network television news, judging from the *Television News Index and Abstracts*. A large proportion of earthquake stories were about earthquakes in other countries, reflecting the greater frequency of damaging earthquakes outside the United States. In general, earthquake news (to the extent that one can generalize about it based on three nightly network news broadcasts) reflects three themes, judging from the types of people appearing in it.[9] One is the theme of personal suffering and loss, reflected in the standard inclusion of disaster victims who tell of their experiences. Another is government as the principal agent of restoration, symbolized by the routine appearances of politicians inspecting damage, commiserating with victims, and assuring everyone that better times lie ahead. Third, the earthquake threat is a scientific story; our future is in the hands of technical experts. When the earthquake threat is dealt with in the news—as over against a specific earthquake disaster—television news organizations turn overwhelmingly to earth scientists to explain why earthquakes occur and what the future will hold.

THE COMPOSITION OF THE "EARTHQUAKE ESTABLISHMENT"

Information in Table 3.3 provides a general picture of the people engaged in claims-making on behalf of the earthquake treat on a national level in the United States. The data were compiled by combining the names, organizational affiliations, and, where available, job titles of

Table 3.3. Claims-Makers by Type (*N* = 329)

	Frequency	Percentage of category	Percentage of total
Academics	92	100.00	28.05
Earth science	33	35.87	10.06
Engineering	19	20.65	5.79
Social/law/economics/policy	20	21.74	6.10
Other	20	21.74	6.10
Federal government	111	100.00	33.84
Geological Survey	22	19.82	6.71
National Science Foundation	12	10.81	3.66
FEMA	20	18.02	6.10
Small Business Administration	4	3.60	1.22
All other federal agencies	53	47.75	16.16
State/local governments	34	100.00	10.37
State	25	73.53	7.62
California	17	50.00	5.18
All other	8	23.53	2.44
Local (including regional)	9	26.47	2.74
California	7	20.59	2.13
All other	2	5.88	0.61
International agencies	8	100.00	2.44
Total public sector (all levels)	153	100.00	46.65
Nonprofit sector	41	100.00	12.50
Professional associations	28	68.29	8.54
Red Cross	8	19.51	2.44
Other	5	12.20	1.52
Private sector	35	100.00	10.67
Politicians	8	100.00	2.13
Congressional	2	14.29	0.30
State	3	42.86	0.91
Local	3	42.86	0.91

earthquake experts and safety advocates appearing in the three major national arenas (i.e., the expert panel, the congressional hearing, and the television network news broadcast) into a single list.[10] The resulting list contains slightly more than three hundred names. The total number of entries in Table 3.3 is actually about 10 percent greater than this due to double-counting. For example, some people "wore two hats" (e.g., the engineering professor invited to testify because he was also chairing the California Seismic Safety Commission at the time). Others held more than one job during the study period (e.g., an academic who accepted an administrative position with a federal agency).

The data in Table 3.3 show that the individuals most frequently involved in the arenas where the earthquake threat is defined have been bureaucrats. Nearly half (47 percent) are affiliated with some local (including regional), state, federal, or international public organization. The largest contingent of these (nearly three-fourths of the people in this category) are employed by agencies of the federal government. In fact, federal officials make up more than one-third (34 percent) of the total number of names on this list. The Geological Survey, FEMA and its predecessors, and the National Science Foundation are the three most frequent agencies with whom these people are affiliated. However, representatives of a wide array of federal agencies are included in the earthquake establishment, as reflected in the large proportion (17 percent) of people on the list affiliated with other federal agencies. These include, to name only a few, the National Aeronautics and Space Administration, the National Oceanic and Atmospheric Administration, the Army Corps of Engineers, the National Institute of Standards and Technology, and the Federal Insurance Administration.

More than a quarter (28 percent) of those on the list are academics. More than half of these (57 percent of the academic category) are in the earth sciences and engineering. Somewhat surprising is the large proportion of social scientists, economists, and policy analysts in this category. This subcategory comprises 22 percent of the academic contingent and 6 percent of all those on the list.

Actually, the number of academics on this list seriously understates the size of the "technocratic" wing of the earthquake establishment. (By technocrat, I mean all those technical people—scientists, engineers, social scientists, economists, and policy analysts—whose special expertise is deemed relevant for reducing the risk of earthquakes.) Many of the individuals in the bureaucratic, nonprofit sector, and private-sector categories are also scientists or technical people with advanced degrees in fields such as geology, geophysics, and engineering. For instance, most members of the Geological Survey appearing on this list are earth scientists. Likewise, many if not all representatives of the National Science

Foundation are either engineers or specialists in some other scientific field.

A better sense of the proportion of scientists and engineers who make up the earthquake establishment, therefore, is produced by combining the academic subtotals for these categories with Geological Survey and National Science Foundation subtotals. A fairly large percentage of individuals in the private sector category are also technocrats. Including as a rough estimate one-third of the total in the private-sector category (geologists and structural engineers), one-fourth of the total from California (which includes several state geologists and other earth scientists who serve on the California Earthquake Prediction Evaluation Council), and one-fourth from the professional-association subcategory of the nonprofit sector (technocrats representing scientific and academic associations) yields 111 individuals, 33 percent of the total number of names on the list. In other words, I estimate that one-third of the claims-makers promoting the risk of earthquakes over the years have been technocrats, chiefly earth scientists and engineers.

Three other generalizations emerge from Table 3.3. First, the vast bulk of the participants in these national arenas from state and local (including regional) governments have come from California. Although state and local people make up only 10 percent of these national claims-makers, Californians make up 71 percent of them. This is not surprising. Even though the earthquake threat has been defined as nationwide in scope in recent years, the bulk of experience with the earthquake threat still comes from California.

Second, the extensiveness of involvement of representatives from the nonprofit and private sectors is somewhat surprising. Combined they make up 25 percent of the names on the list. Three things may account for this total. Participation by representatives of the insurance industry has increased in recent years; many claims-makers from the engineering professions are either self-employed or are affiliated with for-profit engineering firms; and many parties interested in earthquake risk promotion are represented by their professional associations (the National League of Cities, the U.S. Conference of Mayors, the National Association of Counties, the National Governors' Conference, the Council of State Governments, and the American Institute of Architects, to name only a few).

Third, politicians are seldom directly involved in promoting risk in these three national arenas, at least not in the same way as other claims-makers. The invisibility of members of Congress in Table 3.3 is understandable. Their role is to draft legislation and to negotiate its passage. They seldom sit in front of the microphones at the witness table. Only one senator (Cranston from California) appeared on the list as a result of doing this. Somewhat surprising, however, is the lack of involvement of state and local politicians. Less than 2 percent (six) of the names on the list were elected politicians, and half of them were participating by virtue of their having been elected head of a professional association (National League of Cities, U.S. Conference of Mayors, National Governors' Conference, etc.).

The numeric data in Table 3.3 show the composition of the earthquake establishment from only one angle. They suggest the range of people involved with the threat, and the list of names from which the data are derived comes close to being a sampling frame for the "universe" or "population" of active participants at the national level. Put differently, these data suggest patterns of participation but not patterns of influence. One way to identify who has had the greatest opportunity to influence the definition and redefinition of the earthquake threat is to identify the individual claims-makers who have appeared repeatedly over the years on panels, at hearings, and in news reports. Repeated participation suggests two qualities. One is that the individual is among the elite within the earthquake establishment. The other is that the points of view that such individuals represent reflect the more stable elements of the definition of risk.

To identify some of the elite within the earthquake establishment, I first visually inspected the list of three hundred names. Individuals on this list seemed easily divisible into two categories: those whose names were associated with only two or three activities (i.e., panel participation, hearing testimony, network news interview) and those whose activity list was much more extensive. Extensive lists of activity also meant repeated appearances over a period of time since there are relatively few opportunities in any given year. I arbitrarily chose a total of six activities as a criterion for distinguishing the more frequent from the less frequent participants. Second, I eliminated representatives (usually the head or the deputy director) of federal agencies whose activity lists were made extensive by repeated appearances before congressional committees to defend the past performance of their agencies in the aftermath of earthquakes. While also arbitrary, this criterion was intended to reduce the weight given to unique issues associated with past disasters and to increase the weight of appearances defining present and future risks.

These criteria produced a short list of twenty-two experts who, based upon their professional reputations alone, would be among the "Who's Who" of earthquake risk promoters if there were such a thing (Table 3.4). There are some well-known individuals who are not on this list. For one thing, the selection process screened out long-time earthquake safety advocates who have concentrated their efforts at state and local levels. (Chapter 4 introduces some of the people operating primarily in these

Table 3.4.   Short List of Claims-Makers, 1964–1992

Name	Degree Field	Affiliation(s)
Allen, Clarence A.	Earth science	Caltech
Beavers, James E.	Engineering	Private sector
Bernstein, George K.	Law	Fed. Insurance Agency
Bolt, Bruce A.	Earth science	UC-Berkeley
Cluff, Lloyd	Earth science	Private sector
Degenkolb, Henry J.	Engineering	Private sector
Haas, J. Eugene	Social science	U. of Colorado
Hamilton, Robert M.	Earth science	Geological Survey
Housner, George	Engineering	Caltech
Jahns, Richard H.	Earth science	Stanford U.
Kunreuther, Howard C.	Economics	U. of Pennsylvania
Lyons, John W.	Physical science	Nat. Bureau of Standards
McKelvey, Vincent E.	Earth science	Geological Survey
Newmark, Nathan M.	Engineering	U. of Illinois
Peck, Dallas L.	Earth science	Geological Survey
Press, Frank	Earth science	MIT/White House/NAS
Scott, Stanley	Social science	UC-Berkeley
Steinbrugge, Karl	Engineering	UC-Berkeley/private
Thiel, Charles C., Jr.	Operations research	NSF/private sector
Turner, Ralph H.	Social science	UCLA
Wallace, Robert	Earth science	Geological Survey
Wright, Richard N.	Engineering	Nat. Inst. Std. and Tech.

arenas.) For another, it favored people active during the peak period of federal earthquake-related policymaking in the late 1960s and early 1970s (due to the greater number of opportunities) over people active since that time. Also missing are individuals whose efforts in these national arenas were directed toward some type of hazard other than earthquakes (e.g., floods). Nevertheless, while one might quibble about whether this or that individual should have been included, the more important point is whether these are the *types* of people who make up the elite within the earthquake establishment. The short list "feels right" on that score.

Earth scientists (nine) and engineers (eight) have been the most frequent participants in these three national arenas by these criteria. Combined, they make up 77 percent of this short list. Half are academics or were academics at some point during the study period. Forty-one percent are or were at one time employed by agencies of the federal government. About one-fifth have worked in the private sector in engineering or related fields. The presence of a surprising minority of social scientists (18 percent) again underscores the fact that, whatever "skewing" exists in the image of risk in favor of the earth sciences and engineering, social scientists nevertheless have been frequent participants in national-level risk-defining activities.

CONCLUSION

This chapter contains a description of the people who have contributed to claims about the risk of earthquakes. Some—perhaps a majority— might not think of themselves as claims-makers or promoters of risk. Yet each has participated in one of the three major national arenas in which public images of the causes, solutions, and rationales associated with the earthquake threat have been shaped and reshaped over the years. Two things remain to be done. First, the identity of these claims-makers needs to be placed in some sort of context. One way of doing this is to observe what kinds of people are *missing* from the descriptions of claims-makers presented here. Second, some conclusions about what difference the composition of the earthquake establishment has made for the career of the earthquake threat can be offered.

Many of the people at the forefront of doing something about the threat that earthquakes pose to the nation have been what I call technocrats. They are the earth scientists and engineers who have described some of the causes of great earthquakes and championed some solutions for reducing their destructive potential. Some have been academics (e.g., Clarence Allen, Bruce Bolt, George Housner); others have spent the majority of their careers in federal agencies like the Geological Survey (e.g., Vincent McKelvey, Barry Raleigh, Robert Wallace) while others have moved back and forth from academia to government service (e.g., Frank Press) or between academia and the private sector (e.g., Karl Steinbrugge). A small but surprisingly robust proportion of the nation's earthquake elite have been social scientists (e.g., Ralph Turner, Howard Kunreuther). Another large segment consists of all the employees of federal agencies whose missions encompass the earthquake threat. These are agencies like FEMA, the Geological Survey, the National Institute of Standards and Technology, and many more.

Several other types of actors have played either an intermittent role or an increasingly frequent one in recent years. These are representatives of occupational and professional associations (e.g., the International Conference of Building Officials, the Council of State Governments); nonprofit organizations and institutes (e.g., Earthquake Engineering Research Institute, the American Red Cross); the private sector (especially the insurance industry, most recently through The Earthquake Project); and members of Congress (e.g., Alan Cranston, George Brown) who have sponsored earthquake hazard reduction legislation. The earthquake establishment until recently has had a decidedly West Coast—especially California—flavor. Many of its academics still are affiliated with research universities like the University of California at Berkeley, Stanford University, and the California Institute of Technology. A number of the agency people are based in California, such as the Geological Survey employees who work in Menlo Park (northern California) and Pasadena.

This is all well and good, but what does it tell us about claims-making? More importantly, what does it say about the consequences of claims-making for transforming the earthquake threat into a social problem? The answer to both questions becomes clearer when the kinds of people who are missing from the list of claims-makers are noted. Specific *kinds* of people who have been involved in promoting other social problems are conspicuous by their absence in the descriptions presented in this chapter.

Most conspicuous is the absence of *victims* and *relatives* of victims within the ranks of earthquake safety advocates. Victims or their relatives are usually among the most tireless and outspoken claims-makers in the social-problems process. This was certainly the case in two of the social problems that "came of age" in the 1980s. Candy Lightner, mother of a teenager killed by a hit-and-run driver who was legally intoxicated at the time, created a nationwide organization, Mothers Against Drunk Drivers (MADD), and became its most prominent and visible spokesperson (Reinarman 1988:96–100). John Walsh, father of Adam who was murdered in 1981, was an impassioned witness who testified at several congressional hearings on missing children in the 1980s (Best 1990:22–40).

Victims and their relatives have not played a part in promoting the risk of earthquakes. Their absence is not explained by the criteria I used to generate the list of national claims-makers. The rule that I used was to omit from these lists the names of anyone who did not appear more than once in the three public arenas. Victims as a *category* testified frequently at congressional hearings, especially lessons-learned hearings conducted near the site of damage and destruction. They could be seen routinely on television news broadcasts about earthquake disasters. Their plight was often tragic, and their grievances were real, but their function was more that of "stage prop" than claims-maker. They were chosen by reporters, congressional staff members, and other "gatekeepers" as symbols of disaster rather than as new champions of a cause. There are no Candy Lightners and John Walshs within the earthquake establishment. Significantly, I could find no victims listed as members of expert panels, commissions, and committees.

Victims and relatives of victims are not the only types of people noticeably absent from the ranks of claims-makers. With only one exception, there are also no lawyers on the lists described in this chapter.[11] Some of the higher-level people representing federal agencies were undoubtedly law school graduates, and legal advice, especially on matters of liability, is always close at hand where public policies are concerned. However, there are no individuals among the earthquake risk promoters whose legal interests or careers have led them to play active roles in this public issue. Lawyers as claims-makers (rather than litigants) have been involved in other safety issues such as those related to product liability, the safety of the workplace (e.g., Draper 1991:141–74), and the antismoking movement (Troyer and Markle 1983). Other occupational groups are absent as well. Stockbrokers, financial investment councilors, and business and economic leaders in general have had little to contribute to the promotion of the earthquake threat. They have been opponents of specific "solutions" to this threat at various times, however.

Given these patterns of participation in claims-making, some conclusions can be drawn not only about why some claims but not others have been advanced about the earthquake threat but also about why claims have been advanced in some ways but not others. It is clear that claims-making on behalf of the earthquake threat has been carried out by "insiders." It is in the hands of experts. The process has not encompassed "amateurs" and ordinary citizens. These insiders and specialists have not run off everyone else. On the contrary, they would most likely welcome some forms of assistance by "outsiders." Few people have been interested enough to participate, however. Experts have assumed ownership of the promotion of risk by default. The result is a definition of risk, including both causes and solutions, that now makes it difficult for ordinary citizens to join in.

Gatekeepers of the national arenas (e.g., members of Congress and congressional committee staffs, news reporters and news researchers) in which claims-making takes place by and large share this insider definition of risk. Their decisions regarding appropriate expert witnesses and relevant news sources select in the people who have shaped this definition and screen out those who have not. The primary role assigned to ordinary citizens is to be prepared. If promoting the earthquake threat were a war, experts would be the frontline soldiers and everyone else would be a civilian on the home front supporting the war effort.

Whether they be earth scientists, engineers, bureaucrats, or social scientists, people who promote the risk of future earthquakes share three common characteristics. They are people of reason. They are people who work within the system. And they are people who are relatively powerless.

Earthquake claims-makers are people of reason in the sense that their worldviews are grounded in a rational approach to problem-solving. Earth scientists, engineers, and social scientists work within deductive systems of logic in which hypothesis, research design, data, and laws of probability are the basis for reaching rational conclusions. Career bureaucrats calculate odds, select strategies (political ones, of course), and apply cause-effect logic to achieve the objectives in what is essentially a political universe (see Nakamura and Smallwood 1980). For all of them, rationality demands that, once solutions to a problem have been identified, they must be implemented in the public interest. Facts suggest "the right thing to do." To fail to do so is to act "irrationally."

The absence of victims from the ranks of claims-makers means that the rhetoric of risk usually lacks the passion displayed in the promotion of social problems. Scientists and federal officials may be enraged by actions that they define as creating rather than reducing risk, but their rage is directed at acts of irrationality and stupidity. Theirs is not the moral outrage frequently found in the rhetoric of social problems associated with the "evils" of alcohol, drugs, or life-style (see Gusfield 1981:173–85; see also the discussion of rhetorical idioms in Ibarra and Kitsuse 1993:35–41).

Claims about the risk of earthquakes are statements about safety. They describe the issue as one in which lives, property, and personal well-being are all at risk. Solutions include knowledge, public policy, and voluntary preparedness by individuals. These are rational approaches, and appeals on their behalf are rational as well. In other words, these claims feature what Best (1990:43–44) calls the rhetoric of rationality. Best argues that claims-makers who use the rhetoric of rationality assume that their audience is a persuadable one; it can be won over with well-reasoned arguments. It is also an audience that is assumed to be nonhostile. In contrast is what he calls the rhetoric of rectitude. This form promotes claims in terms that are moralistic in nature. The rhetoric of rectitude is directed at an audience assumed to be hostile or at best indifferent; it highlights basic values in order to outrage the uncommitted into action. In claims-making about the risk of earthquakes, the rhetoric of rectitude is virtually absent. The rhetoric of rationality predominates. The claims-making "style" (Ibarra and Kitsuse 1993:49–53) is consistently scientific.

Second, claims-makers are insiders in the halls of government. Bureaucrats obviously are insiders by virtue of being public servants employed by the government. Scientists are insiders in two senses. They are part of a government-funded research establishment, receiving grants and participating in peer review of their fellow scientists' grant proposals to agencies such as the Geological Survey and the National Science Foundation. They are also insiders in the sense that they are part of the science advisory apparatus that is called upon (and often calls upon itself) to shape government policy. Many of these policy advisory efforts have occurred through ad hoc committees organized by such executive-branch departments as the Office of Science and Technology Policy. Other policy-related activities have been part of the ongoing advisory role of the National Academy of Sciences and the National Academy of Engineering. More recently, a National Earthquake Hazard Reduction Program advisory committee has been created, half of whose members are earth scientists and engineers. In other words, these claims-makers do not have to set fire to police cars in order to gain access to the policymaking process.

On the other hand, having access to policymaking arenas and having influence over policymakers are two different things. Earthquake safety advocates on the whole are a relatively powerless lot. Scientists may have impressive credentials and appointments at prestigious universities, but they have never had much political clout in the United States. Civil servants by law work for politicians and are expected to be nonpartisan in order to be able to work with whichever party controls the White House and Congress. Even after attention-focusing events such as earthquakes, claims-makers have difficulty being heard. Typically, politicians swamp legislative arenas after earthquake disasters with their own proposals, burying claims-makers' more carefully crafted legislation (May 1985; Mittler 1991). California's recently scuttled earthquake insurance program, created amid the legislative avalanche following the Loma Prieta earthquake but canceled when analysts showed it to be badly underfunded (Mulligan 1992), is just one example. Recognizing that they are at a political disadvantage, claims-makers tread lightly when promoting policy proposals that they perceive can mobilize opposition from well-connected constituents (e.g., real estate developers, insurance industry representatives).

In sum, most of those promoting the risk of earthquakes are insiders. Their occupations and outlook have shaped the content of claims in ways that make it difficult for a broad-based constituency to join the "cause." Their insider status has given them access to policymaking arenas without the support of any outside power base. The advantages and disadvantages of claims-making under these circumstances is revealed in an examination of the arenas in which claims are made.

NOTES

1.   Clearly, descriptions and accounts of past events create images of what earthquakes are like. However, eyewitness accounts, etc., only become part of

the claims-making process when they are used to promote future threats, by the eyewitnesses themselves or by others who use their accounts in promoting risk.

2.   I have selected documents that both reflect and determine how the threat is viewed in general within the earthquake establishment. Collectively, they represent something akin to a "collective definition of the situation" even though it is not universally shared.

3.   The RANN program funded research whose results were deemed vital to practitioners regardless of the scientific priority of such projects within academic disciplines.

4.   My files contain a list of 159 such hearings identified through the *CIS U.S. Congressional Committee Hearings Index*.

5.   Many of the seventy or so hearings omitted from consideration here are tangential to claims-making about the earthquake threat though they may be significant in other respects. For example, I have omitted several hearings by both House Ways and Means and Senate Appropriations Committees dealing with "routine" affairs such as the budget of the Geological Survey and the National Science Foundation. Numerous other hearings dealt with federal disaster relief policy and with reauthorization of the Earthquake Hazard Reduction Act during the 1980s. Matters raised in these hearings that affect claims about the risk of earthquakes will be introduced where relevant.

6.   The name had been changed from the Office of Emergency Planning following a reorganization of the Executive Branch in 1968.

7.   To follow the career of this agency within the federal government, including the changes in its name that resulted from each new reorganization, see May (1985:49–56).

8.   These abstracts do not cover the entire study period, having first been compiled in August 1968. In addition, the television news abstracts give no indication of which persons reporters or researchers might have consulted in preparing their stories but did not interview on camera.

9.   One often overlooked trait of news organizations increases my confidence in the representativeness of the patterns of news participation described here. This is the tendency for news organizations to cover each other better than any other segment of society. Put differently, when a story appears in one place (say, *Newsweek* or on the NBC "Nightly News"), there is a high probability that the same story also will appear in other media (say, *Time* magazine or the CBS "Evening News"). Even though the same individuals may not be interviewed, it is highly likely that the same *type* of individuals will be used by several news organizations. These three news organizations may not be "typical" of all news media, but their news products are probably as representative as any of the ways earthquake news is covered in the United States.

10.   As mentioned elsewhere, people testifying as disaster victims at congressional hearings were not included unless they appeared at more than a single hearing. Thus, the list is biased intentionally in favor of "professional" claims-makers and away from "amateurs" advancing local grievances.

11.   George Bernstein, trained in law and a Federal Insurance Administration administrator for many years, is the lone exception.

4

Public Arenas and the Promotion of Earthquake Risks

Claims-makers use public settings to promote claims about putative conditions such as the risk of earthquakes, but they do not control any of them. People other than the claims-makers themselves control access to such arenas and, to a certain extent, manage what goes on in them. The gatekeepers and managers of the various public arenas have interests of their own that are seldom identical to the interests of claims-makers. Furthermore, the nature of the arenas themselves—not only their carrying-capacity (Hilgartner and Bosk 1988:58–61) but also their structure and culture—both facilitates and constrains the claims-making process. Public arenas, in other words, are not merely empty canvases on which claims-makers paint at will. Arena gatekeepers and managers make it either easy or difficult to advance particular causes, rationales, and solutions related to the earthquake threat. Hence, the definition of risk visible in one arena—television network news, for instance—may differ from the definition that prevails in another such as a congressional hearing.

Hilgartner and Bosk (1988) present an explicit model showing how characteristics of public arenas affect the careers of social problems. Ibarra and Kitsuse (1993:53–56) propose that claims-making is "context sensitive" and call for examination of the ways in which settings (e.g., media, legal-political, and academic) affect the social-problems process. Taking a similar tack, I argue that the promotion of risk emphasizes some elements rather than others as a function of the arenas or settings in which claims-makers either choose or are forced to operate. I will begin to explore the influence of public arenas on claims-making by revisiting the three national arenas already introduced (i.e., expert panels and committees, congressional hearings, and television network news). The focus this time will be on the arenas themselves and how they produce an emphasis on some aspects of risk but not others. Then I will examine some of the other arenas in which definitions of risk

emerge. These include state and local government, television documentaries, and popular-entertainment movies.

NATIONAL-LEVEL ARENAS

The only characteristic noted about the public arenas examined thus
far was that they are all nationwide in scope. That is, the products of
expert panels, congressional hearings, and network news are aimed at
the nation as a whole (e.g., an evening news broadcast, a federal statute,
or a set of policy recommendations for reducing the nation's exposure to
risk). Arenas as processes of activity bounded in time and space are not
autonomous. They are controlled by organizations whose purposes are
usually quite different from those who participate in them. For example,
the evening news consists of a series of stories woven from text and
pictures for the purpose of chronicling selected events of the day, for
competing with other news organizations, for advancing the careers of
reporters, etc. The individuals and groups featured in the news have
little or no interest in these objectives. People who manage public arenas
make choices about whom they allow to participate and about what
participants will be invited to contribute. Exactly how participants and
participation are managed affects the claims-making process and its
prospects for successful social-problem promotion.

The Expert Panel as Arena

Expert panels that examine policy issues for the federal government
do not originate in the personal concerns of scientists and mid-level
bureaucrats. They are usually initiated by "higher-ups" within the executive branch. Examples such as Lyndon Johnson's launching of several
panels, including the Ad Hoc Interagency Working Group for Earthquake Research, after the Alaska earthquake in 1964, and Jimmy Carter's
creation of the Committee on Assessment of Consequences and Preparation for a Major California Earthquake in 1980 are unusual only in the
personal involvement of the two presidents. Members of the White
House staff may be involved in setting broad outlines for a panel's objectives, but specific decisions about whom to invite and what specific tasks
they are to undertake are usually in the hands of the managers of administrative departments and agencies. Many of the organizations handling
the details of these arrangements are dominated by physical scientists
and engineers (e.g., the Office of Science and Technology Policy, the

National Academy of Sciences, the National Academy of Engineering), and physical scientists and engineers usually make up a majority of panel participants. However, the choice of participants also reflects the prevailing conventional wisdom about what disciplines and areas of expertise will be required to produce a final product. Therefore, economists, legal scholars, social scientists, and policy analysts may also be included in combinations that vary with the specific topic to be investigated.

The way in which the expert panel as an arena is managed has a number of consequences for claims-making about the earthquake threat. Even though ultimate control of this process rests with political appointees, earthquake panels in general are not political affairs. Quite the contrary. They are among the most apolitical, nonpartisan activities in government service. They have political consequences precisely because they are apolitical. That is, the conditions of their formation and the auspices under which they work limit the process to scientific, technical, and public-policy matters. A case can easily be made that one of the chief functions of the expert panel is to maintain the nonpolitical status of natural hazards such as the risk of earthquakes. If scientific and technological solutions for reducing risk could actually be found, then political fallout from a future catastrophic event would be eliminated. If not, at least the administration had put "the nation's best minds" to work. In short, it is not that this arena is politicized. On the contrary, by providing a boundary around what is acceptable, the process keeps the focus on scientific and technical elements of the earthquake threat. The likelihood of causes or solutions emerging that would damage the party in control of the White House is highly unlikely.

The fact that these panels and committees in effect are part of the federal government also has consequences for promoting the risk of earthquakes. As both "host" and sponsor of these expert panels, the federal government, implicitly or explicitly (e.g., through agenda control) casts itself in the role of "solution." If there are "problems" that interfere with its ability to reduce risk, then they must lie elsewhere. For example, the federal government is a major sponsor of research on the science and engineering aspects of earthquakes. The results of this research are intended to be one of the solutions to the threat. If it is perceived that research findings are not being put to use, then those who are ignoring research results must be causing the unacceptably high levels of risk. This conclusion is made more likely by the presence on the panels of representatives of the agencies that both fund and conduct such research. Because they are users rather than producers of research, state and local governments often become one of the causes of the "problem" from the perspective of the federally sponsored expert panel.

At the same time, panel members tend to be polite to their federal hosts. Their final reports are more likely to politely recommend "increasing commitment" for research and development on the part of the federal government, for example, than to condemn it for a lack of commitment in the past.

The point is not that experts' judgments are compromised by the fact that panels and committees are launched by political appointees. Rather, the arena in which panelists participate invites them to see conditions one way (i.e., from the standpoint of what benefits the country as a whole) rather than another (e.g., what would benefit only a single state).[1] In fact, most federal officials engaged in reducing the risk of earthquakes would welcome greater direct involvement in the threat by presidential administrations. The general absence of interest at the very highest levels is signaled by how far agency people sometimes have to go to make it appear otherwise. For example, the Office of Emergency Preparedness played up Richard Nixon's commitment to hazard reduction in the preface to its 1972 report by quoting from the president's most recent state-of-the-union message. In the quotation the president seemed to pledge to undertake "new or accelerated activities aimed at . . . reducing the loss of life from earthquakes, hurricanes, and other natural disasters" (Office of Emergency Preparedness 1972:ii, ellipsis in the original). Actually, the two parts of this quotation were several pages apart under the heading Science and Technology in the written version of the speech. Most of the president's address dealt with new roles for research and development as the country moved from a wartime to a peacetime economy with the Vietnam War winding down. The president made no mention of disasters in the speech he actually gave to Congress. The quoted materials appear only in the written version (Nixon 1974).

The expert panel influences claims-making about the threat of earthquakes in two ways. First, panels and committees typically produce a report describing the causes of the threat and offering recommendations for reducing it. The prestige of the organizations issuing the report (e.g., the National Academy of Sciences) confers legitimacy on both causes and recommendations. Second, members of these panels—especially the chairs of the panels—become more likely than other claims-makers to be invited to appear in other arenas as a direct result of their panel participation. The gatekeepers of other arenas such as congressional staff members (who prepare lists of potential expert witnesses) and television news producers identify experts on the topic through their service in this arena. In general, the products of and participants on expert panels perpetuate an image of risk that is generally acceptable to the people who manage this arena. While not claims-makers themselves, political appointees and career bureaucrats influence claims-making by selecting participants and setting agendas.

The Congressional Hearing as Arena

The basic features of this arena are well-known. Congress is one of three branches of the federal government. The executive branch oversees the myriad agencies and departments (the federal "bureaucracy") that implement its policies. Policies are formally adopted in Congress, where an array of committees and subcommittees, each having responsibility over specified policy areas, does much of the early formulation of legislation. Congress is a representative body, meaning that it is appropriate for constituents to expect their elected representatives to work on their behalf. Under the Constitution, the federal government has limited powers and authorities; power is divided among federal, state, and local governments. Precedent is an important value as it is in other arenas; Congress is more likely to entertain policies for which a precedent already exists in the United States Code. Finally, Congress's willingness to provide goods and services directly is constrained by the principle of "market failure" (Mittler 1992). That is, public "solutions" tend not to emerge when alternatives are provided by the private sector.

Less well understood are the ways in which these features shape claims-making about the earthquake threat. In fact, they are a major reason why the definition of risk in this arena stresses four themes that are less evident in others: (1) earthquakes threaten the nation as a whole; (2) earthquake prediction is a major "solution" for dealing with the threat; (3) the earth sciences and engineering should share most of the federal research dollars; and (4) earthquake mitigation is the preferred strategy for reducing risk. They also account for why other strategies such as earthquake insurance and mandatory seismic renovations are less well established in the federal approach to the threat.

The risk of earthquakes has been on the federal government's agenda with fluctuating levels of priority since the Alaska earthquake in 1964. More often than not it was a low salience, back-burner issue in so far as congressional committees were concerned (Wright and Rossi 1981). A federal policy specific to the threat finally emerged in 1977. One reason for the length of time before such a policy was adopted is the nature of Congress as an arena for claims-making. For a federal policy addressing a putative condition like the threat of earthquakes to be adopted, two questions must be answered: Why is this a matter for federal policymaking? Why should individual members of Congress support a policy once it has been formulated?

Scientists provided the rationale for both questions in the 1960s; it is shown pictorially in the 1969 seismic risk map of the U.S. prepared by the Geological Survey (Algermissen 1970). Federal policymaking was justified because the putative condition is national, not local. It is not a matter for which California alone is responsible. Major seismic risks exist in western Washington State, the Salt Lake City area, the mid–Mississippi River Valley, most of South Carolina, and eastern Massachusetts in addition to most of California and Nevada, according to earth scientists.

Congress's view of the earthquake threat did not automatically change because scientists published a map. The information provided by such a map had to be used by sponsors of federal earthquake hazard legislation to legitimate policy proposals and gain support for their passage. The California Democratic congressional delegation made sure that its colleagues, including Republican colleagues, knew about the national scope of this putative condition. Senator Tunney developed one argument for why the federal government had a stake in the earthquake threat following the San Fernando earthquake in 1971. The following exchange took place between Tunney and George Bernstein, then the federal insurance administrator, over the issue of government versus private-sector responsibilities in providing earthquake insurance:

> Senator TUNNEY. ". . . Do you suggest that we ban California because it has an earthquake problem?"
> Mr. BERNSTEIN. "No, sir; but I do suggest that Nebraskans or New Yorkers or anyone else should not run to Washington expecting funding on private problems—problems which are very often local and self-imposed by locational and structural decisions; that they do the best they can to protect themselves. . . ."
> Senator TUNNEY. "Well, of course, you are talking about one-tenth of the population of the United States when you are talking about California; so it is more than just a local problem in the sense of your use of the terminology local." (U.S. Senate 1971:324)

Tunney's argument was in effect that federal policy was appropriate whenever a substantial proportion of the nation's total population (10 percent, in this case) was affected, regardless of where such people were located.

Claims-makers from California provided additional ammunition that contributed to expanding the scope of the threat beyond that state's boundaries, thus making it a national issue. Most did so by expanding the geographical scope of the condition, emphasizing that greater risks existed in other parts of the country than in California. For example, Karl Steinbrugge testified in 1976:

It is my personal point of view that the single greatest disaster to strike the United States, from the point of view of earthquake, will not be in California. It will be in the east of the Rocky Mountains. Larger life loss and property damage will occur in the area where these is no preparedness at all. And it will be catastrophic, far greater here in the East, than it will be in the West. It is a national problem. (U.S. House of Representatives 1976:170)

Testifying later at the same hearing, an engineering professor from the Massachusetts Institute of Technology agreed, calling the loss potential in the East and Midwest "staggering" (U.S. House of Representatives 1976:217).

The nationwide scope of this putative condition was not introduced unilaterally by earth scientists and engineers, however. Many expert witnesses were explicitly asked to testify about the existence of risk outside California. For example, the chair of the House subcommittee that held hearings in 1976 was from Missouri. His staff invited a geophysicist from Saint Louis University to testify: "At the request of the Honorable James W. Symington, Chairman of the Subcommittee on Science, Research and Technology, my description will concern earthquakes in the eastern and midwestern United States" (U.S. House of Representatives 1976:155). Later, this same earth scientist added: "Although large earthquakes occur relatively infrequently east of the Rocky Mountains, no state is free from suffering some effects of earthquakes" (U.S. House of Representatives 1976:155).

Part of the congressional maneuvering to establish a federal earthquake hazard policy required that Democrats win over as many votes as they could among their Republican colleagues. A key to this effort was to line up support for such legislation from members of Congress *outside* California. Democrats' efforts to change the localized image of the threat stressed both geographical and economic dimensions. The transcript of the 1977 Senate hearing illustrates how successful the California delegation had been. Adlai E. Stevenson, a Democrat from Illinois and chair of one of the subcommittees holding hearings in 1977, remarked to Frank Press: "I was surprised to find Illinois in your 39 States that have been mentioned as subject to seismic risks. I think all my constituents would be surprised" (U.S. Senate 1977:30). Even conservative Republican Senator Barry Goldwater asked:

Senator GOLDWATER. "One question. I wonder if you could furnish the committee with a list of the States that might expect earthquakes, and also a list of those that do not face this problem. Could such a list be prepared? Or, are we all exposed to possible earthquakes—I know in my State of Arizona, we say that we can't have earthquakes, but I remember three pretty good ones."
Dr. [Frank] PRESS. "Arizona does fall in the earthquake category." (U.S. Senate 1977:32–33)

Press subsequently sent committee staff the seismic risk map of the United States from the 1972 Office of Emergency Preparedness report to Congress (Office of Emergency Preparedness 1972:Volume 1, Figure 3, p. 75). Finally, Ernest Hollings, Democratic senator from South Carolina, stated on the Senate floor during debate on S. 126: "one thing I learned is that the risks from earthquakes are not just a local problem, occurring in California and Alaska" (*Congressional Record* 123, May 12, 1977:14523).

Not surprisingly, the Findings section of the Earthquake Hazards Reduction Act of 1977 (42 U.S.C. 7701) reads in part:

> The Congress finds and declares the following:
> (1) All 50 States are vulnerable to the hazards of earthquakes, and at least 39 of them are subject to major or moderate seismic risk. . . . A large portion of the population of the United States lives in areas vulnerable to earthquake hazards.

Neither politicians nor earth scientists invented the nationwide scope of seismic risk for political purposes. Mapping of risks was a product of ongoing activity by earth scientists at the Geological Survey and elsewhere. However, federal policies are made in arenas that are political, not scientific. The formal definition of risk emphasized its nationwide scope because politicians used scientific products to solve practical problems associated with formulating public policy.

A similar explanation accounts for the centrality of earthquake prediction among the solutions to the earthquake threat despite the lack of success to date in achieving a routine prediction capability. Most earth scientists were optimistic that prediction capability was right around the corner as the 1970s began. However, their enthusiasm alone would not have had the impact on policymaking that it did without considerable assistance from some members of Congress. Senators Tunney and Cranston in particular expressed a clear desire to develop an operational earthquake prediction system. Their questions of experts during numerous hearings often led witnesses beyond the carefully qualified positions in their prepared statements. What Senator Tunney had in mind in 1971 was a short-term warning system that would provide an alert twenty-four hours before an earthquake so that people could be evacuated, gas and water mains could be drained, and the water levels in dams and reservoirs could be lowered (U.S. Senate 1971:7).

California Institute of Technology seismologist Clarence Allen agreed that earthquake prediction, and even earthquake modification and control, were "legitimate and exciting research objectives" and should be a national goal (U.S. Senate 1971:565–66). On the other hand, he stressed that achieving this goal was a long way off. He called the idea of twenty-four-hour predictions "completely unrealistic" (U.S. Senate 1971:566).

Robert Wallace, earth scientist with the Geological Survey, attempted to lessen some of the committee's fixation on earthquake predictions:

> Dr. WALLACE. "If I may back up, you [Senator Tunney] keep emphasizing 'predictions,' and this is one of the elements available for earthquake hazard reduction.
>
> "There are other things like engineering, development of building codes, development of methods of land-use zoning, as well as prediction. But the whole range of things certainly has to be tackled one of these days, or we will have another great catastrophe, or a series of them." (U.S. Senate 1971:647)

Like most of their fellow earth scientists, however, both Allen and Wallace agreed that whether or not the ability to predict earthquakes would ever be realized, more money for earthquake prediction research over a ten-year period would produce a beneficial increase in basic scientific knowledge.

Throughout the premarkup hearings of the 1970s, most earth scientists offered a more balanced and cautious assessment of earthquake prediction than those of the senator and his congressional colleagues. For example, Clarence Allen appeared before the House subcommittee in the summer of 1976, this time as a result of his having chaired the National Academy of Sciences' Panel on Earthquake Prediction:

> Dr. ALLEN. "The stakes in earthquake prediction are exceedingly high; most seismologists feel that now is the time to make a national commitment to a long-term program aimed at developing a reliable and effective operational earthquake-prediction capability.
>
> "Let me try to respond to your chairman's specific questions. 'What is the present status of earthquake predictions?' There is no question but that earthquake prediction is still in the research phase, and although a few earthquake predictions have already been successful in a scientifically meaningful way, tremendous amounts of basic and applied research must be carried out before we can develop a system that permits socially meaningful predictions on a routine basis. Most, but not all, seismologists agree, however, that this is an attainable goal.
>
> 'How do you believe earthquake prediction will develop in the next few years?' Given adequate funding, it is my guess that we will be successful in predicting an earthquake in the magnitude 5 range in California within the next 5 years.
>
> "However, my own estimate is that we are at least 10 years away from the time when we shall be in a position to implement a system of routine earthquake predictions with an acceptably low false-alarm and failure rate.
>
> "In my opinion, the apparent public impression that routine prediction of earthquakes is imminent is not warranted by the present level of scientific understanding. We have a long way to go, particularly in areas involving very basic research, before an effective earthquake-prediction system will be operative or even capable of being planned in detail . . .

"It is my opinion that a truly effective earthquake-prediction program will require an annual expenditure of at least two to three times that at present, amounting to at least \$25 million per year for the next ten years." (U.S. House of Representatives 1976:143–45)

Even at the final hearing before passage of S. 126, the bill that established the earthquake hazard reduction program, earth scientists and politicians were looking at prediction capability differently. Harrison Schmitt (Republican senator from New Mexico) wondered why it would take so long to have a system up and running and expressed this concern to Frank Press, Carter administration science adviser and long-time champion of earthquake prediction:

Senator SCHMITT. "I am very curious, Mr. Press, frankly, about the length of time that you say we are talking about to begin to implement a major program. Ten years seems like an awful long time considering the kinds of things that this country has done in the past and the length of time that has been required to do them.

"For example, given the existing technology and capability for earthquake prediction, don't you think that a bright group of young men and women sitting down for about 6 months could design a precursor system, or a preliminary system that could be on the ground and implemented within a year in areas of particularly high risk such as the Palmdale area [of southern California] or places such as San Francisco or otherwise? Coming from the world that I came from, that doesn't seem to be too unreasonable, considering what is possible at least to get started on this project."

Mr. PRESS. "Senator Schmitt, I think we don't know enough right now to design and install an operating system of the kind that you suggest." (U.S. Senate 1977:27–28)

Earthquake prediction as a solution to reducing the risks of earthquakes enjoyed several advantages in this arena. First, it offered an option that Congress was fully familiar with, that is, the funding of basic and applied scientific research. There was ample precedent for federal involvement in this area, and no new organizational infrastructure needed to be erected. Second, it enjoyed the support of policy advocates both inside and outside the federal government. Task forces in the 1960s, including one headed by Frank Press, and National Academy of Sciences committees in the 1970s recommended a national commitment to it. The research community was described as ready to take up the challenge when additional funding became available. Third, a prediction system, when it was up and running, would increase the pressure on local governments to do the things the federal government was unable to force them to do under the federal structure of shared governance. A highly publicized, scientifically credible prediction would turn the public spotlight on a specific local government and on what it was or was not doing to reduce risk. The following findings in the Earthquake Hazards Reduction Act of 1977 (42 U.S.C. 7701) therefore come as no surprise:

(4) A well-funded seismological research program in earthquake prediction could provide data adequate for the design of an operational system that could predict accurately the time, place, magnitude, and physical effects of earthquakes in selected areas of the United States.
(5) An operational earthquake prediction system can produce significant social, economic, legal, and political consequences.
(6) There is a scientific basis for hypothesizing that major earthquakes may be moderated, in at least some seismic areas, by application of the findings of earthquake control and seismological research.

Congress is an intentionally political arena. Republicans and Democrats occupy different sides of the aisles of both chambers, symbolizing the differing interests of their respective parties. Part of the disagreement between the Ford administration and the California Democratic congressional delegation on earthquake legislation involved competing plans for rearranging the relationships among federal agencies. The White House had a reorganization plan to streamline the federal bureaucracy, but legislation to establish a national earthquake policy called for different relationships than those envisioned in the administration's plans. The White House was also interested in cutting overall federal spending, but the proposed earthquake program called for increased spending for research over a long period of time. Administration witnesses unanimously opposed all versions of the proposed legislation in 1976. The director of the Geological Survey, Vincent McKelvey, testified at the last hearing held during the Ford administration:

The Department is sympathetic to the general objectives of [the three major bills] and is actively involved in the administration's program to accomplish the objective of reducing risks from earthquakes. However, we would point out that the objectives of the bills can be accomplished under the existing authorities already available to Federal agencies. Indeed, as [the president's science adviser] has indicated [in his testimony], the National Science Foundation and the Geological Survey are identifying types of earthquake research and their practical applications in developing a research program plan to provide the underlying knowledge to deal with earthquake hazards. (U.S. House of Representatives 1976:32–33)

However, members of California's House delegation, including some from the president's own party, were unimpressed. Representative Barry Goldwater, Jr. (Republican-California), a member of the full committee but not a member of the subcommittee although he actively participated in the hearing, confronted the Geological Survey director:

> Mr. GOLDWATER. "Why does the administration come up with a program that obviously does not address the question? Why don't you and [the president's science adviser] and who else [*sic*] get together and come up with a comprehensive program, not just prediction and warning, but research, the whole program?"
>
> Dr. McKELVEY. "Part of the program is under development. And as [the science adviser] and I indicated, the administration will come out with it."
>
> Mr. GOLDWATER. "I do not think the program is under development. You have a study out which talks about one aspect of it. You are talking about USGS and National Science Foundation in the area of research and dollars and predictions and scientific work. But you have talked here with respect to the question Mr. Mosher [Representative Charles E. Mosher, Republican-Ohio] asked you, are you satisfied that we have a program? You said no and then you went on to enumerate numerous areas that were not adequately treated.
>
> "Now this study you have out is not going to address all of those areas."
>
> Dr. McKELVEY. "It is not presently addressing the coordination problem. But, as I indicated, I think that this is an extremely difficult problem and one that needs to be looked at."
>
> Mr. GOLDWATER. "It becomes less difficult when you begin addressing it." (U.S. House of Representatives 1976:47)

This exchange between Goldwater and McElvey alludes to two other aspects of the earthquake threat shaped by features of this arena. The operational arm, so to speak, of the federal government is the numerous departments and agencies within the executive branch that implement public policy (the Department of Defense, the Department of State, the Environmental Protection Agency, etc.). These agencies and their supporters in Congress comprise unique organizational "infrastructures" with their own interests in legislation (Heclo 1978). Lack of resolution of some of the "turf battles" among federal agencies was one of the early stumbling blocks to an earthquake hazards reduction policy.

In working out the interagency relationships and responsibilities, members of Congress and the executive branch were in effect deciding who "owned" the earthquake threat (Gusfield 1981:10). The Geological Survey retained primary responsibility for basic research in the earth sciences, including research on earthquake prediction. The National Science Foundation concentrated on programs to fund earthquake engineering studies. (The Geological Survey and the National Science Foundation were recipients of an additional appropriation of $102.5 million each to carry out their new responsibilities under the Earthquake Hazard Reduction Act of 1977.) The National Institute of Standards and Technology was given responsibility for developing and promoting seismically safe design and construction standards. FEMA retained its responsibility for providing financial and technical assistance to state and local governments for earthquake preparedness and mitigation programs. This compromise over turf also crystallized the basic components of a definition of risk (e.g., earthquake prediction, engineering, and mitigation).

Interorganizational problems nevertheless remained after passage of the Earthquake Hazards Reduction Act in 1977. Amendments were added in October 1980 (P.L. 96-472) in an attempt to clarify the situation by naming FEMA the "lead agency," making it responsible for implementing the National Earthquake Hazards Reduction Program (NEHRP).[2] Basic federal solutions to the earthquake threat parallel the missions of the agencies involved. They include: more research on the dynamics of earthquakes, including the search for changes that might signal that one is imminent (the Geological Survey); research and testing to design and construct buildings that have less likelihood of collapse (the National Science Foundation and the National Institute of Standards and Technology); and getting local jurisdictions to mitigate, prepare for, and educate about the threat (FEMA). The three-pronged attack of the earthquake threat is not simply the result of agencies "protecting their own turf" or "feathering their nests," however. More fundamentally, the federal government had the capacity to do certain things at the time a national earthquake policy was being developed, and that policy—including the image of risk described in it—reflects what its organizations were and were not capable of doing.

Another characteristic of the federal government as an arena is reflected in the image of the earthquake threat. Local government has always been the "first line of defense" in the event of disasters, but the federal government, because of vast resources produced by its greater taxing capability, has always been close behind to provide funds for rebuilding and recovery. After two decades of expansion of the amount and type of aid available to local jurisdictions (May 1985:17–47), federal officials have been trying to increase local governments' commitment to keeping the amount of potential damage and loss to a minimum (May and Williams 1986:2–11). Under shared governance, the ability of the federal government to force local governments to do this is severely limited. The term *mitigation* is not merely a heading for policy tools such as zoning ordinances and building codes. It is a code word for conflict between federal and local governments over "acceptable costs." By stressing mitigation as a high-priority solution to the earthquake threat, federal policymakers were trying to put more pressure on local and state governments to make decisions that would reduce the need for federal disaster aid in future earthquake disasters.

The emphasis on mitigation is not unique to claims-making about the risk of earthquakes. It spilled over from a debate about disaster relief taking place at the same time that the California delegation, led by Senator Cranston, was beginning to push for a national earthquake program. Several individuals in Congress and in the Nixon administration were alarmed by the increasing generosity of disaster relief legislation written by a Democratic-controlled Congress in the 1960s (e.g., P.L. 91-606 carried by Indiana Democrat Birch Bayh). Many felt that local jurisdictions were intentionally exposing themselves to risk knowing that "Uncle" and his "deep pockets" would come to their aid if disaster ever struck. A series of disasters between 1964 and 1974 that included hurricanes, floods, and the earthquakes in Alaska and Los Angeles prompted another look at federal disaster relief policy. The Senate Public Works Committee's Subcommittee on Disaster Relief held an amazing total of six hearings at five different locations around the country over a twelve-month period (U.S. Senate 1973–1974). The result was a new piece of enabling legislation, the Disaster Relief Act of 1974 (P.L. 93-288).

Just how effective the 1974 act was in curbing Congress's "generosity" is debatable as losses eligible for federal aid continued to expand after its passage (May 1985:23–27). One thing the act did do was codify the word *mitigation* in discussions of disasters of all types. Section 101(b)(5) of the Disaster Relief Act encouraged "hazard mitigation measures to reduce losses from disasters, including development of land use and construction guidelines" and made future federal assistance contingent on local mitigation efforts (Section 406). It reemphasized what had been the case since 1950, namely, that federal aid after a disaster was supplemental to aid from other sources (e.g., state and local governments), although May (1985:26–27) concludes that the full implications of this term were not pursued in 1974. Local and state governments, through their representative associations, lobbied successfully to minimize even more disadvantageous (to them) increases in the state and local shares of post-disaster costs (May 1985:27).[3]

The conflict between federal and local governments over who pays what share of the costs of disasters and where responsibility lies for controlling those costs spilled over into policy formulations for dealing with the earthquake threat. Bills introduced by Senator Cranston and others before the adoption of the new disaster relief act in 1974 (e.g., S. 3173, S. 3392, and S. 3584, all introduced in the second session of Congress in 1972) make no mention of mitigation. After 1974, a later version of Senator Cranston's bill (S. 1174, introduced in the first session of the 94th Congress) was titled the "Earthquake Disaster Mitigation Act of 1975." Eventually, the Earthquake Hazards Reduction Act of 1977 gave high priority to mitigation though without including the term in its

The relatively low levels of concern about the risk of earthquakes outside California is by now an accepted truism within the earthquake establishment.[4] Rossi, Wright, and Weber-Burdin (1982:39–67) documented the lack of perceived seriousness among state and local elites.[5] Compared with other problems in twenty states, earthquakes averaged a 1.44 rating on a scale of 1 to 10 where the score 1 meant "no problem at all" (Rossi et al. 1982:40, Table 3.1 and footnote b). Among local elites, earthquakes compared with other concerns received an even lower average rating, 1.18. Absence of concern within the public at large is continually documented in nationwide samples of households (see Chapter 1). Indeed, most federal officials take for granted "the low priority given to the earthquake hazard by the many state and local governments, many private-sector entities, and the public at large" (Office of Earthquakes and Natural Hazards 1993, "Executive Summary," p. vii).

Claims-making activity is present in many state and local jurisdictions, however, despite its apparent lack of success. The question here is about how claims-making is affected by the characteristics of these two arenas. Two examples, one from Los Angeles and one from St. Louis, bring several features of these local arenas to light.

Los Angeles and the Creation of Division 88

California is usually cited as the state where claims-makers have had the most success in getting local government to deal with the earthquake threat. That assessment is certainly accurate relative to the other forty-nine states. However, California's reputation obscures the many defeats claims-makers have experienced along the way and the unevenness of their influence across the state's nearly four hundred local jurisdictions. The City of Los Angeles stands out as one that has been responsive to claims-makers demands. In particular, it has been an exemplar for programs dealing with unreinforced masonry buildings, a particularly troublesome earthquake safety issue in the eyes of insiders. The Los Angeles Building Code is regarded within the earthquake establishment as a seismic "success story," especially Division 88. Division 88 is a section of the local building code requiring the retrofitting of essential and high-occupancy buildings constructed before seismic provisions took effect in October 1933. Division 88 was one of the earliest efforts to deal with structures considered to be the most dangerous in earthquakes and has been a model for other cities around the state. This seismic success story took eight years to write, however. (The account that follows is based upon Alesch and Petak 1986:57–79.)

The story begins two years after the earthquake in the San Fernando

Valley. Los Angeles City Council member (later mayor) Tom Bradley in 1973 introduced an ordinance to study the feasibility of creating a seismic rehabilitation program like the one implemented two years earlier by the city of Long Beach. Initial attention focused on run-down movie theaters, partly because they were "high density, public assembly buildings" often filled with children and—paradoxically—partly because many were places where pornographic movies were shown (Alesch and Petak 1986:58). A proposed 1974 ordinance targeting these buildings for seismic upgrading or demolition drew strong opposition from the Association of Motion Picture and Television Producers and from the California Society of Theater Historians (many old movie theaters in Los Angeles are quite ornate and have interesting histories). Their opposition forced the city's Building and Safety Commission to hold a series of public hearings at which building owners complained about the absence of any provision for financing the required repairs.

A revised proposal was eventually trotted out in 1976 that added to the previously targeted theaters all pre-1934 buildings with a potential occupancy of one hundred or more people. This proposed ordinance was supported by the city's building department staff, the Structural Engineers' Association of Southern California, the state's newly formed Seismic Safety Commission, and many academics. Increased safety for building occupants was the primary issue for these advocates, but the financial burden on owners for repairs and the possibility of secondary repercussions (loss of housing stock, business flight to other cities in the region, etc.) was on everyone's mind. While possible financing mechanisms were being explored, the city council's Building and Safety Committee proposed that warning signs be posted on potentially hazardous buildings until they were either rehabilitated or torn down. Opponents mobilized almost immediately, including the Hollywood Chamber of Commerce (many of the targeted structures were in Hollywood), the Apartment Association of Los Angeles County headed by Howard Jarvis (soon to organize the successful property tax limitation initiative known by its number on the ballot, Proposition 13), and owners of commercial property. A key argument of these opponents, stressed by Jarvis, was, "Costs of repair would be an amount equal to 80% of the replacement cost of the entire structure" (quoted in Alesch and Petak 1986:64). Another opposition argument was uncertainty: "Now I've heard everything! Our brilliant City Council is going to tear down 14,000 buildings because there *might* be an earthquake that *might* knock these buildings down and the people *might* get hurt" (from a citizen's written comments to the Building and Safety Committee, quoted in Alesch and Petak 1986:66, emphasis in the original letter).

Supporters of the proposed posting ordinance, including the Los An-

geles Chamber of Commerce, the State Historical Building Code Advisory Board, and engineering faculty from a local university, argued that
the safety of occupants outweighed the economic concerns of building
owners. Their argument was summed up several months later in a letter
to the city council from Charles Richter, California Institute of Technology earth scientist and creator of the scale expressing the amount of
energy released by earthquakes: "I do not overlook problems of relocat-
ing present occupants, nor the loss of income to property owners; but
these points are secondary to the obvious issue of life and death" (quoted in Alesch and Petak 1986:70). Earthquakes were an especially salient
issue in southern California in 1976 (Turner et al. 1986:25–60) with the
public disclosure of the land uplift known as the Palmdale Bulge, the
Whitcomb "earthquake prediction hypothesis test" (see Chapter 3), and
the prediction of an earthquake by amateur scientist Henry Minturn (see
Chapter 6). Still, opposition to the several proposed ordinances based
upon projected costs of repairs resulted in another feasibility study but
no additions to the building code after four years of effort.

Supporters of an ordinance for seismic rehabilitation received welcome news in 1980. Results of studies commissioned by the city showed
the average cost of earthquake strengthening to be 20 percent of replacement costs, not 80 percent as Howard Jarvis and other opponents of
earlier proposals had argued. Compromises soon were reached on related issues such as what to do about buildings with cultural or historical
value and how much time building owners would be given to make
repairs. An environmental impact report prepared by the city's planning
department identified significant negative impacts of the proposed rehabilitation ordinance, but the department cited reducing loss of life as an
"overriding consideration" and supported the newest proposal: "The
hazard to life in the event of a major earthquake would be substantially
alleviated, with perhaps a five-fold reduction in anticipated casualties"
(cited in Alesch and Petak 1986:75). Earthquake safety advocates in city
government, including successive heads of the Building and Safety Department and the city council member chairing the Building and Safety
Committee, continued to work behind the scenes. The National Security
Council assessment of likely deaths and injuries in a catastrophic southern California earthquake (FEMA 1980) was cited by these and other
supporters during council debate on the latest proposed ordinance.
Finally, despite repeated complaints from property owners about the
costs of rehabilitation and the absence of financing, the Los Angeles
City Council passed the ordinance creating Division 88 in January 1981
by a vote of eleven to three. Mayor Tom Bradley signed it into law almost eight years to the day after his original motion for a feasibility
study.

The City of St. Louis vs. the Department
of Housing and Urban Development

Earth scientists, members of Congress, and federal bureaucrats may see the earthquake threat as a nationwide condition, but outside California local governments and citizens alike act as though they were unaware of any seismic risks threatening them. Scientists some time ago identified the mid–Mississippi River Valley as an active fault zone, naming it after the town nearest the epicenter of a series of spectacular earthquakes in 1811–1812. The city (and county) of St. Louis is the largest city in this New Madrid Fault Zone and has the greatest concentration of older buildings considered most susceptible to failure in an earthquake. In the 1970s the city's building code was based on BOCA (Building Officials and Code Administrators) Zone I standards, which meant in effect that there were no seismic safety requirements for either new construction or existing structures. Concerned about the possibility of damage and loss in St. Louis in the event of a catastrophic earthquake on the New Madrid Fault, the federal Department of Housing and Urban Development (HUD) notified the city in 1976 that it would require seismic rehabilitation of older buildings as a precondition for any FHA (Federal Housing Authority) or VA (Veterans Administration) loan. (The following account is based on Drabek et al. 1983:93–99.)

The fight in St. Louis technically was over two sets of building codes, the BOCA Zone I standards with nonexistent seismic requirements (defended by the city) and the UBC (Uniform Building Code) Zone II standards, which had specific seismic requirements for existing structures (favored by HUD). The city opposed the tougher UBC Zone II standards on grounds that they would harm an already depressed local economy. The city received support from local members of the American Society of Civil Engineering, who agreed that the BOCA Zone I requirements were sufficient for the St. Louis area. St. Louis County opposed the new standards because it viewed them as the first step toward seismic requirements for new construction, a move that it feared would slow county development. The few local earth scientists who supported the new standards came under heavy pressure from opponents; one was publicly labeled "a traitor to the City of St. Louis" by a city official (Drabek et al. 1983:96). The strength of local opposition caused a split within the HUD ranks over the merits of insisting on the new standards. Supporters of the tougher standards within HUD viewed the conflict as a life-or-death struggle for its national earthquake policy. They feared that losing in St. Louis would undermine HUD's ability to implement that policy elsewhere.

HUD officials pressed their argument that the proposed UBC Zone II standards were needed to reduce loss of life and property damage. They imported earth scientists from California to speak in favor of their proposal. Local engineers continued to speak in opposition and argued that seismic safety objectives could just as readily be achieved under existing BOCA Zone I code requirements. Housing and development interests complained that the proposed standards would be a "deathblow" to their industries. City officials challenged the certainty of the risk of earthquakes in the St. Louis area. They argued that inclusion of the city in the New Madrid Fault Zone was actually a mistake that had occurred as the result of a map-maker's error, that the average time interval between earthquakes in the fault zone was not known with certainty, and that the damage potential of a repeat 1811–1812 earthquake was unknown. Opponents of UBC Zone II appealed directly to the HUD secretary to exempt St. Louis from its national policy, solicited assistance from the Missouri congressional delegation (which it received), and welcomed additional pressure on the HUD secretary from the Council of Mayors, the National League of Cities, and the Home Builders' Association. City officials interviewed by Drabek and members of his research team were convinced that the city would be better off in the long run if it did nothing about earthquake rehabilitation and let federal disaster aid pay for any damage resulting from a future earthquake (Drabek et al. 1983:99). In the end a compromise of sorts was worked out. HUD excluded St. Louis from its new national policy, but later insisted that UBC Zone II be applied to multifamily housing units before FHA and VA loans would be guaranteed.

Other State and Local Arenas

State government except in California has not been a setting that has seen a lot of claims-making about the risk of earthquakes. State governments seem to confine themselves to relatively noncontroversial threat-related activities such as maintaining an emergency management organization responsible for disaster planning, calling out the National Guard if disaster strikes, and handling the paperwork for requests for federal disaster aid submitted by local governments. Most states delegate earthquake matters to local jurisdictions and provide few resources to assist them. A recent examination of earthquake policymaking and programs in six states other than California considered to be at risk by earth scientists (Massachusetts, Missouri, South Carolina, Tennessee, Utah, and Washington) found few existing programs as well as budget constraints that make new ones unlikely (Building Technology, Inc., 1990:61–67).

California is the "star" among the fifty states in terms of earthquake consciousness. Its creation in the 1970s of a group of advisers made up

of earth scientists from around the state to evaluate the merits of earthquake predictions for the governor's office is frequently offered as an
example of its responsiveness to the threat. More importantly, the state
has provided three platforms that have institutionalized claims-making
as a publicly supported activity. First, its university system, early on in
Berkeley and more recently in La Jolla and elsewhere, has housed laboratories and departments where basic data gathering and research on
earthquakes and earthquake engineering take place. Second, the Institute of Governmental Studies on the Berkeley campus has been a continual sponsor of reports and seminars on the earthquake threat, especially
in the San Francisco Bay area. The Institute's assistant director (Stanley
Scott), together with colleagues from across the campus and public officials from around the Bay area, have been long-time advocates for increasing awareness of the threat and for earthquake safety policies.
Third, the legislature created a permanent base for claims-making within the state when it turned a legislative committee on seismic safety into
a public commission. The California Seismic Safety Commission currently is made up of seventeen members appointed by the governor to
represent state and local government, relevant professions, and the private and nonprofit sectors. Its staff is headed by an executive director
who is in effect the state's full-time, officially designated earthquake
threat claims-maker. The commission and its staff work closely with
earthquake safety advocates in the state legislature (such as state senator
Alfred Alquist) to craft legislation. Much of its legislative effort has been
directed at local jurisdictions that, even in California, have seldom initiated any seismic-related activities on their own.

Overall, states are in a position that is similar to the federal government. Although they possess much of the formal authority that would
seemingly make them the focal point for those demanding action on the
earthquake threat, they have delegated much of that authority to local
jurisdictions. On top of this, states have fewer financial resources than
the federal government. Their stake in the earthquake threat is further
diminished by the fact that federal disaster relief policies have included
aid for repairing and replacing damaged state property ever since Congress voted funds for the repair of flood-damaged public roads in 1930
(May 1985:21–25). States are in competition with each other for attracting
and retaining industry and commerce (i.e., jobs). Policies that can be
portrayed by opponents as obstacles to those objectives are not popular
in state legislatures. Thus state government in general has not been an
arena where earthquake claims-makers have had their finest hour.

Even the possibility of earthquake prediction, in particular short-term
and middle-term predictions, was not welcome news to state and local
governments in the 1970s.[6] Commercial real estate interests were less

than thrilled. The California Business Properties Association warned, "It is quite possible that the consequences of the announced service [i.e., routine earthquake prediction capability] could be more damaging, socially and economically, than the earthquake" (Cook 1975:1). Alarmed, the mayor of Los Angeles created a twenty-five-member task force on earthquake prediction with seven separate subcommittees to prepare a plan for the city (see Dunne 1978). Karl Steinbrugge, testifying at a 1976 congressional hearing in his role as chair of the California Seismic Safety Commission, pointed out some of the negative aspects of earthquake prediction from the viewpoint of local government:

> Current research studies on earthquake prediction indicate that a substantial life saving will result from a successful prediction, but that the overall financial impact could be worse [than an actual earthquake].
> As a result from the State's point of view, a reliable earthquake prediction capability may have some of the aspects of a mixed blessing.
> Whenever a high confidence prediction is made for a major catastrophe, State and local government responses can be drastic and expensive. For one State and local government action, hundreds of thousands of people may be removed from homes, hospitals, factories, offices, and the like, thereby resulting in loss of income, costs of temporary housing, and other social, economic, and political problems which could cost billions. The State does not have the resources. (U.S. House of Representatives 1976:168)

He singled out the likelihood of false alarms (predicted earthquakes that failed to occur) before the technology was perfected as especially troublesome:

> [A] false prediction would be very costly—let us take the case of moving all of the people out of San Francisco's Chinatown or all the poor people out of the Tenderloin [two sections of that city with older structures and high population density] and the State not having the funds to take care of this problem. This will cause political ramifications as well as economic problems. (U.S. House of Representatives 1976:169)

Local governments like their state counterparts have always been more comfortable with solutions to the risk of earthquakes such as planning, preparedness, and public education. An infrastructure supporting these activities was created by the federal government in the 1950s under cold war civil defense programs. The Defense Civil Preparedness Agency (another predecessor of FEMA) provided money for the salaries of local civil defense directors and required the creation of local plans for nuclear attack (and later, for natural disasters).[7] Drills and exercises at that time simulated enemy attacks; now the same exercises simulate natural disasters such as earthquakes. These local programs were inexpensive (the federal government picked up the tab), they were politically safe (no powerful local interests were severely antagonized; most supported a strong defense posture anyway), and they provided a certain amount of protection for local jurisdictions from liability.

Disaster preparedness and planning continue at local and state levels but without the emphasis on nuclear attack. Earthquake preparedness as a focus of these activities varies considerably. It is found in some jurisdictions but not in others, including jurisdictions in areas designated at risk by earth scientists (Building Associates, Inc., 1990:68). Structural arrangements for local preparedness and planning activities range from having a full-time emergency management director to having an assistant fire or police chief devoted part-time to these duties (Quarantelli 1975; Anderson 1969). The same people are usually responsible for the other major weapon in the local earthquake arsenal, public education. In California, public education usually consists of emergency preparedness specialists speaking to civic groups or other assembled bodies, often joined by earth scientists or earthquake engineers who narrate a series of pictures showing damage to buildings, highways, and utilities. Preparedness tips are a major theme of these presentations.

Public education is an important vehicle for local claims-making about the earthquake threat in California. Consciousness-raising is a major ingredient in these efforts. The educational message typically is prefaced by a summary of scientists' expectations about the likelihood of an earthquake of a certain magnitude (e.g., 8.3 or greater) within a certain period of time (e.g., the next twenty years). The theme of the message is that families and workers should prepare for an inevitable earthquake. Emphasis is on being self-sufficient for the first seventy-two hours following impact. An example of this message appeared in the *Los Angeles Times* in midsummer 1992 following two large earthquakes and a series of aftershocks in the desert east of Los Angeles near the San Andreas fault system.[8] The *Times* printed a full color, half-page insert containing a checklist of "Things to Do" before, during, and after earthquakes. The insert was titled "Planning for the Big One":

> If the earthquake known as the Big One does strike along the southern San Andreas Fault or in parts of the Los Angeles–Orange County metropolitan area, vital services by firefighters, paramedics, health care professionals and police may not be available for several hours or days. Moreover, in the hardest-hit areas there may be no water, gas, electrical or phone service for several days. Many freeways and roads may be impassable and strong aftershocks could hamper aid efforts. (*Los Angeles Times*, July 27, 1992)

In an insert listing supplies to keep on hand, the theme is repeated: "You should have enough emergency supplies for at least 72 hours."

Generally speaking, much of the load of claims-making at the local level is carried by emergency services professionals. In some jurisdictions these are full-time emergency management directors, while in other jurisdictions they are administrators from police or fire departments. They promote individual preparedness by speaking to small groups and by providing information to news reporters. Their primary efforts are directed at maintaining the readiness of local emergency response agencies. This is in line with conventional public safety functions emphasizing reducing life loss and property damage. They are not only relatively low-cost activities, they are noncontroversial as well. They are undertaken in a manner that emphasizes voluntary cooperation rather than confrontation or conflict.

PUBLIC TELEVISION DOCUMENTARIES ABOUT THE EARTHQUAKE THREAT

Public television is another arena where descriptions of the risk of earthquakes appear. The Public Broadcasting System (PBS) occasionally addresses the threat as part of its public education mission. One example was an installment of the weekly science program, "NOVA." An episode called "Earthquake!" aired in 1990 not long after the earthquake in the San Francisco Bay area. Produced by Boston public television station WGBH, the program dealt with the recent history and current state of the art of research on earthquakes in typical public education fashion. It featured several "visuals" of the San Andreas fault, the 1906 San Francisco earthquake and fire, and the 1989 Loma Prieta earthquake. Videotape recordings made during the 1989 earthquake captured some of the drama at the moment of impact. Viewers saw falling ceiling panels in a college classroom and swaying lights followed by darkness in a gymnasium at the University of California–Santa Cruz. Security cameras recorded bartenders and customers fleeing a tavern with glassware and bottles crashing all around them. Tape of rescue efforts on the collapsed double-decked freeway in Oakland, a car plunging almost in slow motion through an opening in the Bay Bridge connecting San Francisco and the East Bay cities, and structure fires in the Marina District of San Francisco also were shown.

"NOVA" focused on the science of earthquakes, including the status of earthquake prediction and earthquake forecasting. It documented successes as well as failures and aired interviews in which researchers listed some of the major technical problems in earthquake prediction research (such as measurement error and very small samples of very large earthquakes). There were on-camera interviews with leading earthquake researchers from the California Institute of Technology, the Geological Survey, and the seismological observatory at Columbia University. Two themes the program stressed were the great risks associated with catastrophic earthquakes and the slow, diligent progress being made by scientists to reduce our ignorance of the mysteries of the earth. The program ended with the head of the Geological Survey's seismology branch recommending that, with the seriousness of the risks involved, viewers act *as if* all the uncertainty associated with the earthquake threat did not exist.

There were very few hints in the sixty-minute broadcast that earthquakes were anything other than a scientific problem. Early in the program while scenes of destruction in downtown Santa Cruz were on the screen, the narrator mentioned in passing that at the time of the 1989 earthquake the city had not reached agreement with property owners on a local ordinance for dealing with the older brick buildings that could be seen in damaged condition. Later, the Bay Bridge with its disappearing section of roadway and the collapsed double-decked freeway in Oakland were both described with a touch of irony as having been built to the latest earthquake safety codes in place at the time. Near the end of the program, as an aerial view of homes built of pillars resembling giant stilts on the side of foothills in Los Angeles appeared on the screen, the narrator reported that existing earthquake forecasts provided enough time for local governments to make necessary changes in land use patterns and construction practices.

A scientific viewpoint clearly dominated this documentary. The narrator contributed to the learned tone by speaking in a deep, precise, and authoritative voice. He carefully pronounced technical concepts; he introduced viewers to a "great" Japanese scientist who had been ahead of his time and to an "epic" scientific study in this country. Colorful computer graphics and restrained instrumental background music underscored the rationalistic motif. The program was about the world of science, not about the other worlds (the political, the economic, etc.) in which science exists. The controversies dealt with in the broadcast were scientific controversies, that is, intellectual disagreements about such things as the prospects for ultimately predicting earthquakes.

Two other PBS programs echo the scientific style (Ibarra and Kitsuse 1993:49–53) used by "NOVA." An episode of "Newton's Apple," taped in 1985, contained a ten-minute segment on predicting the Big One. Hosted by public broadcasting's science expert, Ira Flatow, the segment dealt with questions and answers about the science of earthquake prediction. Allan Lindh of the Geological Survey who was interviewed on

camera described earthquake prediction science as "very new" and explained that one of the problems in this field was the necessity of relying
on indirect measurements of movements taking place six miles deep in
the earth. A 1992 installment of the thirty-minute PBS science program
"Earth Revealed" dealt with the Parkfield (California) earthquake prediction experiment (see Mileti and Fitzpatrick 1993), a project that coincidentally was directed by Allan Lindh. Once again, the focus was on
hard science involved in unraveling the mysteries of nature with special
emphasis on techniques of data collection (e.g., creep meters and the
information they supply). There were on-camera interviews with a variety of personnel from the Geological Survey who made the point that,
while predictions were still decades away, earthquake forecasts were
already a reality. The program concluded by equating knowledge of
earthquakes with the "power to survive" in earthquake country.

A different but complementary focus is present in "Surviving the Big
One," produced by Los Angeles public television station KCET. Hosted
by Los Angeles City Fire Department safety specialist Henry Johnson, the
theme of this local documentary is that even the Big One (an 8.3 Richter
magnitude earthquake on the San Andreas Fault) is survivable. The
emphasis throughout is on personal and family safety with special attention to children and their emotional needs in earthquakes. The hour-long
program takes viewers into every room in the home, showing ways to
prevent personal injury and reduce property damage (such as by install-
ing baby latches on kitchen cabinets to prevent the contents from spilling
out); discusses safety tips and survival equipment for the office; and even
what supplies and equipment to keep in the trunk of the car.

"Surviving the Big One" is the prototypical preparedness presentation. Its grass-roots approach is oriented to middle-class families living
in suburban, single-family tract homes. (A brief discussion of the safety
of condominiums and apartment buildings constructed had to be updated to explain the loss of life in the Northridge Meadows Apartments
unit in the 1994 earthquake.) Its emphasis is on voluntaristic "solutions"
that families can undertake such as storing bottled water and keeping
fresh batteries for portable radios with a dash of items that are easy to
overlook [e.g., extra supplies of pet foods, sufficient cash for a week or
so in case the networks of automated teller machines (ATMs) and computers leave banks closed due to a lack of electricity]. Most striking is the
program's avoidance of any explicit recommendations about individual
earthquake "solutions" that are at all costly or controversial. This means
that the program has to go out of its way, even in its 1994 postearthquake
updated version, to avoid taking a stand on aspects covered by the term
mitigation.

For example, Fireman Johnson spends a good deal of time (perhaps five minutes or so in a one-hour program) talking about the issue of earthquake insurance for the home. He asks how many viewers have earthquake insurance and notes that coverage is indeed expensive and deductibles equal to 10 percent of the value of the house are standard. Furthermore, he reports that "some studies" show that the insurance industry would be $22 billion underfunded in the event of a major earthquake. On the other hand, he recounts the experience of one home owner in Whittier whose home received $144,000 in damages during the 1987 earthquake but who wound up paying only $14,400 for repairs because he had earthquake insurance. His strongest statement, made more than once, is that purchasing earthquake insurance is "something that really should be considered." His treatment of automatic gas shutoff valves (devices that shut off the flow of natural gas to homes when ground shaking exceeds a certain intensity) is similar. He notes that they can be purchased, that they are not cheap, but that all new fire stations in the City of Los Angeles have them, and that fire following earthquakes is a major concern. The program avoids altogether three other potentially controversial issues that arise. A discussion of problems with mobile homes during earthquakes notes only that they "move around" but does not recommend specific forms of anchoring devices. During an excursus on the Great Alaska earthquake, the likelihood of landslides is introduced and documented with aerial photographs of the Turnagain Heights (see Office of Emergency Preparedness 1972:Vol. 3, p. 81, Figure 9), but there is no mention of how zoning and land use controls could address this phenomenon. Finally, a discussion of safety at the office during and after an earthquake deals only with drop-and-cover as a way to reduce the likelihood of being injured by flying glass or falling objects; the discussion omits any reference to what office workers might demand that employers or building owners do to reduce such risks (such as coating glass with a safety lining or rearranging office furniture and wall decorations).

In sum, "Surviving the Big One" is as good an example of the preparedness message at the local level as is available. Firefighter Johnson speaks calmly about the practical dos and don'ts of earthquake survival, allowing that even to talk about earthquakes at all is "controversial." He concludes the broadcast with a heavy dose of moral suasion in an effort to get members of the viewing audience to implement his safety recommendations: "If you don't do something within twenty-four hours after seeing this program, you'll slip back into your old life-style" and will always regret, when the earthquake strikes, "what you should have done to protect yourself and your family."

EARTHQUAKES "AT THE MOVIES"

Earthquakes in movies are about heroism and heroic struggles. Rather than heroic scientists matching wits with inscrutable nature, Hollywood's heroes confront the horrors of actual earthquake disasters. Charlton Heston, in perhaps the best-known of these movies, the 1974 film *Earthquake* (Universal Studios), single-handedly saves several lives including that of his character's father-in-law (played by Lorne Greene). More recently, Ruben Blades and Sandy Duncan play characters who overcome personal and family tragedies in the 1993 made-for-television film, *Miracle on I-880.*

Earthquake is the prototypical disaster movie. Its themes are those of heroism, strength, and overcoming calamity, both personal and social. Most of the images of the earthquake threat are projected through various visual materials rather than through dialogue. The film's special effects, cinematography, and physical action express the nature of risk. Many of its special effects clearly are modeled after the 1971 San Fernando earthquake. For example, a cattle truck plunges off a collapsed freeway overpass; office buildings are damaged but remain standing; a major dam is damaged both by two strong foreshocks and finally by the Big One itself; etc. The cinematography establishes the threat of dam failure as the movie's unifying theme. The film opens with aerial shots over a dam that appears to be in a rural area, but the helicopter-mounted camera maneuvers to reveal the city of Los Angeles laid out below, framed between the steep walls of a canyon. Throughout, the threat of a dam break is like a ticking time bomb. In the end, the several subplots are resolved in an underground parking structure flooded when the dam finally does give way.

Earthquake contains a mixture of science and pseudoscience. There is a short-term earthquake prediction advanced by a graduate student at the fictitious California Seismological Institute. Based upon his analysis of a pattern of foreshocks (two occur on the same day as the Big One), the student predicts that a severe earthquake will occur during the next twelve to forty-eight hours (a time window that is much smaller than anything earth scientists were hoping to achieve at the time). The student's prediction quickly encounters the professional jealousies that exist in science; the head of the seismological institute (played by Barry Sullivan) rejects his analysis as the work of a "mere graduate student" and lectures the student about the consequences of a false alarm, reminding him that a "foolproof" prediction system is four to five years away (both are points that most claims-makers at the time would have agreed with, although the term foolproof undoubtedly would have made many earth scientists cringe). Yet the institute director keeps the student's computer printouts for further study, and, after a senior researcher is killed during another foreshock predicted by the student, the director takes the prediction to the mayor of Los Angeles (played by John Randolph). The mayor is reluctant to issue an earthquake warning. He fears setting off a panic by issuing a public announcement (a common concern among elected officials at the time). He also fears political repercussions because he and the governor of the state are from different political parties. Eventually he "does the right thing," issuing a public warning and convincing the governor to call out the National Guard.

Other aspects of risk also show a pattern of mixing elements generally accepted within the earthquake establishment with others that most insiders would dispute. For example, there are scenes showing animals sensing the Big One before it happens (a controversial but discredited idea among claims-makers). There is also a scene depicting panic flight by moviegoers attending a matinee (a behavioral response refuted by social science research even at the time). On the other hand, the film's handling of looting is complex and not as inaccurate as one might have expected. Convoys of National Guard troops are seen moving into the city in advance of impact to provide extra security. The one instance of actual looting shown is not the stereotype of rampaging hordes making off with goods but a rather complicated scene in which two brothers return to a pawn shop to retrieve something they had previously pawned. There is also an overzealous National Guardsman who tries to take advantage of the situation but is stopped by a passing policeman (played by George Kennedy). Images of damage are not entirely inaccurate either. Special effects show a high-rise office building suffering serious damage (e.g., an elevator full of people hurtles down its shaft, stairwells break away from the structure, glass showers onto the street), yet the building remains standing. On the other hand, the movie's final scene shows the entire city of Los Angeles in ruins but showing signs of life at dawn on the day after (insiders believe that pockets of damage within largely untouched areas are more likely).

The focus of the movie is on the star, a macho hero (Stu Graff) played by Charlton Heston. Stu is a former local college football hero who keeps himself in shape with rigorous daily workouts and who drives around town in a souped-up sport-utility vehicle. Now a successful and highly respected civil engineer, Stu is about to become president of his father-in-law's high-powered engineering firm. His status in the engineering profession is established early in the film by a young engineering graduate who is flying to Los Angeles to interview for a much sought-after job with the firm at the time of the earthquake. Stu is not only famous, he is also principled. He refuses to work on a big project for an important client until the client agrees to build in excess of existing seismic code requirements. After the earthquake and several strenuous rescues, Stu expresses anger and remorse for having participated in building forty-story high-rise office buildings "here," meaning where the risk of earthquakes is so great. In the end, he atones for his two "sins" [his infidelity to his wife (played by Ava Gardner) for his affair with the widow of a former employee (played by Genvieve Bujold) and his infidelity to the people of Los Angeles for his role in constructing many of the buildings that have killed people]. Faced with the choice of saving himself and rejoining his mistress or plunging back into the flooded parking structure to try to save the drowning Ava Gardner, Stu opts for one more heroic rescue and perishes in the torrent of water released from the badly damaged dam.

Like *Earthquake* released twenty years earlier, *Miracle on I-880* is also an action film that is incidentally about earthquakes. It follows two families affected by the loss of a family member in the Loma Prieta earthquake. One is the family of Buck Helm, the longshoreman who was rescued after being trapped in his car for four days on the collapsed freeway in Oakland. Helm died in the hospital several days after being rescued. The other is a Hispanic family whose son and daughter were rescued from the car in which their mother and a neighbor had died. Doctors had to amputate the little boy's leg to free him from the wrecked vehicle.

Miracle on I-880 is a character-strengthening story. Ordinary people whose lives are touched by disaster summon up inner strength that they did not know they had. For example, a warehouseman risks his personal safety by climbing up onto the damaged freeway in search of survivors. Reporters pass up the opportunity for a scoop on a good story out of respect for the feelings of victims. Courageous doctors and paramedics do miraculous things under the worst circumstances. Families pray together. Buck's wayward eldest son rejects his evil ways and returns to the family circle. Emergency service workers shake hands with volunteers as the rescue effort is winding down. The father whose children were rescued inspires everyone listening to his thank-you speech at the hospital entrance. People find the strength to go on; a new day dawns, and life in the big city goes on.

The themes here are courage, inner strength, and altruism, not public policies or risk reduction. Earthquakes are once again acts of nature that have to be dealt with and overcome. They may be dark moments, but thanks to the ability of ordinary human beings to call upon extraordinary resources a better future is assured.

SUMMARY

Several points were raised in this chapter regarding the nature of public arenas that have implications for claims-making about the earthquake threat. Claims-makers have enjoyed their greatest access to national expert panels, commissions, and committees. Most of the expert bodies are organized or sponsored by agencies and departments within the executive branch of the federal government. Issues of science and technology are predominant in the reports they produce. Political questions are sidestepped. Federal bureaucrats, as might be expected, are highly visible in congressional hearings. Although the earthquake threat would seem to be a consensus issue (no one argues for more and bigger earthquakes), proposed solutions to the threat bring out underlying differences and conflicts. Some of these involve relationships among federal agencies, while others center on the different interests of federal versus local governments. The committee structure itself, with several different committees and subcommittees having responsibility for various programs, agencies, and aspects of the threat, maintain the complexity and potential contentiousness of solutions. Earthquakes are frequently defined as an economic threat, with bureaucrats and some politicians attempting to contain costs to the federal government while other politicians work to retain politically popular disaster relief programs.

Network television news highlights the drama of earthquakes and to a lesser extent the scientific aspects of the earthquake threat. The requirements of story suitability (Gans 1979) used by news organizations produce an underexposure of the majority of people who deal with the threat on a daily basis. The everyday routines of hazard reduction provide no action, little controversy, and none of the scandals that are the raw material for so much of the news (see Molotch and Lester 1974). For instance, building departments may be understaffed, overworked, and lacking in seismic specialists, but these are easily explained by budgetary constraints (another impersonal label for aggregated human choices) rather than corruption. Contractors may cut corners to save money during new construction, but this is "economic reality," not scandal. Because claims-making contains no villains, there are no scandals, no corruption, and no cover-ups available for the news—and for news consumers. There is no opportunity to turn loose investigative reporters to dig up stories of injustice perpetrated by building owners and concealed by co-conspirators in government. There are several potential negative symbols here—slum lords, real estate conglomerates, "shady foreign investors," and "crooked politicians" on the take. However, the earthquake threat as a news story has always been one about the "wonders of science" rather than a story of intrigue, conspiracy, or scandal.

State governments in general have not been the site of many great accomplishments by claims-makers. Things recently have begun to change somewhat. Historically states have had little interest in the earthquake threat, have devoted few resources to it, and generally have passed on responsibility to local governments. What state governments have done, first in California and more recently in the Midwest and the East, is to provide an institutional base for claims-makers. The earliest of these were academic and university service programs; more recently, a number of publicly supported consortia have been formed.

Local government is the arena in which safety concerns dominate. Traditionally these have manifested themselves in preparedness and planning activities by emergency response agencies. In the area of building practices, reducing life loss is a perennial argument of local earthquake safety advocates. Public education messages stress it as well in identifying what people should do to survive the shaking of a severe earthquake. Economic arguments are advanced by opponents of local mitigation solutions. Any financial loss that may occur in an earthquake is assumed to be covered by outside aid especially federal disaster relief.

Most other arenas afford even less opportunity for claims-making about the earthquake threat. For example, there is little secondary claims-making about the risk of earthquakes in popular culture because there is little action to dramatize (cf. Best 1990:112–30). The absence of villains and the emphasis on science makes it difficult to construct heroes—people of action—whose struggles can entertain readers of novels, moviegoers, and prime-time television audiences. Earthquakes and other disasters have been dealt with in commercially produced films, but all the action takes place after impact. Heroes and heroines struggle mightily against the consequences of earthquake disasters, not against the risk of future earthquakes. Earthquakes build character as ordinary human beings discover hidden strength to confront their post-earthquake futures. Heroic struggles against the social trends and economic forces that increase exposure to harm in the first place, as claims-makers see it, are apparently not "good box-office." And documentaries, especially those shown on educational channels of broadcast and cable television, promote science not risk. Claims-makers often have major roles in them as technical advisers and as on-camera subjects, but claims-making takes a back seat to the promotion of scientific literacy.

CONCLUSION: THE INFLUENCE
OF ARENAS ON CLAIMS-MAKING

The concept of a public arena, especially as Hilgartner and Bosk (1988) systematically link it to the careers of social problems, has been an important recent addition to the development of a theory of social problems. The term calls our attention to the setting in which claims-making takes place. It compels us to examine how the characteristics of these settings such as their "carrying capacity" constrain the claims-making process (see Ibarra and Kitsuse 1993). Best's (1990:176–88) use of the term "marketplace" further highlights the omnipresent competition with other claims-makers also operating in these arenas. This chapter has dealt with a fundamental question: How does the nature of the various public arenas to which earthquake-risk claims-makers have had access affect the process of making claims about the earthquake threat? Stated differently, What differences are there in causes, rationales, and solutions for dealing with the threat in different arenas, and how can we explain these differences? The answers lie in the relationships among the people associated with each arena: those who manage or attempt to control the arena; claims-makers who participate in the arena; and other participants and potential participants.

One potential drawback of the arena metaphor is that it can cause us to overlook how what takes place in them is influenced by the gatekeepers and managers of arenas. Performers do not "book" themselves; they are selected by arena managers and invited to participate based upon their reputation for previous performances. Using another metaphor, public arenas are like carefully planned cocktail parties. A "host" prepares a "guest list" with a particular type of gathering in mind, plans the refreshments, arranges the furnishings and decorations, and extends invitations to the right mix of guests to make the party a success. While the host does not dictate everything that happens during the evening, the party takes place on the host's terms. The outcome of the party (for example, whether it is a "success" or a "boring evening") usually depends on how well the host has organized and orchestrated the festivities. Uninvited guests (party crashers) are screened out; invited guests who do not contribute to a successful evening are not likely to be invited back to subsequent parties.

Thinking of claims-makers as invited guests at a party is one way of focusing attention on the relationship between those who manage public arenas (the hosts) and those who participate in them (the claims-makers). Guests may be more "famous" than their hosts, but their "attendance" is nevertheless by invitation. Indeed, the decision to give a party in the first place rests with the hosts. Deciding what kind of party it will be, when it should be held, and how long it should last also are prerogatives of the hosts. So are deciding how lavish a party it should be and what entertainment will be provided.

Arenas therefore do not influence the claims-making process in some abstract or supernatural sense. The people who manage them do.[9] An examination of the influence of arenas, therefore, is an examination of hosts and what they expect from the parties they give. Just as conversation at a party is likely to be constrained to a small number of appropriate topics, participants in claims-making arenas are not free to talk about any aspect of risk they might choose. Thus it is the interests of arena managers that make it easier to promote some aspects of risk (e.g., solutions) than others. Nichols (1991; see also Nichols 1990), for instance, uses the term "certification ceremony" in describing congressional hearings to emphasize his contention that one outcome of such public events is the transformation of points of view held by committee staff members into public "facts" through the invited testimony of witnesses. Points of view at wide variance with those of gatekeepers are not likely to be legitimated. A congressional committee is unlikely to allocate many minutes to a witness who proposes that the federal government take over all zoning decisions in a state, a local building commission is unlikely to devote much time to a speaker proposing to make areas being considered for development free from the threat of earthquakes by performing an ancient pagan ritual, and a movie studio executive is unlikely to even meet with a screenwriter with a proposal for a documentary about an honest, overworked building inspector trying to save his city from an earthquake that may or may not ever happen. Successful proposals are those that take the interests of arena managers into account. Some proposals never get made because promoters lack access to the appropriate arena.

In general, earthquake claims-makers seem to have relatively greater access to and influence over the products of public arenas with very small audiences. Experts have a relatively free hand in fashioning policy and funding recommendations in the final reports issued by panels and committees, but the readership of these reports is vastly smaller than the audience of a nightly television news broadcast. At the other extreme, very few experts are involved in the creation of a made-for-television movie about earthquakes and have little control over the final product. Yet even the lowest-rated movie on network television has a significantly larger audience than the typical expert report on earthquakes. The result is that claims-makers have few opportunities to directly define risk for the public at large.

Claims-makers generally have greater access to arenas whose managers define the risk of earthquakes as almost certain. (Certainty and relative priority are two different things, but they are related; where certainty is low, arena managers are likely to assign the issue low priority.) Nevertheless, the certainty rationale is more easily argued in some arenas but not others. Even if the certainty of future events (i.e., earthquakes) is accepted, the certainty of the consequences of those events may be challenged. Federal officials mostly share a belief in both the certainty of events (a future severe earthquake) and the certainty of the consequences (major impact on one of the nation's most important regional economies). Local governments, on the other hand, can challenge the federal government's estimates of the probability of future earthquakes, as in the example from St. Louis in the 1970s. Or, local officials may accept the certainty of future earthquakes but not the certainty of catastrophic consequences, as in Oroville, California, in the 1970s (Olson and Olson 1993).

Arena managers also differ in their beliefs about the nature of the threat posed by earthquakes. Some are more concerned with threats to life and property while others worry more about threats to commerce and economic stability. Access to arenas is greater when arena managers share the concerns of claims-makers. For example, local officials who accept the certainty of earthquakes and their consequences worry about life loss and property damage, spurred in part by concerns about liability. Claims-makers have stressed this theme more consistently before city councils and local planning commissions than in congressional hearings. There the themes of life loss and damage reduction have shared time with the goals of reducing economic and social disruption.

Despite the potential mutual concern for safety between local arena managers and claims-makers, other participants in local policymaking arenas have had little trouble defining risk reduction proposals as economic threats (e.g., preventing economic growth, increasing unemployment, driving out business to other jurisdictions). This presents a difficult challenge for local arena managers, most of whom are elected officials. Power at the local level is based upon the operation of a growth machine (Logan and Molotch 1987). Safety advocates and local power elites hold conflicting views of place. Logan and Molotch (1987:1–2) portray the difference as a contrast between the use value of property and the exchange value of property. Use values are the nonmonetary benefits that property provides such as shelter, comfort, and a place to raise a family. Included here also is safety, as in safety in the event of an earthquake. Exchange values are the monetary benefits property brings when it is exchanged (i.e., bought and sold) in the marketplace.

At the local level, Logan and Molotch argue, the power of those who share an interest in the exchange value of place vastly exceeds that of those who hold the use value of place more highly. Therefore, claims made using the rhetoric of safety (barring development in certain areas, mandating rehabilitation of older structures, etc.) are proposals for increasing the use value of place but are easily portrayed as attacks on the exchange value of place. Home owners, unlike owners of rental property, have an interest in both use and exchange values, which is one reason for their lack of enthusiasm for mitigation measures that may increase the former but not the latter. Recognizing that safety is a "hard sell" at the local level because of the nature of the opposition and of the relationships between opponents and local arena managers, claims-makers have been searching for an economic rationale to justify hazard reduction measures (economists call them "incentives").

A further disadvantage is that the arenas to which claims-makers have greatest access are those for which their professional skills are not well suited. These include the arenas ultimately managed by politicians (for example, congressional committees, local building and zoning commissions, the city council, and even to some extent the nationwide panels of experts). Successful claims-making in these arenas requires not only good "front-stage" performances but powerful "back-stage" maneuvering as well. Scientists and technocrats in general are at a disadvantage, especially when it comes to back-stage maneuvering. Bureaucrats fare somewhat better, being exposed daily to "bureaucratic politics." In general, earthquake risk promoters lack the lobbying, negotiating, and bargaining skills that increase the probability of successfully promoting one's point of view. The same is not true of those who are capable of opposing these claims-makers. Therefore, claims-makers usually are at a disadvantage in most of the arenas in which they participate. Not only is their message an unpopular one but also their ability to deliver it is constrained by their professional training and outlook. Trained to present "facts" that speak for themselves, earth scientists especially are out of their league when it comes to political maneuvering. Not surprisingly, studies of successful local earthquake safety efforts usually show that the presence of an inside policy advocate (a member of the local city council, for example) is a necessary condition (Alesch and Petak 1986; Olson 1985; cf. Olson and Olson 1993). Access to an arena and successful claims-making within it are two quite different things, in other words.

Finally, the multiplicity of arenas in which claims about the earthquake threat are presented ensures that a heterogeneous rather than uniform image of risk is created. The causes of earthquakes described by earth scientists may be widely accepted, but little else about the earthquake threat is. The meaning of the consequences of earthquakes varies from arena to arena as do the rationales for taking action. In some it is a' reminder of God's power, in others it is another breaking news story, and so forth. Solutions in one arena are the problems to be overcome in others. For example, a city that decides to let the normal course of building replacement be its solution to the earthquake threat becomes a problem for the federal government, which sees the continued existence of older structures as an increase in the potential demand for disaster aid.

An examination of these public arenas suggests that claims-makers are more like guests invited to a party than possessors of truth who present unquestioned facts. They are permitted to perform a public service only when invited to present expert testimony or to answer questions from television news reporters. They have little opportunity to take their case directly to the people. They have a hard time getting on television except after a damaging earthquake. They have not had to build a grass-roots power base in order to gain access to policy makers.

Overall, the record seems at best mixed. The science but not the politics of the earthquake threat is presented to mass audiences. The proposed solutions and policy recommendations have been gratefully accepted—and largely ignored. An obvious question is: Would the status of the earthquake threat as a social problem be the same if a different claims-making process were to be created? For example, what if claims were presented in different arenas? What other claims could be advanced in the arenas to which access has been customary? These questions are pursued in Chapter 8. Before that, I examine how earthquake disasters as "unscheduled events" simultaneously turn the spotlight on claims-makers and alter the claims-making process.

NOTES

1. The federal commission responsible for deciding which military bases the country could do without in the post–cold war era is an example of a panel specifically instructed to place the nation's "needs" above those of the communities where existing bases are located.

2. For a history of this program, see Mileti and Fitzpatrick (1993:20–26). See also May and Williams (1986:95–97).

3. Recent amendments to this legislation require a 75 percent–25 percent sharing of aid between federal and state governments. A major reworking in 1988 (P.L. 100-707, the Stafford Disaster Relief and Emergency Assistance Act) reiterated that local jurisdictions receiving federal disaster aid must undertake mitigation measures to reduce losses from future disasters.

4. I say *relatively* low levels because, as discussed in the next section, it is easy to overstate the level of concern among both elites and the public at large in California.

5. There is some disagreement about this lack of concern. Mittler (1989) reanalyzed the Rossi et al. data and found more pockets of support for earthquake hazard mitigation than the earlier researchers originally described. He also questioned the importance of support by elites for the success of local claims-makers.

6. Although it is not a prediction as such, most people treat the inevitable catastrophic earthquake in California as the equivalent of a long-term prediction.

7. Remnants of these programs wound up in FEMA, which is one reason the agency has come under attack from congressional critics such as Senator Barbara Mikulski (Democrat from Maryland) for still being too "cold war" oriented (Risen 1993).

8. Neither earthquake qualified as the Big One because of their rural location.

9.   The choice of a verb for this sentence is driven by how strong an hypothesis one wishes to make about the influence of the "gatekeepers" of public arenas.
Arenas would seem to vary in terms of the degree of control gatekeepers exert
over them. For example, television news programs and motion pictures may be
controlled (by producers, writers, editors, etc.) to a greater extent than expert
panels and congressional hearings. While "control" may vary, all arenas have
people who attempt to "manage" what takes place within them.

CHAPTER

5

Changing Typifications of the Earthquake Threat

There is no single definition of the earthquake threat. Beliefs about what kind of risks earthquakes pose and why, what should be done to reduce those risks, and why action is necessary vary from one public arena to another. One reason for this variation stems from the differing characteristics of arenas in which claims-makers operate and how those characteristics influence the claims-making process.

Definitions of the earthquake threat have also changed over time. Most obvious are changes across long sweeps of history. For example, the ideas of the ancient Greeks about what causes earthquakes seem quaint and unrealistic compared to contemporary scientific models. However, changes have also occurred over relatively short periods of time. Many alterations in the characterization of the earthquake threat have occurred in the aftermath of damaging earthquakes. Although actual earthquakes and the threat of future earthquakes are two different things, there is an important connection between them. Stated in the language of constructionist theory, typifications of earthquakes and typifications of the earthquake threat are related. The lessons people draw from their experience in an actual earthquake shape and reshape what they think future earthquakes will be like. Each earthquake leaves its mark, but a few have had major influence on conceptions of risk. Karl Steinbrugge succinctly makes the point in his description of the earthquake hazard in the San Francisco Bay area: "It is more pertinent to study the occurrence of *great* earthquakes than of the more frequent moderate shocks, because the great earthquake defines the full scope of seismic risk" (Steinbrugge 1968:7, emphasis in the original).

The question addressed in this chapter is: *How can we best explain changes over time in typifications of the earthquake threat?* One explanation for why people's thinking about the nature of the earthquake threat changes stresses the continual accumulation of new knowledge about earthquakes acquired through scientific research. Another quite different explanation emphasizes the importance of new groups and their cultural authority. The first, or scientific view, holds that nature reveals a little more of itself each time an earthquake occurs. Students of earthquakes—earth scientists, engineers, social scientists, and others—apply the research tools of their disciplines and come away with new data that partly reinforce and partly change the image of what future earthquakes hold in store. The second, or cultural-authority hypothesis, implies that this explanation is too simple. For instance, the choice of topics for postearthquake research is not merely a scientific decision; it is also affected by the involvement of new groups recognized as legitimate "stakeholders" by members of the earthquake establishment. Representatives of these groups help construct the "lessons learned" from earthquakes by calling attention to new forms of harm. I prefer the cultural-authority explanation because it seems less naive and more complete than the scientific explanation.[1] The material presented in this chapter should demonstrate why.

The next section reviews some premodern theories about earthquakes and compares them with currently accepted scientific explanations. It also describes the contemporary mixture of coexisting scientific, religious, and mystical views of earthquakes in American culture. The recent confrontation in the earth sciences between those who believed in "the stability of the continents and the permanence of ocean basins" (Stewart 1990:xi) and those who subscribed to continental drift theory, an antecedent of the current theory of plate tectonics, also is described. Each of these descriptions in one way or another involves a comparison of what have been called "paradigms" (Kuhn 1962, 1970). A paradigm becomes dominant when its adherents gain control of the institutions that create and maintain the "public consciousness" (Gusfield 1981:27–50) about earthquakes. In earlier periods, religious interpretations were dominant. Currently the theories of earth scientists dominate, but not without occasional challenges.

Typifications of threats can change in important ways while dominant paradigms remain more or less intact. Three different types of changes in typifications of the earthquake threat are described in the third, fourth, and fifth sections of this chapter. Two forms of change represent variations on a theme. The first I will label *domain elaboration*, and the second I call *domain expansion* after Best (1990:74–86). Examples of domain elaboration include identification of new aspects of the threat such as so-called secondary and tertiary effects (for example, the failure of earthen dams or the loss of major electrical distribution systems). Domain expansion involves the "discovery" that some previously overlooked segment of the population—the non–English speaking, the disabled, and the hospitalized, for instance—is especially vulnerable in the event of a catastrophic earthquake. A more fundamental form of change I call *retypification*. More than increasing complexity or expanding boundaries is involved. Retypification denotes a fundamental change in the way some people think about a threat, including its nature and its consequences. Two examples described in this chapter are the emergence of earthquakes and other natural disasters as psychological hazards and more recently their retypification as economic hazards. The final section of the chapter returns to the question of why typifications change.

CONTRASTING PARADIGMS IN TYPIFYING THE EARTHQUAKE THREAT

The threats of earthquakes and other natural disasters are not just seen as threats to our well-being and to our possessions. They are also viewed as threats to some of the basic myths that make human existence possible. Among the most important of these myths is that life is orderly and predictable, if not always fun and games. Natural disasters can undermine the myth that we control our own destiny (Hewitt 1983). All cultures have sets of beliefs that provide an explanation for why such troubling events occur. Explaining trouble gives meaning and order to what otherwise would be a chaotic and unpredictable universe. These sense-making, meaning-giving, and order-restoring theories make up part of what may be called worldviews or paradigms. They emerge within and are refined, taught, and defended by representatives of the dominant institutions at any given time. In simpler societies, a single worldview may remain unchallenged for centuries. In more complex societies, different perspectives may exist side by side or compete for supremacy. The content of these worldviews and the institutions from which they emanate have changed over the centuries, but their function remains the same. They contain theories of why earthquakes happen and point to actions that humans can take to reduce risk, both individually and collectively.

Ancient Earthquake Theories

Many of the earliest theories of earthquakes that we know about seem quaint by late-twentieth-century standards. John Fried (1973) describes several in his book, *Life Along the San Andreas Fault*. He calls the oldest of these "gods-and-serpents theories" (p. 25). Tribes in central Europe, for example, held to a theory that earthquakes occurred when the water buffalo that carried the earth on its back paused to shift its enormous load. The Algonquins of North America had a similar theory except that they believed a giant tortoise rather than a water buffalo supported the weight of the world. The ancient Greeks believed that Poseidon, god of the seas, produced earthquakes whenever he was seriously displeased with mortals. Their "earthquake hazard reduction strategy" was to place shrines glorifying Poseidon all around the Mediterranean. Bruce Bolt, the noted University of California seismologist, begins his widely read primer (1978:2–3) by describing an ancient Japanese legend that attributes earthquakes to giant catfish that thrash about inside the earth whenever the god assigned to keep them quiet (with a huge hammer, if necessary) isn't paying attention.

None of these contemporary authors means for us to take these early theories about the nature of earthquakes seriously, of course. Each only uses them by way of contrast to introduce explanations of the structure and dynamics of the earth produced by twentieth-century earth scientists. Bolt (1978:3), for instance, is already on to the first "nonmystical treatment of earthquakes" by the second paragraph of his opening chapter. Fried (1973:28) arrives at modern science on the sixth page of his book after a few additional paragraphs on ancient Greek philosophers, the Enlightenment, and science in the nineteenth century. What one society knows about earthquakes can become myth and superstition when judged from the vantage point of other societies. We do not know how widely these early earthquake theories were believed or whether they were challenged at the time by competing theories. We presume that these were structurally simple societies with a homogeneous belief structure maintained by a single, overarching power structure. Many contemporary societies are quite different. Consequently, we expect a different configuration of ideas about earthquakes in them.

Multiple Contemporary Paradigms

In structurally complex, heterogeneous societies such as the industrialized nations, it is not uncommon for several belief systems to exist side by side. Each system can vary from individual to individual, ranging from total acceptance to skepticism to those who are unaware. Many individuals adhere to two or more belief systems without being at all troubled by what outsiders might see as contradictions among them. One example of currently contradictory but coexisting belief systems is that of religious and scientific theories about the origins of human life, known as creationism and the biological theory of evolution, respectively.

Nothing quite as controversial exists regarding beliefs about earthquakes. However, different belief systems do currently coexist. Ralph Turner and his colleagues report data from a random sample of 1,450 adult residents of Los Angeles County surveyed in the winter of 1977

(Turner, Nigg, and Paz 1986:19–20). Respondents were asked a series of questions about the frames of reference with which they viewed and understood earthquakes. The investigators sought evidence for the existence of three different frames of reference: physical or natural, in which earthquakes were understood as products of natural forces; mystical or magical, which see earthquakes as the work of a sorcerer, for example; and teleological or religious, wherein earthquakes were part of some grand design, punishment for sins, or signs of a coming utopia on earth. Almost all the responses (93 percent) from those surveyed attributed earthquakes to physical causes. Only seven percent were mystical or religious explanations (pp. 259–60). However, these data showed considerable overlap between scientific and nonscientific explanations. Some of the physical earthquake triggers mentioned (e.g., drilling and digging in the earth, underground nuclear testing) are not "scientifically accepted," suggesting a moralistic framework in which some disapproved form of human activity (e.g., developing nuclear weapons) was held causally responsible (p. 261). Also, when respondents rather than responses were compared, only one-third discussed earthquakes solely in natural or physical terms (p. 262).

Turner and his associates probed the relationship among these frames of reference with additional questions and analytical techniques. They noted that a large minority of their respondents (31 percent) believed that people other than scientists (mostly psychics, mystics, and occultists) could tell when an earthquake was coming, and a majority believed that unusual animal behavior, unusual weather patterns, and premonitions and instincts—all hypotheses disparaged by earth scientists—were valid precursors of impending earthquakes (pp. 262–63). In addition, nearly half of the respondents who reported that religion was very important in their lives also described earthquake dynamics in exclusively natural terms and subscribed only to scientifically approved earthquake precursors (pp. 268–69). The authors conclude that scientific and nonscientific views of earthquakes not only coexist but also are interwoven (pp. 262, 267). There may be

> a segment of the very religious who see the world through a frame of reference that is incompatible with science who are skeptical of scientific claims and aspirations. But they are not in active confrontation with science, and they may not even realize the incompatibility of their perspectives. (p. 269)

And

> Although a great majority of our respondents said that religion was important in their lives, very few of them suppose that religious leaders can

forecast earthquakes and few tried to explain earthquakes in religious terms. It is the secular mystics rather than the religious mystics who today offer an alternative to scientific prediction of earthquakes. (p. 275)

In short, scientific theory may provide the dominant explanation for earthquakes, but it has not completely replaced other explanations. Earth scientists do not have a monopoly on answers to the questions posed by nature. A sizable portion of the public at large believes that many people without advanced university degrees understand the dynamics of earthquakes. Actually, within the earth sciences there has been considerable change in the commonly accepted understanding of the earth and earthquakes. Different theories have come and gone over the last century. The theoretical model that most contemporary earth scientists work with emerged only in the late 1960s.

The Emergence and Acceptance of Plate Tectonics

At the end of the nineteenth century, a number of ideas existed among scientists about the formation and structure of the earth's surface. Most practicing scientists at the time accepted some form of *contraction theory*. This theory held that oceans, mountains, and continents formed as a result of the gradual cooling of the earth. Cooling produced shrinkage in the earth's surface, and through various processes (there were many ideas about this) this produced both mountains and earthquakes. A smattering of scientists, mostly amateurs, had challenged this dominant contractionist idea as early as 1858, but it was the German scientist Alfred Wegener who offered the most complete description of and the most systematic argument for a competing theory known as *continental drift* (Stewart 1990:28–29).

Wegener (1924) argued that the continents as we know them formed when a supercontinent broke apart, that the oceans emerged as a result of this separation, and that mountain ranges were produced when these floating continents bumped into each other (Stewart 1990:29–30). Wegener's continental drift theory failed to impress earth scientists in the United States and fell out of favor completely after coming under attack at a symposium in New York City in 1926 (Stewart 1990:35–39).[2] After World War II, there was a surge of interest in empirical research in the earth sciences, especially in the fields of oceanography and seismology. The explosion of studies produced many anomalies, things that existing theoretical models did not seem to explain satisfactorily. Stabilist theory—a general label for several different models having in common the view that the continents had remained in fixed positions over recorded history—remained the dominant theoretical paradigm (Stewart 1990:69–71).

By the end of the 1960s, a descendant of continental drift theory, the theory of plate tectonics, had replaced stabilist theory and was accepted by all but a handful of American earth scientists (Stewart 1990:96–121). The change was a remarkably rapid one. Several empirical investigations in the mid-1960s of a hypothesis about the spreading of sea floors produced findings more consistent with drift theory than stabilist theory. Data on patterns of earthquakes worldwide also supported drift theory. These data were presented in a series of four influential articles published in 1967, which collectively elaborated the plate tectonic model and raised the possibility that earthquakes could be predicted (Stewart 1990:96–103).

The acceptance of plate tectonics among North American earth scientists, especially among geophysicists, was rapid and extensive. This scientific "revolution" was over by 1970. In 1976 the category "Plate Tectonics" appeared for the first time in the *Bibliography and Index of Geology* with references to 750 articles for that year alone. The following year 1,100 articles were listed in the index with joint references to over 200 different subheadings, indicating the extent of diffusion across scientific specialties (Stewart 1990:111). By this time there were only a handful of stabilist holdouts among earth scientists in the United States. It took longer for plate tectonics to win over scientists in Europe and Japan, and, for a variety of reasons, the Soviets took even longer before embracing the theory (Stewart 1990:108, 116).

Implications

It would be incorrect to conclude from these descriptions of premodern ideas about earthquakes, multiple frames of reference in our own time, and competing scientific theories that there is a right and a wrong way to explain earthquakes. What I think they show instead is that ideas about the earth and the earth itself (the subject of those ideas) are two different things. Ideas about earthquakes have come and gone, while the dynamics of earthquakes apparently have remained virtually unchanged for thousands of years. There is another implication of these descriptions. Ideas about earthquakes tell us something about the social circumstances in which those ideas exist. The theories of the ancients could have survived only if they met with the approval of tribal elites. Therefore, they tell us not what everybody at that time believed but rather what elites of the day found acceptable. Unacceptable ideas have a much lower chance of being preserved as part of the historical record. Similarly, not everyone in southern California today thinks that earth scientists are the only ones who know something about earthquakes, but the scientific worldview with its emphasis on natural forces and cause-effect relationships is nearly universal within the public at large. This tells us that science as an institution dominates the way we currently view nature. The history of continental drift reminds us that to challenge ideas is also to challenge the people who control particular institutions (that is, people who make hiring and promotion decisions, organize conferences, allocate research funds, edit and referee professional journals, etc.). The hypothesis that the sun, not the earth, is the center of the universe was not just "ivory-tower" speculation during the Middle Ages; it was religious heresy because it challenged the teachings of the dominant institution at the time, the church. Kuhn's use of the term "revolution" to describe the ascension of new theories in science (1962, 1970) captures the sense that major intellectual debates are also power struggles.

The main implication is this: If ideas tell us about the distribution of intellectual authority among groups at a given time, then the emergence of new ideas must signal the emergence of new groups, or a reconfiguration of intellectual authority among existing groups, or both. The fate of ideas, whether about earthquakes or any other putative condition, and the fate of groups struggling to gain acceptance and attain credibility are interrelated. Therefore, in examining the changing definition of the earthquake threat over the past three decades, the arrival on the scene of new groups such as new academic disciplines, specialized fields within disciplines, occupations and professions, and professional associations should be highly correlated with the "discovery" of new facets to the risk of earthquakes. The more successful a new group is in acquiring intellectual authority, the greater should be its impact on the definition of risk.

DOMAIN ELABORATION

The role of groups in redefining risk is especially visible in the aftermath of earthquakes. The composition of research teams and investigation panels indicates what areas of expertise are considered relevant at the time. Their research reports and official findings identify the lessons learned from the earthquake. In this way, each new earthquake, especially a major one, leaves distinctive fingerprints on the process of claims-making. Often a new aspect is added to the definition of the earthquake threat, showing it to be a more serious concern than previously believed.

"Made" Land

The term *made land* was used extensively in the report of the investigation commission looking into the San Francisco earthquake in 1906 (State Earthquake Investigation Commission 1908–1910). Previous earthquakes in northern California had indicated that buildings erected on fill dirt from the San Francisco Bay and on naturally occurring deep alluvial soils experienced especially heavy damage. After the 1906 earthquake, soil was officially identified as a new aspect of risk. Neither the amount of energy released nor the proximity of buildings to earthquake faults could completely account for the pattern of damage. By 1908 geologists were convinced that the character of soil was part of the problem:

> This investigation has clearly demonstrated that the amount of damage produced by the earthquake of April 18 [1906] in different parts of the city and county of San Francisco depended chiefly upon the geological character of the ground. Where the surface was solid rock, the shock produced little damage; whereas upon made land great violence was manifested. (State Earthquake Investigation Commission 1908:241; quoted in Steinbrugge 1968:23)

The authors of this section of the report were geologists, people who study soil. Ground failure hazards have since become an established aspect of the earthquake threat. Liquefaction (sudden increase in the permeability of soil exposed to seismic tremors), landslide, and land subsidence are part of the lexicon of earthquake professionals. Soils analysis, slope stabilization, and grading regulations are part of the building construction process. Specialists such as geologists and soils engineers are needed to provide geotechnical and engineering information to developers in many local jurisdictions (Mader and Tyler 1993).

Lifelines

Lifelines are "the basic installations and facilities on which the continuance and growth of a community depend, and without which the high standard of living enjoyed today would vanish" (Buckle 1993:39). Lifelines include water and sewer systems; transportation facilities (highways, railroads, mass transit systems, ports, and airports); electric power transmission systems; gas and liquid fuel transmission systems; and communication systems (p. 39). The "lesson" that lifeline damage is a major element of risk is drawn repeatedly after major earthquakes. Sometimes it is the failure of lifelines to withstand the intense shaking that drives the message home. At other times it is the success with which specially designed facilities withstand extreme forces that makes the same point. It would be a distortion to single out a particular earthquake disaster as a turning point in the inclusion of this new aspect of risk. However, the photographic record of one disaster is used so frequently to illustrate what can happen to unprotected lifelines that it has made a special contribution to the claims-making process.

The 1971 San Fernando earthquake was a moderate one as far as energy levels go (Richter magnitude 6.6). The number of deaths and injuries was light for such a heavily populated area, due in part to the fact that the earthquake occurred at 6:00 A.M. However, it had a lasting impact on redefining the risk of future earthquakes. The pictorial record preserved the effects of this earthquake on lifelines. The Sylmar Converter Station, a nearly completed facility for converting direct current (DC) electrical power into alternating current (AC), was heavily damaged by ground vibration and landslides. Federal and local agency photographs captured toppled oscillators, looking like giant robots resting on their sides with four legs sticking in the air (see Office of Emergency Preparedness 1972:76, Figure 5). Other photos showed porcelain insulators strewn about like broken toys, the result of "inadequate anchorage" (Steinbrugge, Schader, Bigglestone, and Weers 1971:63). The lesson learned was this:

> Countless failures of brittle ceramic electric insulators resulted in a loss of millions of dollars at the Sylmar Converter Station. In a great earthquake, the power outages could be catastrophic. Obviously, this should be the subject of a high priority research project. (p. viii)

Dam Failures

The San Fernando earthquake also solidified the place of the potential for dam failures in the image of future earthquakes. Much of the water supply for California's major urban areas is stored behind earthen dams owned by various public and private water suppliers. In 1971, dam failure became a prominent feature of the earthquake threat with the near collapse of the Lower San Fernando Dam in the Van Norman Reservoir Complex. (The threat of dam failure is a major theme in the movie *Earthquake*; see Chapter 4.) The Pacific Fire Rating Bureau report quotes extensively from the official investigation by the California Division of Safety of Dams:

> The embankment including the parapet wall, dam crest, most of the upstream slope, and a portion of the downstream slope, for a length of about 1800 feet, slid into the reservoir. . . . At the time of the earthquake the water level in the reservoir was about 35 feet below the crest, leaving about 4 feet of soil as the remaining freeboard. Eighty thousand (80,000) people living

downstream of the dam were immediately ordered to evacuate and steps were taken to lower the water level in the reservoir as rapidly as possible. (Steinbrugge et al. 1971:58–59)

The summary of this same report concludes:

The near catastrophic failure of the older hydraulic fill (earthen) Lower and Upper San Fernando Dams have [sic] required a detailed re-evaluation of a number of similar dams throughout California, and pose a special [insurance] underwriting problem for structures below these dams. This problem also must be faced in all states where an earthquake potential exists. (Steinbrugge et al. 1971:viii)

"Fire Following"

One aspect of the current earthquake threat is concern that fires may be a serious problem. Residential fires are expected to occur if gas hot water heaters topple, breaking the gas line; escaping gas could then be ignited by the small flame of the gas pilot. The 1994 Northridge earthquake added some new dimensions to the threat. Especially vulnerable were mobile homes, which were knocked off their supports, breaking gas lines and starting several fires. Even homes with secured hot water heaters were not spared; many caught fire when the earthquake moved the entire structure off its foundation, rupturing gas mains and producing fires. If water service is lost due to earthquake damage, any resulting fires could spread unchecked.

When earthquake safety advocates refer to *fire following*, two earlier disasters are the prime symbols of such conflagrations. One is the great Kwanto earthquake of 1923 in the Tokyo-Yokohama area, in which nearly 40 percent of the 143,000 deaths were officially attributed to the firestorm that followed. The other is the San Francisco earthquake and fire of 1906. Reexaminations of losses suffered in 1906 conclude that only 20 percent of the half-billion (1906) dollars in damages resulted from the earthquake itself. Eighty percent of the losses were attributed to the fires that followed the earthquake. The fires that burned much of downtown San Francisco lasted seventy-four hours. Within fifteen minutes after the earthquake struck at 5:12 A.M., fifty fires were burning out of control in the downtown area. The three-day bonfire reduced nearly five downtown acres to rubble, an area of 521 city blocks. One myth about this disaster is that there was no water left in the city's reservoirs to fight the fire. In fact, fire-fighting efforts were hampered by damage to the pipes and other equipment making up the city's water distribution system (Steinbrugge 1968:45).

This disaster has been referred to for a long time as the Great San Francisco Fire: "[I]n the years that followed it became 'proper' to call the event the 1906 *fire*, and to omit any reference to the earthquake" (Steinbrugge 1968:45, emphasis in the original). The typification of this as a fire disaster was probably influenced by the concerns of insurance underwriters before the earthquake. In a report completed in 1905, the National Board of Fire Underwriters (now the American Insurance Association) identified several features of the city that made its potential for a fire disaster exceedingly high and concluded: "San Francisco has violated all underwriting traditions and precedent by not burning up" (quoted in Steinbrugge 1968:45). The fact that the insurance industry treated this 1906 earthquake as a fire disaster rather than as an earthquake disaster had important consequences for the city. Fire insurance policies written at the time excluded damages caused by earthquakes from the coverage they provided. Nevertheless, insurance companies paid for claims of damage that covered 75 percent of the total losses in this disaster. Mittler (1991:161–62) argues that had insurance companies enforced the clause that excluded claims for losses from fires following earthquakes the city would have had a very difficult time recovering.[3]

Some Special Concerns of Disaster "Insiders"

Not all of the changes over time in the definition of the risk of earthquakes are visible to the public at large. Some are added worries that affect mainly earthquake disaster insiders such as emergency managers. These potential consequences of earthquakes are visible only to people who are likely to play specific official roles in future disasters. However, the consequences are not physical ones such as dams collapsing or fires breaking out. They are in a sense social consequences, because they involve anticipated behavioral reactions to future earthquakes.

News Media as an Aspect of the Earthquake Threat. Members of the news media have a love-hate relationship with their audiences at the end of the twentieth century. On the one hand, we depend on the news media to keep us informed of the important events of the day and, to a lesser extent, to explain what they mean. On the other hand, many Americans believe that the news they receive is distorted by an ideological bias on the part of reporters or by the profit maximization motives of news executives. For earthquake professionals, the news media are a source of concern, part of the threat that future earthquakes pose.

The threat that the news media pose is twofold. One part is organizational. With reporters expected to descend in a "feeding frenzy," emergency managers fear being so overwhelmed that they will be unable to perform their jobs effectively. The Seismic Safety Commission's official report on a moderate earthquake in the small central California town of Coalinga (1980 population 6,953) includes a photograph of reporters, audio technicians, and cameramen milling about. The report contains the following description:

> Media representatives came from literally all over the world, taking photographs, interviewing emergency responders and residents, and hiring aircraft to fly over the damaged area. The presence of so many media workers added to the burden of emergency response agencies, and residents deeply resented the behavior of some reporters. (Tierney 1985:34)

Yet disaster personnel count on the news media to inform the public at large of many aspects of the disaster process. Hence, the second part of the threat is that the media "won't get it right." That is, media reports will be sensationalized, inaccurate, or worse. Accuracy of news content is worrisome at all stages, from issuing predictions and warnings to coverage of relief activities.

Concerns about the impact of media coverage of disasters, and more recently of risks of all types, have provided a research agenda for communications scholars (e.g., Scanlon, Alldred, Farrell, and Prawzick 1985). Both the U.S. and Canadian governments have funded research projects, conferences, and public information programs aimed at promoting the accurate portrayal of risk. The National Science Foundation funded a National Academy of Sciences Committee on Disasters and the Mass Media. Chaired by Everett Rogers, an internationally known communications scholar, the committee included leading researchers on mass media and disasters, producing a report that was partly an overview of existing research and partly a listing of topics for future research (Committee on Disasters and the Mass Media 1980). Other agencies concerned with other types of threats, such as the Environmental Protection Agency, have funded risk communication research (e.g., Sandman, Sachsman, Greenberg, and Gochfeld 1987) as well as numerous workshops (e.g., Rogers 1988). Research on the mass media in disasters and on risk communication are now established subfields in communications studies (e.g., Walters, Wilkins, and Walters 1989), although researchers in these fields more often study controversial chemical and radioactive accidents than earthquakes (see Wilkins 1987).

Fear of Crime as an Aspect of the Earthquake Threat. The threat of earthquakes for disaster professionals also raises the possibility of mass evacuations. This was one of the "lessons" of the San Fernando earthquake of 1971 in which eighty thousand people were evacuated from homes that would have been in the path of a wall of water had the damaged

Lower San Fernando Dam failed. The prospect that thousands of damaged buildings will stand vacant, their contents exposed, until building inspectors verify their soundness (or lack of soundness) creates concern that security will be a major problem in a catastrophic earthquake. Fear of looting and other antisocial behavior is widespread despite research reports that conclude that they basically do not take place following natural disasters (Quarantelli and Dynes 1972; Wenger, Dykes, Sebok, and Neff 1975).

The probability of looting and other forms of criminal behavior in the aftermath of a great earthquake disaster is a "lesson" that local law enforcement officials learn in a variety of other types of emergencies. The looting of stores during riots and disturbances is a reminder of the scope of the potential problem. Absence of looting and lawless behavior in disasters is explained by the fast work of law enforcement agencies in setting up security perimeters and implementing systems of passes for legitimate residents. The persistence of this aspect of the risk of earthquakes—the risk of being victimized by criminals taking advantage of the situation—ironically is reinforced each time a news report of the latest disaster describes the deployment of security forces to *prevent* looting. Especially convincing are reports of arrests for *suspicion* of looting. The fact that most suspects are later released without charges being filed is seldom reported.

Fear of Emergent Groups as an Aspect of the Earthquake Threat.   Another aspect of the threat that future earthquakes pose for public officials and disaster professionals, especially at the local level, is that of being "shown up" by amateurs. Disaster planners in the 1950s, with the threat of nuclear attack always clearly in mind, based emergency preparations on the assumption that survivors would be dazed, docile, childlike, and unable to function. Social scientists studying dozens of disasters in the 1950s and 1960s reported instead that civilian survivors were the first to act following impact. Survivors were typically the first to enter damaged buildings to search for victims trapped under debris, and they transported the injured to hospitals in private vehicles without waiting for paramedics or ambulances to arrive.

Self-help efforts frequently resulted in hard feelings between members of these newly emerging groups and local authorities. Emergent group leaders often felt that, since they had been on the scene before emergency personnel arrived, they had a better idea about what needed to be done and where resources should be allocated. However, managers of public emergency response agencies considered themselves to be the experts on such matters and could not understand why these emergent groups did not dissolve once the professionals had arrived. The lesson learned by emergency responders and public officials was that at best these emergent groups can get in the way and at worst their appearance might be seen as a sign that local government had failed to deal adequately with the situation. Thus, many disaster professionals anticipate that a future catastrophic earthquake will contain challenges to their authority from emergent citizens groups.

In general, elaboration of the meaning of the earthquake threat is not a function of what happens in an actual earthquake. Nor is it a product of individual experience. Rather, images of what the future will be like reflect the interests and points of view of those select few who evaluate the implications of each new disaster.

DOMAIN EXPANSION

New things to worry about are continually being added to the threat of future earthquakes. I used the term *domain elaboration* to describe the addition of some of these new aspects to the definition of risk. Domain elaboration consists of the identification and official acceptance of some "new" type of situation that the earthquake establishment comes to expect in a future earthquake disaster. Most of these new situations involve some type of damage that is expected to be more troublesome in the future than in past earthquakes, or some type of behavioral response associated with an earthquake disaster that could pose headaches for disaster professionals.

Another type of change in the definition of risk involves the "discovery" that previously overlooked segments of the population are especially vulnerable to the effects of earthquakes. If my hypothesis that the lessons of earthquake disasters result from the concerns of newly accepted stakeholders and not from the event itself, then we should find a connection between the recognition of new categories of potential earthquake victims and the emergence of groups promoting an awareness of the special problems of such people in general. I will borrow the term *domain expansion* to describe changes in the typification of the earthquake threat that involve the recognition of new types of victims with special needs.

School Students

An early example of recognizing the special vulnerability of specific segments of the population is associated with the Long Beach (California) earthquake of 1933:

In the immediate aftermath of the 1933 Long Beach earthquake, architects, engineers, and other professionals formed teams to investigate the effects of the earthquake and to determine the reasons for the extensive loss of life and property. Their purpose was to develop steps to be taken to minimize the effects of future earthquakes. Among other findings, it was noted that more than half of the 3,417 damaged buildings in the City of Long Beach had been constructed with unreinforced masonry walls. Eighty-percent of the unreinforced masonry buildings affected by the quake failed in some way. (Alesch and Petak 1986:6)

The lessons learned in this earthquake were twofold. One, as noted in the quote, was the special vulnerability of unreinforced masonry buildings. Changes in building codes after the earthquake addressed new construction, but buildings completed before May 23, 1933 (the date the Riley Act, affecting future construction, became law in California), continue to be objects of concern to this day.

The other lesson of this earthquake was that school children were especially vulnerable in earthquakes. Many of the masonry structures that failed were school buildings. The official committee investigating this earthquake concluded: "[T]here should be no delay in making these buildings—particularly school buildings—safe" (Joint Technical Committee on Earthquake Protection 1933, quoted in Alesch and Petak 1986:9). In fact, the Long Beach earthquake is known to many as the "schoolhouse disaster," and photographs of earthquake-damaged schools have long been the icon for this earthquake (the Alesch and Petak monograph has a close-up of one on its cover). The Field Act required that plans for all new public school buildings be approved by the California Division of Architecture, which would also be responsible for supervising all school construction.

The Hospitalized

School children are considered vulnerable not only because of the structures they inhabit but also because of their dependent state in a world of adults, including teachers and principals. Dependency of a different form was discovered in 1971. The San Fernando earthquake put the special vulnerability of hospital patients on display, especially in dramatic scenes of rescue efforts on national television. If the 1933 Long Beach earthquake was the schoolhouse disaster, then the San Fernando earthquake was the "hospitals disaster." Its icons remain the photographs of the sagging Medical Treatment and Care Building at Olive View Hospital and of the totally collapsed central building at the Veterans Administration Hospital. In all, seventeen hospitals were damaged or destroyed and numerous nursing homes and privately owned medical and professional buildings were damaged (Steinbrugge et al. 1971:41).

Like the Long Beach earthquake four decades earlier, the San Fernando earthquake left its fingerprints on public policies. Within a year, the State of California enacted a Hospital Seismic Safety Act mandating standards for hospital construction. Another lesson learned is anticipated in the executive summary of the Pacific Fire Rating Bureau's report:

> It is of utmost importance that hospitals and other structures vital to public need after a disaster, including public utilities, remain functional after an earthquake. In the instance of four major hospitals, clearly they did not remain functional. Unfortunately, in spite of the potential hazard known to many knowledgeable persons, there is no legal restriction which will prohibit the construction of hospitals or other vital facilities on known earthquake faults. (Steinbrugge et al. 1971:vii–viii)

At the same time the state legislature dealt with hospitals, it passed a bill restricting development within specified distances of known earthquake faults.

The Non–English Speaking

It is probably not accurate to conclude that the special difficulties of disaster victims whose native language is not English were discovered in the San Fernando earthquake. However, issues arose during the Los Angeles area earthquake that had not been faced in the 1964 Alaskan earthquake, due in part to the relative homogeneity of the population of Anchorage.[4] Complaints about the handling of the 1971 disaster came from many low-income disaster victims and the spokespersons for groups representing them. In fact, an entire day of the three-day 1971 Senate subcommittee hearing was arranged through a Catholic priest and held in the recreation hall of Santa Rosa Catholic Church in a low-income neighborhood in Sylmar.

Several barrio residents testified, some through interpreters, about problems they had encountered in the aftermath of this earthquake. Some of these special difficulties were specific to Spanish-speaking residents, over and above the problems associated with low income and the absence of financial resources. Father Luis Valbuena, pastor of Santa Rosa church, testified in his own imperfect English:

> [W]e have 40 percent of Spanish speaking community. The SBA sent people to San Fernando Junior High—San Fernando Park, excuse me. They were receiving on the average of 300 applicants every day. Out of those three or five, not percent, but people, there were no Spanish speaking and a lack of communication was very obvious and yet nobody moved to do something about it until we called Washington and then they moved. . . . [T]here was a lack of sensitivity as far as Spanish-speaking

people were concerned. Their forms are still only in English and they are very very complicated. No. 2, no radio—there was no information available in Spanish on the radio or television or in the papers until we asked for it. (U.S. Senate 1971:776)

Particularly contentious was the lack of bilingual assistance in explaining what would and what would not be covered by federal disaster aid.

Concerns about the special status of non-English-speaking populations in disasters grew as anticipation of routine earthquake prediction rose in the years following the 1971 earthquake. A National Academy of Sciences' committee focused on the issue:

> *Recommendation 12*   Careful attention should be paid to the problems of communicating to segments of the population that might otherwise receive only last-minute warnings. These segments include such groups as foreign-speaking minorities. (Panel on the Public Policy Implications of Earthquake Prediction 1975:11)

Until recently, this special concern meant paying attention to the Spanish-speaking in Los Angeles and to Hispanics and Chinese-Americans in San Francisco. As immigrants to California from other parts of the world not only grew in number but, more importantly, gained their political voices, concern grew to include the Vietnamese, the Thais, people speaking only Tagalog, and so forth. The 1994 Northridge earthquake reinforced these concerns. FEMA personnel counted seventeen different languages spoken by applicants for disaster assistance (Miller 1994). Most visible in the news was a group of elderly Armenians who occupied many damaged apartment buildings in Hollywood (Nazario 1994).

The "arrival" of new aspects of the earthquake threat is usually followed by funding of policy-relevant research by the National Science Foundation's societal response to natural hazards program. Thus, a grant from the National Science Foundation to the Battelle Human Affairs Research Centers in the late 1970s for a study of the special problems of minorities, especially Hispanics, served to legitimate this new phase of domain expansion (see Perry, Greene, and Mushkatel 1983; see also Perry, Lindell, and Greene 1980). Later studies of a similar nature were funded following the Whittier Narrows (Nigg and Tierney 1990; Bolton, Liebow, and Olson 1993) and Loma Prieta earthquakes (Comerio et al. 1994).

The Disabled

The emergence of concerns for the disabled as a new aspect of the earthquake threat has a history similar to that of the non–English speaking. One difference is the spillover from a growing body of research sponsored by the federal government on behavior in fire disasters (see, for example, Pearson and Joost 1983). Fire research and the special threat of fires for the disabled had become linked by the early 1980s. Only a slight nudge was needed to expand these concerns to the situation facing disabled persons in an earthquake disaster.

That nudge occurred in 1983. The author of the California Seismic Safety Commission's report on the 1983 Coalinga earthquake became part of a research team at the University of Southern California studying "Physical Disability and Earthquake Hazard Mitigation" with funds from the National Science Foundation. This project involved several different tasks, including interviews with disabled persons who had experienced the earthquake in Coalinga as well as separate interviews with nursing home administrators in the Los Angeles area. The preface to the final project report begins with the following:

> The project summarized here is the first study to focus on how earth-quake hazards affect the large and growing segment of the population that is disabled. One of our initial discoveries in conducting the research was that there is very little solid data available on the topic. Disabled people are an invisible population in the disaster research literature, just as, until recently, they have been in society. (Tierney et al. 1988:iii)

While this monograph established the special circumstances involving the disabled as a legitimate aspect of the threat of earthquakes, its authors were not optimistic that these concerns would be aggressively pursued:

> At present, stakeholder mobilization with regard to the issues discussed in this report appears to be very low. In order to lobby effectively in their own behalf, disabled persons must be aware of the earthquake hazard and organized as a constituency, and this has not yet occurred. (Tierney et al. 1988:104)

Minorities

That minorities were a segment of the population especially vulnerable to the effects of natural disasters predates the San Fernando earthquake. It was one of the lessons of a series of hurricanes along the Gulf Coast, including the devastating Hurricane Camille in 1969. That hurricane killed nearly three hundred people and inflicted $1.5 billion in damage (in 1969 dollars), mostly in the South (in Mississippi, Alabama, and Louisiana but also in West Virginia and Virginia). This was the post–civil rights movement South, and the complaints of angry blacks about favoritism given to white neighborhoods in rehabilitation efforts, about the inade-quacies of emergency housing arrangements for minorities, and about recovery in general were heard very clearly in Washington, D.C.

The social science research community at the time was focusing al-most exclusively on the period of immediate impact in disasters. Since the issues of concern to minorities, especially to African-Americans, arose much later in the disaster process, questions involving the special problems facing minorities did not arouse any research interest until a few years later. (It should also be noted that there were extremely few African-American social scientists doing research on natural hazards at this time.) In the meantime, federal emergency managers were becom-ing increasingly concerned about the "instant integration" that occurred when blacks were given temporary disaster housing in all-white neigh-borhoods (see Drabek and Key 1984). Another concern was the ability that federal disaster relief officials had to desegregate whole commu-nities simply by refusing to pay for reconstruction (of public housing, for example) in hazardous areas such as floodplains. Building elsewhere could mean developing low-income minority housing in previously all-white neighborhoods. The authority to refuse reimbursement grew out of an increasing emphasis on mitigation and the effort to eliminate the federal government's obligation to subsidize what it deemed poor loca-tional decisions by local governments.

Social scientists did not begin to study minorities in disasters until the focus of their research broadened to include the rehabilitation and recov-ery phases. Robert Bolin (1982) in particular took an interest in the ability of families to recover from disasters, and race became an important independent variable in these studies (e.g., Bolin and Bolton 1986). Mi-nority problems in all phases of disaster were the focus of research carried out at the Battelle Human Affairs Research Centers (Perry et al. 1983), again funded by the National Science Foundation.

The Homeless

Special problems of the homeless as an aspect of the earthquake threat are not yet fully established as part of the definition of risk. They are currently in process, so to speak, due largely to one of the lessons of the San Francisco Bay area earthquake in 1989. The homeless had not arrived as an especially vulnerable population in the mid-1970s when the Nation-al Academy of Sciences' panel was examining special problems in issuing earthquake predictions and warnings. In its Recommendation 12, where the panel identifies segments of the population that could easily be left out of the warning process, the NAS report states:

These segments include such groups as foreign-speaking minorities, the physically handicapped, tourists, and the socially isolated. (Panel on the Public Policy Implications of Earthquake Prediction 1975:11)

In the body of the report similar language is used.

Special efforts should be made to reach underprivileged groups, including the more isolated ethnic, religious, non-English-speaking, aged, and non-mainstream groups in the community. (Panel on the Public Policy Implications of Earthquake Prediction 1975:129)

The homeless could quite easily be considered among "the socially isolated" and "nonmainstream groups in the community." However, the fact that the homeless are not specifically named suggests that this particular set of potential earthquake victims had not forced its way into the collective consciousness of the earthquake establishment at the time.

The homeless are a special concern to emergency shelter managers such as the American Red Cross and to FEMA because of the roles these agencies play in providing temporary housing after disasters (see also Rubin and Popkin 1991). One concern is the volatility of the relationship between the homeless and other displaced people in such temporary housing arrangements. Another concern, reflected in a class action suit filed against FEMA in the aftermath of the Loma Prieta earthquake, is the failure of federal agencies to meet the unique needs of homeless and transient populations. How important this special population becomes in the definition of the risk of earthquakes will be a function of how persistent and effective groups representing the homeless, the transient, and low-income tenants are.[5]

A Negative Case: Inmates in Correctional Facilities

My hypothesis that changes in the earthquake threat over time result from recognition of new stakeholder groups by the earthquake establishment is also supported by the *absence* of certain elements in the definition of risk. Over the years, several so-called captive populations have been identified as especially vulnerable in the event of an earthquake. Captive populations involve people who are unable to function independently during or immediately after the impact of an earthquake. Examples include school-age and preschool children, the disabled, hospital patients, and residents of nursing homes. Missing from this list of captive populations is the incarcerated.

Inmates in prisons, jails, and juvenile detention facilities are as dependent during the onset of disaster as any of the captive populations listed, but special concern for them is not part of the definition of the risk of earthquakes. This lesson could have been learned in some of the earthquake disasters described above. For example, dealing with prisoners from the city's jails was one of the concerns during the San Francisco earthquake and resulting fire in 1906. The journalistic account by Thomas and Witts (1971) provides some details:

> All morning [of Wednesday, April 18, 1906] the fearful din continued in the city jail, unchecked. To the prisoners the building seemed on the verge of collapse, as it creaked and groaned like a worn-out sailing ship in a storm. Then a chilling rumor swept through the cell block. San Francisco was being evacuated—but they would be left to die as an object lesson to future sinners. (pp. 106–7)
>
> Late in the afternoon it [i.e., help] came. From the Hall of Justice, where he had been in conference with the other leading citizens, Judge John Hunt arrived and ordered the prisoners to be taken outside. The cell doors were swiftly unlocked. The inmates, watched by the detachment of soldiers who had guarded them all afternoon, were herded out into Plymouth Square. . . . Fifty-five hours passed before they were safely behind bars again. They were ferried across the Bay to San Quentin Prison, and were refused admission because "they were federal prisoners in the charge of troops." The steamer returned to San Francisco, received new orders, and made the shorter crossing to Alcatraz Island. There, before being locked up, they got their first real meal in over two days. (p. 136)

Part of the dilemma was the conflicting jurisdictions of various governmental entities. The prisoners were inmates of the *city* jail but were guarded by *federal* troops whereas San Quentin is a *state* penitentiary.

The dilemmas were not limited to prisoners. Another captive population proved difficult to deal with as well:

> At the State [Insane] Asylum of Agnews [near San Jose], Sheriff Ross and twenty deputies from San Jose surrounded the wrecked buildings and began to advance on the scene that Ross later testified "had never before been seen in an asylum. The moans of the dying were terrible. To add to the horror of the situation many lunatics had broken from the rubble and were trying to escape. They were wild and rushed to and fro, attacking everyone who came in their path. The question of what to do with them arose. There was no building nearby in which they could be confined, and as they were violent, it was necessary to restrain them in some way. A doctor suggested that they be tied to trees."
>
> Ropes were procured and the acutely disturbed were bound hand and foot to small trees which surrounded the hospital and miraculously remained standing. (p. 82)

This lesson was available for learning once again in 1971. Both the Karl Holton Boys Camp and the Sylmar Juvenile Hall were extensively damaged by landslides caused by the San Fernando earthquake. Each had to be evacuated. The juvenile hall received more attention from postearthquake commissions than the more remote camp. Though built of sturdy reinforced concrete befitting a structure for incarceration, several of the buildings were extensively damaged. Inmates had to be moved outside onto the grounds only after those who were trapped in their cells by jammed cell doors—with the strong smell of natural gas filling the air—were freed (Stallings and Freeling 1977).

Inmates, whether juvenile or adult, have never become one of the captive populations of special concern that comprise the earthquake threat. One of the most important reports on the San Fernando earthquake, the one by the Pacific Fire Rating Bureau, does not even mention problems at the Sylmar Juvenile Hall in its summary of major findings. The report itself deals with the facility only as one of the "Special Cases of Damage," not as an instance involving an especially vulnerable population:

> The special *engineering* and *insurance* problem [sic] here is the need to identify similar conditions elsewhere. Earthquake induced landslides on slopes this gentle have not been considered a general problem in the past. Additionally, buildings are not designed to withstand landslides such as these without incurring losses which probably would make the costs of reconstruction prohibitive. The special *soil liquefaction problem* identified here may have many counterparts in the soft alluviums throughout the earthquake prone areas of western United States. (Steinbrugge et al. 1971:61–62, emphasis added)

The lesson here is about unexpected soil failures and special engineering and insurance issues, not the risks faced by a different type of dependent population. In fairness, one could argue that this report is intentionally about engineering and insurance aspects of this earthquake disaster. However, in other sections of the report dealing with hospitals and dam failures, for example, there is ample concern for potential human victims. The report by the county's own official earthquake commission treats the issue of the inmate population in the same way, that is, by not mentioning it in its conclusions and recommendations and citing concern only for ground deformations in the body of its report (Los Angeles County Earthquake Commission 1971:3–5, 25–26).

Twenty years later, inmates are still invisible as a special aspect of the earthquake threat. Undoubtedly those responsible for managing penal facilities in areas known for their earthquake risks like California have plans and procedures for what to do in a disaster. California's Disaster Act, for example, does describe authorities and responsibilities for the state's prison administrators. However, within the earthquake establishment, the potential vulnerability of inmates is not a special concern. One could offer several hypotheses about why this is so. They would include the belief that running jails, prisons, and penitentiaries is someone else's responsibility; inmate facilities are built to be secure, therefore they will withstand the forces of earthquakes; inmates are too big a strain on public finances as it is; if anything, it is not the exposure of inmates to the earthquake threat but the exposure of society to the threat of escaping inmates after an earthquake that is the real issue. I would simply offer a single hypothesis as an alternative to this list. Inmates as a special at-risk population in the event of earthquakes is a nonissue because there is no interest group or social movement organization championing this issue. Target populations lacking social standing and political power in general receive few benefits in the policymaking process (Schneider and Ingram 1993).

RETYPIFICATION

There is a more fundamental form of change in the typification of the earthquake threat than either increasingly complex consequences or identification of segments of the population with special vulnerabilities. The change is more fundamental because it involves seeing the threat in an entirely new light, as a threat of a different nature. The change represents a growing consensus within the earthquake establishment that the *consequences* of earthquakes are not limited to personal injury and property damage. The earthquake threat is undergoing retypification, being recast as a qualitatively different type of condition. Two forms of retypification are the emergence of earthquakes as psychological hazards and as economic hazards. The earthquake as an economic threat has had the greater impact on risk promotion.

Partial Retypification and the Mental Health Movement

The Disaster Relief Act of 1974 (P.L. 93-288) expanded the scope of federal aid in the aftermath of major natural disasters such as earthquakes to include funds for a new type of assistance. The change is described in Section 413 of the Act (42 USC 5183):

> The President is authorized (through the National Institute of Mental Health) to provide professional counseling services, including assistance to State or local agencies or private mental health organizations to provide such services or training of disaster workers, to victims of disasters in order to relieve mental health problems caused or aggravated by such major disaster or its aftermath.

The inclusion of this section, while only fifty-eight words in a bill running nearly eighteen pages long, indicates that earthquakes and other
natural disasters had become more than medical and engineering catastrophes. They had become psychological disasters, and the federal government was officially recognizing the legitimacy of a mental health
perspective. How had this come about?

The aftermath of the San Fernando earthquake provided an opportunity for exposure of a large number of people suddenly and dramatically reminded of the earthquake threat, especially young people, to the
range of mental health services offered in a major metropolitan area.
Especially well situated was the San Fernando Valley Child Guidance
Clinic. The clinic was treating a number of children and their parents
in the aftermath of the earthquake. Its executive director and its director of
clinical services were both invited to testify before the Senate Public Works
subcommittee in June of 1971. The clinical services director testified:

> The incidence of anxiety in the so-called normal population was much
> higher than was expected—most parents were surprised that usually com-
> petent, unafraid children, particularly boys, were affected.
> The large number of parents bringing children to the clinic have shown
> willingness to use mental health services when such are offered in time of
> crisis. This compares favorably with parents of children who have more
> chronic conditions, and suggests that it is in time of crisis that people
> should be reached with an offer of help. . . .
> As a result of the experiences of the clinic with the earthquake crisis, the
> clinic has several suggestions for future action. This is usually in the form
> of a mental health component for disaster planning.
> We would like to add a mental health team to present disaster programs.
> We would like to send teams to local schools to meet with school personnel
> and provide consultation to them in directing discussions centered around
> the disaster.
> We would like to develop training programs in the area of mental health
> for policemen and firemen, particularly stressing an understanding of fear
> reactions and how to counteract them. . . .
> We would like to disseminate the findings of a study based on the present
> earthquake to alert mental health professionals to the highest risk populations.
> We would like to provide a model of intervention where a team of scien-
> tists can move into a community affected by disaster, earthquake, fire,
> flood, immediately after the disaster, to compile important data as to the
> pattern of reaction and degree of effectiveness of the attempted mental
> health intervention.
> Also we would like to prepare a brochure acquainting parents, teachers,
> doctors, et cetera, with children's reactions, in order to prepare them to
> handle such reactions at home during and after the disaster, thus dimin-
> ishing the severity of emotional reactions. (U.S. Senate 1971:756–58)

At least one member of the subcommittee was impressed. Senator John
Tunney thanked the clinical services director for his

> very interesting statement. The tremendous impact that fear resulting
> from a natural catastrophe has on the feelings of children is a very real
> problem and I agree that persons skilled in mental health problems should
> be part of a disaster team. . . .
>
> It would be important to have a mental health component for every disas-
> ter team, and I think the committee should encourage the National Direc-
> tor [of the Office of Emergency Preparedness] to make this a policy at the
> Federal level. (U.S. Senate 1971:758)

More was going on in the mental health field than just this one earthquake disaster, however. Most important for the retypification of the
earthquake threat was a growing concern for the psychological effects of
combat. The Vietnam War was winding down, and mental health professionals were reporting that many returning veterans were having a
difficult time readjusting to civilian life. Symptoms such as depression,
anxiety, alcoholism, and the like were being identified. An emerging
explanation was taking shape; it would come to be known as post-
traumatic stress disorder (PTSD; see Scott 1993, esp. pp. 27–73). With
the large and growing number of mental health professionals and the
increasing acceptance of psychological interventions as part of normal
health care practices, it was inevitable that PTSD would be expected
following other presumably traumatic experiences. Natural disasters
such as earthquakes easily fit the category of a traumatic experience for
survivors who escaped unharmed, for the friends and relatives of victims, and even for those far removed from physical impact but who
nevertheless felt psychologically victimized.

Once again signaling the growing acceptance of a new aspect of the
definition of risk, research funds began to be devoted to the study of the
mental health consequences of natural disasters. Although two decades
of social-science research showed few short-term and no long-term psychological problems attributable to disasters (Marks 1954; Mileti, Drabek,
and Haas 1975; Drabek 1986), program managers within the National
Institute of Mental Health, the principal agency gearing up to fund
research on this topic, were convinced that new studies would find
widespread mental health problems (see Frederick 1977). After all, some
of the studies showing otherwise were rather old and from another era
(e.g., Marks 1954). Most were case studies without the rigorous sampling
designs, standardized measuring instruments, and sophisticated statistical analyses that epidemiologists were accustomed to. A schism was
developing among disaster researchers with sociologists on one side
insisting that negative mental health effects of disasters were blown out of

proportion and psychologists and psychiatrists on the other insisting that the problems were real but had not been found by other researchers.

Support for the mental health position seemingly came in 1972. The collapse of earthen dams in the coal fields of West Virginia released a wall of water that destroyed entire villages downstream. The Buffalo Creek flood drew the attention of mental health professionals for many reasons including the scale of the devastation and the amount of dislocation it produced. It also drew the attention of lawyers who filed suit against the coal company responsible for damming up the river. The Buffalo Creek disaster also aroused the interest of a renowned Yale sociologist, Kai Erikson, who wrote a book about the flood that seemed to contradict nearly a quarter-century of previous research. Erikson (1976) concluded that this disaster had left deep and long-lasting psychological scars on survivors. Mental health experts readily accepted Erikson's findings, but veteran disaster researchers found his study seriously flawed. Erikson's reliance on legal depositions given by victims for the up-coming court case was identified as a major methodological weakness of his study and one reason to be skeptical about of his conclusions (Dynes 1978).

A major sociological counterattack on the mental health position came in the aftermath of a spring tornado that touched down only a few hundred miles from Buffalo Creek. The small city of Xenia, Ohio (population about 28,000 at the time), was extensively damaged in the storm. Xenia was an attractive research site because the percentage of its residents directly affected by the tornado was unusually high, as had been the case in Buffalo Creek. With funds from both federal and state mental health agencies, researchers from Ohio State University tracked down victims and survivors using a complicated sampling design. Their interview schedules included standardized scales for measuring stress and depression (Taylor et al. 1976). The study's findings challenged the image of disasters as serious threats to the mental health of stricken communities (see also Taylor 1977).[6]

Whatever the actual incidence of psychological difficulties following disasters, the belief that mental health services should be available was growing. Consensus was further enhanced by the 1976 crash of a commercial jetliner and a private airplane near Lindbergh Field in San Diego. The condition of most of the bodies of passengers and crew members from the airliner was such that many of the emergency personnel responding to the scene (fire, police, ambulance, and medical personnel) reported psychological problems for a long time afterwards. The movement to provide mental health counseling to emergency responders spread. Both predisaster training and postdisaster crisis management services were increased.

The psychological definition of disasters, including earthquakes, did not replace the prevailing definition of threats to life and health. Analysts continue to compute risk as the probability of being killed or injured in an earthquake rather than as the likelihood of suffering from depression, anxiety, and the like. Still, the mental health movement succeeded in establishing the earthquake threat as a psychological as well as physical threat. Even in California, with its frequent (usually small) earthquakes, the prospect of a future catastrophic earthquake is accepted as a threat to mental health by many:

> For many Southland residents, that air of uncertainty—arguably unlike any potential disaster other than the now-receding threat of nuclear warfare—is difficult to handle.
> UCLA psychiatry professor Dr. Gary Small says the thousands of frenetic calls that government officials are receiving from quaking citizens comprise essential elements of a classic panic reaction.
> "Mass panic is an outbreak of anxiety or fear in a group of people," said Small, who has studied mass hysteria. "The symptom spreads from person to person due to a situation that's anxiety-provoking, such as being in the actual earthquake, or less directly, by telephone after observing media reports or reading about it in the newspaper." (Feldman 1992)

For some, both inside and outside the earthquake establishment, the earthquake threat is a psychological threat above all else.

Retypification and the Ascension of Mitigation

More pervasive has been the shift from earthquakes as causes of suffering and destruction to earthquakes as economic disasters. The most visible indicator of this change is the shift in emphasis from preparing for earthquakes and other natural disasters in the 1960s to earthquake *mitigation* in the 1980s and 1990s. The fundamental difference between these two emphases is the willingness to make human agents at least partly responsible for unacceptably high levels of risk.

The ascension of mitigation reflects a growing economic definition of the earthquake threat. In the 1960s, only a handful of economists were interested in research on disasters. During the cold war, research money was available from the federal government to study events that could be considered peacetime analogs for an enemy attack. The RAND Corporation in southern California, under contract with the Department of Defense, conducted many of the economic studies of the effects of a variety of catastrophes (e.g., Hirshleifer 1966). One of those participating was Jack Hirshleifer, an economist at the University of California in Los Angeles, who maintained a research interest in the economic effects of disasters and intermittently served the earthquake establishment for nearly two decades. The Alaskan earthquake of 1964 brought more economists into the research picture. Howard Kunreuther from the Wharton School led a comprehensive economic analysis of this disaster for the Institute of Defense Analysis (IDA) (Kunreuther and Fiore 1966; Dacy and Kunreuther 1969). Kunreuther's research interests were in private insurance as an alternative to federal disaster relief in recovery from major catastrophes. The first sentence from the preface to one of the Alaska reports makes his position about recovery from disasters clear:

> The main objective of this book is to formulate a clear-cut case for the development of a comprehensive system of disaster insurance as an alternative to the current paternalistic Federal policy. (Dacy and Kunreuther 1969:ix)

Kunreuther maintains his interest in insurance as a mitigation strategy to the present day. George Rogers, an economist on the faculty at the University of Alaska, assisted in the IDA analyses and also participated in the National Academy of Sciences panel as an expert of the economy of Alaska (Committee on the Alaska Earthquake 1970). Jerome Milliman examined economic implications of earthquake predictions for the National Academy of Sciences Panel on the Public Policy Implications of Earthquake Prediction (1975). From the mid-1960s to the mid-1970s, individual economists made contributions to the promotion of the risk of earthquakes. However, these contributions were more a form of domain elaboration, that is, recognizing new aspects of the threat, than a fundamentally different way of thinking about earthquakes.

The ascension of mitigation had more to do with policymaking directed at another type of natural hazard, the threat of floods. The view of risk that emerged in dealing with floods spilled over into claimsmaking related to the earthquake threat. A new strategy for dealing with floods was emerging in the 1970s. It involved a federally subsidized insurance and reinsurance program with strings attached for local participation. The program was called the National Flood Insurance Program and was created by major pieces of legislation in 1968 (the National Flood Insurance Act, P.L. 90-448) and 1973 (the Flood Disaster Protection Act, P.L. 93-234). Both bills escalated the conflict between the federal government and state and local governments over who pays for the costs of natural disasters. The 1968 act required local governments to regulate construction within flood plains as a condition for receiving federally subsidized flood insurance (see Burby and French 1981). The 1973 act closed some loopholes in the implementation of the earlier bill (May 1985:31–38). Together with the inclusion of a section (Section 406) requiring reduction of future risk as a condition for receiving federal disaster assistance in the Disaster Relief Act of 1974 (P.L. 93-288), these policies established the trenches in a battle over acceptable costs. The battle was about saving money.

Retypification of the risk of earthquakes and other natural disasters in economic terms was further aided by the growing influence of specially trained policy analysts within the federal government. Most policy analysts are trained in the theory of microeconomics and in the methods of econometrics. Nowhere in Washington is the prevalence of an economic perspective more evident than in the General Accounting Office (GAO). GAO staff undertake analyses of public policies and policy options at the behest of members of Congress. Several analyses of the federal role in future disasters were carried out in the late 1970s. The following quotation is from the cover page of one of the most important of these. Note in particular the traditional microeconomic emphasis on equity and efficiency as the two main criteria for evaluating disaster assistance alternatives:

> Three forms of assistance are presently available: loans, grants, and insurance. Some tax transfers [also] are a form of assistance which increases the [federal] Government's risk while escaping budget scrutiny.
> In formulating Federal disaster policy, two economic principles should be considered:
> —equity—consistency of assistance among victims, for different disasters, and over time; and
> —efficiency—the influence of the policy on potential victims' willingness to risk disaster losses.
> The policy should embody the notion that those losing the most—proportionately—from a natural disaster should receive the most assistance and that the availability of assistance should minimize the possibility of contributing to poor locational decisions. GAO believes that the most efficient and equitable form of assistance is insurance. (Comptroller General of the United States 1980)

The report itself examines the cost to individuals and to the federal government of these three alternative approaches.

Economic aspects of the earthquake threat currently attract a large share of attention within the earthquake establishment. Five different earthquake insurance bills were introduced in the 102nd Congress (1991–1992), and four more bills were introduced in the 103rd Congress (1993–1994). The insurance industry itself is concerned about its prospects if a truly catastrophic earthquake were to occur. The subtitle of its 1989 report signifies its definition of risk: *Catastrophic Earthquakes: The Need to Insure Against Economic Disaster* (The Earthquake Project 1989). Currently, the National Earthquake Hazard Reduction Program (NEHRP) is organized around six domestic program elements, one of which is "planning and mitigation (including insurance)" (National Earthquake Hazard Reduction Program 1992:ix).

Mitigation currently enjoys a fair amount of bipartisan support in Washington.[7] Clearly the Clinton administration subscribes to the primacy of mitigation as a strategy for dealing with the earthquake threat and with natural hazards in general. In an invited comment in the principal newsletter for the natural hazards research and practitioner communities, the newly appointed (as of April 1993) director of FEMA makes the Clinton administration's position clear. Though couched in the rhetoric of fostering partnerships among levels of government (e.g., "Disasters are about people helping people"), mitigation is the preferred policy alternative.

> Riding above all is the aim of any effective, efficient response—to help victims. Victims must be our first priority.
>
> Yet, because victims are truly our first priority, we must first help people avoid becoming victims. Reducing the risk to people and our society is the best job emergency management can accomplishment. In a program of national emergency management centered on people helping people, mitigation is the principal foundation because it helps reduce the number of victims. And where it cannot prevent a person from becoming a victim, it can help reduce the losses and suffering.
>
> In addition, mitigation should be viewed as the means to decrease demands for disaster response services. It reduces the principal causes— failing buildings and falling debris—of injuries and deaths; it enables quicker lifesaving response and economic recovery because the community infrastructure remains intact; and it reduces the societal impacts of disaster because it results in less disruption of the social environment. . . .
>
> Our recent experience with the National Earthquake Hazards Reduction Program (NEHRP) aptly supports this view. Two recent reports to Congress on the NEHRP state that lack of mitigation know-how is not the principal reason earthquake mitigation has not been widely implemented. Instead, both of these reports conclude that most state and local governments are unlikely to implement thorough earthquake mitigation programs in the absence of stronger federal requirements, guidance, and incentives. . . .
>
> We cannot afford to continue with "business as usual" in the natural hazards field. And because mitigation is to become recognized as the foundation of emergency management, I propose that a national mitigation strategy be designed and adopted. . . .
>
> The cornerstone of this strategy must be real financial incentives to support communities, businesses, and individuals who undertake mitigation actions. In fact, I believe that the issue of financial incentives for mitigation must be given priority. . . .
>
> One avenue that may bear fruit is an all-hazards risk reduction program that uses insurance as an incentive. . . . In order to fit into the [national

mitigation] strategy, I believe there are features it needs to contain: it should result in more effective assistance for disaster victims to rebuild their lives, their homes, and their communities; it should place a priority on risk reduction and supply resources for mitigation activities; it should reduce not only the federal, but also the state and local dollars spent on disaster relief; and it should be fair to the taxpayers across the nation. (Witt 1993:2–3)

The last feature, about fairness, is a layperson's term for the economist's principle of equity.

Two final pieces of evidence show the growing retypification around economic concerns. One is an announcement for a "U.S. Natural Hazards Symposium" distributed via electronic mail by the Natural Hazards Research and Applications Information Center at the University of Colorado in Boulder. Held in Washington, D.C. in the fall of 1993, the scheduled speakers included representatives from the White House, Congress, FEMA, the Geological Survey, as well as the World Bank, the U.S. Agency for International Development, and the National Committee on Property Insurance. Sessions were to focus on "four critical areas: the aggregate threat of disaster to the nation; who is responsible for the financial burden of natural disasters; opportunities for mitigating the risks; and the link between disasters and development." Perhaps more significant than all of the above is the following definition in the glossary of the most recent NEHRP report to Congress. Earthquake risk is defined as "[t]he probability of loss (e.g., *economic loss*, morbidity and mortality, loss of function) of one or more physical element or elements (e.g., buildings, lifeline systems, and contents) exposed to its effects" (National Earthquake Hazard Reduction Program 1992:119, emphasis added). An economic component has become, literally, part of the official definition of the risk of earthquakes.

CONCLUSION

It is time to return to the question posed at the beginning of this chapter: How can we best explain changes over time in typifications of the earthquake threat? First, what kind of changes are we talking about? On the one hand, earthquakes are still earthquakes; the forces that produce them seemingly have remained constant for thousands, perhaps tens of thousands, of years. On the other hand, each new earthquake is unique with an infinite number of idiosyncratic features and with as many personal experiences as there are people exposed to the disaster. What has changed about the nature and meaning of the earthquake threat?

Most evident is the change in worldviews across several centuries. People whose dominant belief system explained the world around them in terms of animals and serpents naturally accounted for earthquakes in the same way. People who believed that disasters represent the displeasure of one deity or another logically tried to reduce future threats by appeasing their gods through religious ceremonies. Other people, whose dominant belief system excludes mysticism and deities in favor of natural forces, explain earthquakes in terms of matter, movement, strain, and sudden energy release.

There are short-term changes as well. Throughout the twentieth century, the "reality" of earthquakes and the meaning of the earthquake threat have continued to change. More and more potential consequences of a future catastrophic earthquake have been added to the claims-making process. The threat of fires, dam failures, damage to life lines, extensive evacuations and the potential for massive looting, and the convergence of news reporters in overwhelming numbers have elaborated the image of the Big One. There has also been increasing recognition that certain segments of the population are especially vulnerable in the event of a catastrophic earthquake. I borrowed the term *domain expansion* to describe the singling out of the non–English speaking (originally only those whose first language was Spanish), minorities in general, and other types of so-called dependent populations whose physical movement would be constrained at the time of impact. Each was at some point one of the lessons learned in an earthquake disaster.

Two other changes have occurred. They represent fundamentally different ways of thinking about the earthquake threat from the conventional focus on loss of life and collapse of buildings. One change retypified the earthquake threat as the risk of psychological harm rather than exclusively physical injury. While only partially successful in redefining risk, this mental health perspective became an established element in earthquake preparedness and postearthquake recovery activities. The other change, more pervasive and continuing to grow as a way of thinking about natural disasters in general, retypified the risk of earthquakes as an economic threat. Saving lives, reducing injuries, and minimizing property damage became not ends in themselves but the means for reducing the economic costs of earthquakes. More fundamentally, the fact that lives can be saved and injuries and damage reduced has underscored a growing belief that potential victims must take responsibility for reducing injury and loss. Put simply, this view holds that nature may cause earthquakes, but people cause the unacceptably high costs of earthquake disasters.

Earlier I contrasted two general answers to the question about why typifications of the earthquake threat change. One explains change in terms of knowledge about objective conditions. For example, scientists learn a little more about the dynamics of earthquakes each time one occurs. Engineers learn new things each time they examine a damaged building. Social scientists identify new aspects each time they examine data from the latest disaster. This explanation asks us to believe that a "new" feature of earthquakes is new because it did not exist in previous earthquakes, or if it did that it did not exist to the same extent. For example, the homeless are just now being singled out as a special at-risk population because there are more homeless now than ever before. The economic definition is growing in importance because structures are more expensive to replace than ever, hospital care is increasingly costly, the American economy is not as robust as it once was, etc.

The weakness of this type of explanation is apparent in the change over centuries from gods-and-serpent theories to scientific models of earthquakes. This change did not occur because researchers, with better measuring devices and better tools for analyzing data, discovered that there were no tortoises holding up the earth or that there was no statistically significant correlation between the level of displeasure of the gods and the occurrence of earthquakes. The change occurred as adherents of a new worldview—a new way of looking at things—challenged the authority of the guardians of the prevailing views. Over time the challengers succeeded in gaining control of idea-enforcing activities such as writing history books, teaching in schools and universities, editing periodicals, and managing libraries. Tortoises and gods were dismissed as part of a revolution in which one entire belief system replaced another, not because a growing body of evidence failed to support these hypotheses.

The cultural-authority explanation, the second answer that I presented earlier, argues that new ways of looking at objective conditions like the causes and consequences of earthquakes *precede* rather than follow the "discovery" of new aspects of those objective conditions. For example, the discovery that variations in soil composition pose a risk in future earthquakes was not the reason geologists were called in to investigate the San Francisco earthquake in 1906. Rather, because geologists carried the major responsibility for the investigative work on this disaster, they collected data that described a relationship between soils and patterns of damage. Geologists were selected for this work because geologic studies and analyses had been institutionalized in both state and federal governments by the turn of the century. Similarly, building practices were the focus of postearthquake inquiries in 1933, not because the Long Beach earthquake was the first in which certain types of structures failed more than others, but because by that time engineers had "arrived" as accepted specialists in governmental affairs (see Layton 1986).

Engineers became partners with earth scientists in ownership of the earthquake threat, and together they produced postearthquake reports that included sections on earth movements, earthquake epicenters, and energy released as well as on structures, design, and construction practices. In other words, domain elaboration is produced by changes in society at large prior to individual earthquake events. Most important has been the emergence of new professions and occupations, the growing number of their practitioners, and the legitimation of their authority to render expert judgments on matters falling within their domain.

Domain expansion and retypification result from similar social changes that range far beyond the world of earthquakes and natural disasters.[8] For example, the special vulnerability of the non–English speaking and minorities was discovered in the late 1960s and early 1970s after more than a decade of civil rights activity. Hispanics and African-Americans were not victimized by disasters for the first time, but issues affecting minorities had newfound status on both public and governmental agendas. That such status eventually found expression in disaster relief policy and disaster research funding in the mid-1970s is not a coincidence. Similarly, the first systematic study of the special problems of the disabled in earthquakes came a few years after major federal policy initiatives aimed at ensuring their rights, which in turn came after years of organizing, consciousness-raising, and lobbying by disabled-rights advocacy groups. On the opposite side, the lack of attention to the incarcerated as a specially vulnerable captive population reflects not only the absence of successful advocacy groups but also the success of groups promoting the rights of victims of crime over the rights of criminal defendants. In the future, not the number of homeless persons but the success of advocates for the homeless will determine whether or not this category is added to the list of concerns in future earthquakes. And an economic definition of the earthquake threat will grow because the rational choice models of policy analysts continue to hold sway in public policy debates regardless of the unemployment rate, growth in gross domestic product, or balance of foreign trade payments.

Two additional points about cultural authority and changes in the typifications of the earthquake threat can be stated. First, gatekeepers of the arenas in which earthquake claims-making takes place simultaneously signal that a new point of view has attained legitimacy and further establish its cultural authority. That is, decisions about whom to include on a commission panel or a postdisaster study team are decisions about which occupational specialties are relevant to earthquakes as much as they are about the professional qualifications of individual specialists. Inviting an economist to take part is a sign that an economic perspective is not only appropriate but also desirable. Of course, the inclusion of the economist ensures that economic aspects will continue to be part of the typification of the risk of earthquakes.

Second, research funded or carried out by federal agencies such as the Geological Survey, the National Science Foundation, and the National Institute of Standards and Technology has a similar effect in legitimating new elements of risk. While emergency service professionals and representatives of social movement organizations may prefer that government funds be spent on "things that need to be done" rather than on "more research," nevertheless the consequences of research can be beneficial for them. Research entrepreneurs are especially adept at translating concerns of advocacy groups into research proposals to investigate the implications of earthquakes for such groups. Regardless of what the results of the research are, chances increase that domain elaboration or expansion will draw attention to a new aspect of risk.

In short, nature may be telling her story in each new earthquake, but who is there to listen and who is not determine the moral of the story. We will discover new things in the future about the earthquake threat as new authorities arrive to interpret for us what lesson nature wants us to learn.

NOTES

1.   Readers who are familiar with social studies of science, especially those produced by European scholars, will recognize that the scientific explanation also can—and should—be transformed into a cultural-authority explanation, thus eliminating this distinction. In other words, science itself is an institutionalized form of cultural authority. I want to retain the distinction, not because I need a "straw man" to make my preference easier to defend, but because the "window pane" theory of scientific discovery (Gusfield 1976, 1981:83–108) remains the most satisfactory explanation of how people explain the earthquake threat.

2.   Even in his native Germany, Wegener, though "an accomplished scientist," was unable to secure a conventional academic position because of his advocacy of continental drift theory (Stewart 1990:29).

3.   A 1989 court decision in California (*Garvey v. State Farm Fire and Casualty Company*) reinforced the insurance industry's general right to deny claims for fire damage when fire results from an initial cause that is expressly excluded under an existing insurance policy, though legislation passed by the California legislature in anticipation of this decision sought to retain the practice of covering fire losses following earthquakes in the state (Mittler 1991:162, footnote 11).

4.   The "native villages" outside Anchorage were another matter. See Norton and Haas (1970).

5.   Following the 1994 Northridge earthquake, homelessness has become a concern of a different sort. Housing officials are worried that pockets of severe destruction affecting low-income housing could create new homeless families if entire neighborhoods cannot be rebuilt. See Colvin and Gordon (1994).

6.   Mental health workers descended on Xenia following the tornado but found fewer residents seeking counseling than they had anticipated. Convinced that psychological damage was widespread, some counselors tried to enlist school children to report "strange" behavior on the part of their parents (E. L. Quarantelli, personal communication, 1980).

7.   In the Congress, Democrats, centrist Republicans, and liberal Republicans are more enthusiastic than conservatives in both parties. Conservatives, especially conservative Republicans who traditionally favor market solutions to the threat of natural hazards, oppose mitigation on grounds that it is an attack on property rights.

8.   For a different view, see May's discussions of the relationship between societal learning and public policymaking (1992). In policy areas such as the earthquake threat, what May (1991:194–97) calls "policies without publics," he argues that changing typifications can only be accounted for by policy "insiders."

6

The Social Organization of Claims-Making

How is the risk of earthquakes promoted in the United States? How is success or lack of success affected by the way claims-making activities are organized? These questions call for an examination of the structure of the earthquake establishment. To carry out such an examination, I will treat claims-making on behalf of the earthquake threat as if it were a social movement. Such treatment should highlight strengths and weaknesses of claims-making groups in maneuvering to create a social problem out of the earthquake threat.

A social movement is an organized attempt to change something, often by using unconventional means. Few if any of the people engaged in advocating earthquake safety, or promoting risk as I call it, think of themselves and their colleagues as constituting a social movement. Most of what we currently think of as social movements—the prochoice and prolife movements, the women's movement, and the gay rights movement, for example—differ in major ways from earthquake risk promotion.

Nevertheless, treating such activities as if they were carried out by a social movement has two important advantages. From a theoretical standpoint, it provides a conceptual framework with which to describe the structure of claims-making activity. In other words, it points us in the direction of attributes that have had an impact on the promotion of other causes. From a practical standpoint, this treatment highlights the fact that promoting change is exactly what earthquake claims-makers are doing. They are trying to raise the level of awareness of the risk of earthquakes (in the context of other social movements, this would be called consciousness-raising); they are trying to change people's behavior; and they are attempting to use government, its policymaking apparatus, and its programs, to alter the state of a putative condition.

The attributes of the social organization of claims-making that I will examine are the structure of the earthquake establishment, that is, the pattern of relationships among its members; the resources that those members have at their disposal in advancing the cause of earthquake risk reduction; and the strategy and tactics they employ in advancing that cause. Social movements do not operate in a vacuum, however. Allies, bystanders, and opponents influence what social movements are able to accomplish. I will examine these external influences in the case of earthquake risk promotion. Finally, the emergence of earthquake predictions by individuals outside the earthquake establishment poses an especially delicate challenge to claims-makers. I will describe two instances of outsider predictions and the way these challenges were met. At the end of the chapter, I will assess what we have learned by treating earthquake risk promotion as if it were a social movement.

THE STRUCTURE OF THE EARTHQUAKE ESTABLISHMENT

In Chapter 3, I identified some of the members of the earthquake establishment and the roles they play in earthquake risk promotion. Now I am interested in the relationships among the members and how these relationships are sustained. These relationships form the structure of the earthquake establishment.

The best way to describe the structure of the earthquake establishment is to characterize it as a loose but stable *network* of individuals, organizational subunits, and organizations. The most noticeable difference between this network and other social movements is the absence of a headquarters and affiliated local chapters. The fact that this movement has no name signifies what is missing. Nothing like "Mothers Against Catastrophic Earthquakes" (M.A.C.E.?) exists in the United States. Instead of a national organization with office space, letterhead stationery, and an annual convention, there are only the working relationships among technocrats and bureaucrats centered on short-term projects such as the International Decade for Natural Disaster Reduction (IDNDR). An announcement for a meeting of the U.S. delegation for this United Nations project, the U. S. National Committee for the Decade for Natural Disaster Reduction, held in the fall of 1993 suggests many of the features of the movement's structure:

> The reconstituted U.S. National Committee for the International Decade for Natural Disaster Reduction (IDNDR) will hold its first meeting October 5 in Washington, DC. At this meeting members will be oriented to the mission and general objectives of the U.S. National Committee and learn about developments in the IDNDR. The meeting will also be an opportunity to discuss preparations underway for the U.S. contributions for the World Conference on Natural Disaster Reduction, to be held in Yokohama next May.

U.S. NATIONAL COMMITTEE FOR THE DECADE FOR NATURAL
DISASTER REDUCTION:

Dr. Walter R. Lynn (Chairman), Professor of Civil and Environmental
Engineering, Cornell University

Mr. J. Bryan Atwood, Administrator, Agency for International
Development

Mr. Lawrence Grossman, President, Horizons TV

Dr. George Housner, Professor of Engineering, California Institute of
Technology

Ms. Shirley Mattingly, Director of Emergency Management, City of Los
Angeles

Dr. Robert Hirsch, Director, United States Geological Survey

Dr. E. L. Quarantelli, Research Professor, Disaster Research Center, University of Delaware

Dr. Kathryn Sullivan, Chief Scientist, National Oceanic and Atmospheric Administration

Mr. James Lee Witt, Director, Federal Emergency Management Agency.
(*Disaster Research* 127, September 29, 1993)

Committees, meetings, and workshops are the glue that binds the elements of the movement together. Participants in these joint activities hold full-time jobs in a variety of organizations, most of which are in the public and nonprofit sectors. The earthquake hazard movement as a social movement exists in and through these extraorganizational activities.

Participation in the earthquake hazard movement varies but generally takes one of four or five different forms. Some participants are public-sector employees who work full-time on the earthquake hazard and other natural hazards. Many are in programs dealing with preparedness and mitigation at various levels of government and work for agencies like FEMA, the Office of Emergency Services in California, and the Department of Emergency Management in the City of Los Angeles. Other participants are academics who are involved in the earthquake hazard movement through their research. Participants from the non-profit sector are a mixed lot including physicians and other medical professionals involved with disaster medicine, the staff and associates of organizations like the Earthquake Engineering Research Institute and the Applied Technology Council, and representatives of professional associations like the American Society of Civil Engineers. There are a handful of participants who can be thought of as full-time, professional claims-makers. These include the executive director of the Seismic Safety Commission in California and the directors and paid staff of regional earthquake consortia in the West and Midwest. Finally, there are a number of participants from the private sector including representatives of utility companies concerned about the lifelines issue (see Chapter 5) and, increasingly, from the news media and the insurance industry.

Involvement in joint activities like the U.S. National Committee for the Decade for Natural Disaster Reduction is the main integrative mechanism of the movement. The electronic newsletter, *Disaster Research*, keeps members of the earthquake hazard movement up to date on a host of committees, conferences, seminars, and workshops taking place continually all over the world. Some recent examples, arbitrarily selected from the September 17, 1993, newsletter, include a conference in London on "Human Factors in Emergency Response: Developments in Evacuation, Escape and Rescue"; a meeting in Mexico City on disaster preparedness sponsored by the Mexican Society of Emergency and Disaster Medicine; a workshop on "Disaster Recovery and Business Continuity Planning" for private-sector firms in New York; and a conference on engineering aspects of the 1993 Japanese earthquake held in Chicago.

New members are recruited for the earthquake hazard movement, but not in ways normally associated with grass-roots movements. There are no massive sign-up drives because this is not a mass-based social movement. New members are welcome, but eligible recruits must possess highly specialized research, managerial, or policy skills. The process involves getting people who already have ongoing careers in related fields interested in working on a rather esoteric set of issues. Many new participants first become involved because their superiors assign them to tasks related to the risk of earthquakes, as when a local police department makes an officer responsible for the department's disaster plan. Most such people at the local level leave the earthquake safety business as soon as they receive their next promotion or job assignment. As a result, there is considerable turnover, especially at the lower levels of the earthquake hazard movement. Movement veterans consequently are on the lookout for the kind of people who seem "genuinely concerned" about the earthquake threat.

Academics are recruited typically while in graduate school. While working on advanced degrees, they are employed as research assistants on projects dealing with the earthquake threat. Though most leave this work behind when they graduate, a few develop an interest that they carry over into their subsequent careers. More formally, funding agencies such as the National Science Foundation, seeking to broaden the research infrastructure, give special consideration to research proposals submitted by young scholars early in their careers. In short, the movement does devote attention to securing new blood to carry on its work. The process involves identifying candidates with certain skills or attributes followed by efforts to nurture their interest in the "cause" of earthquake hazard reduction. There is no effort to recruit or convert masses of people.

Since nearly everyone participating in the earthquake hazards movement is employed full-time and since the major activities of the movement are publicly funded (e.g., through research grants, funds for travel to investigate recent disasters, clerical support for committees preparing reports), "fund-raising" has a different character. Typically social movements have had to confine themselves to activities that participants could pay for out of their own pockets such as traveling to the site of a demonstration. Leaders and supporters would attempt to support demonstrators by organizing vehicle pools to reduce travel costs and by securing donations of local housing where demonstrators could stay. Other movements solicit donations in various ways such as through sales of items or through telephone solicitation. Beginning in the 1960s and early 1970s, support became increasingly available from foundations and from the government, leading to the professionalization of many social movements (McCarthy and Zald 1973).

Fund-raising for earthquake hazard movement activities involves trying to increase budget allocations in various legislative arenas. Program administrators seek additional money to carry out work already authorized and to undertake new projects deemed valuable but not currently funded. Budgets for research are another item for which additional funds are routinely sought. Interestingly, the politics of the public budgeting process disclose some of the "fault lines" within the earthquake hazard movement. Local and state officials plead their case for more federal funding to carry out earthquake programs, while federal officials counter that local governments should divert more of their own resources to such programs. The research wing of the movement and managers of mission agencies disagree about what proportion of the hazards budget should go for research, with agency managers frequently grumbling that all those research dollars could be put to better use to fund program activities. Researchers themselves are divided into "hard" and "soft" science camps, with earth scientists and engineers in the former taking the lion's share of federal research and development (R&D) dollars at the expense of social scientists in the latter camp. Fault lines based on geographical differences have emerged in recent years as the risk of earthquakes became redefined as a nationwide rather than a California-only threat. For example, regional pride and considerable long-term funding were at stake in the acrimonious struggle between New York State and California over creation of the National Center for Earthquake Engineering Research, ultimately located at the State University of New York at Buffalo in 1986.

Normally, the nonproblem status of the earthquake threat makes budgets for disaster-related programs and research vulnerable to budget slashers and their sharp red pencils. Having an earthquake or some other devastating disaster, therefore, can be a real fund-raising opportunity.

More than special appropriations to cover the costs of the unscheduled event are involved. There is increased legitimacy for disaster-related agencies, which, if properly managed (such as by avoiding extensive criticism or "bad publicity"), can be used to bolster claims for an increased operating budget. Research funds for studies related to disasters usually grow in the aftermath of such events as well. The following exchange during a 1971 hearing on the collapse of the Veterans Administration hospital in the San Fernando earthquakes illustrates why:

> Mr. PUCINSKI: "Now, [Mr. Degenkolb] you said in your statement on page—I'm not sure what page it is—that the Office of Science and Technology, the task force on earthquake hazard reduction of the Office of Science and Technology had recommended $1,300,000 per year.
> "And I gather you are saying that we only appropriated $300,000 for this work; is that correct?"
> Mr. Degenkolb: "No. It's a little bit twisted around. They have been spending money at the level of around $300,000 a year. After the last earthquake, there was a large number of recommendations as to future research.
> "This task force I referred to here was charged with the evaluation, to put priorities on some of the research. And the recommendation uniformly was that that should be increased by new money by a million dollars a year.
> "I have hopes that that will be going through, I assume in this next budget period."
> Mr. PUCINSKI: "Right now it is not budgeted?"
> Mr. Degenkolb: "It is not budgeted."
> Mr. PUCINSKI: "$1,300,000, that is not budgeted yet?"
> Mr. Degenkolb: "That is my understanding. At least it was not a few weeks ago."
> Mr. PUCINSKI: "It seems to me that the California delegation has their work cut out for them; don't you think so?"
> Mr. Degenkolb: "I think so."
> Mr. PUCINSKI: "I might suggest that you write to each of us individually. You are bound to get more attention than you might have gotten last year." (U.S. House of Representatives 1971a:146)

The earthquake hazard movement has no national convention such as the ones held around the country by the more established social movement organizations. However, there is an annual event that has similar significance. This is a workshop organized annually by the Natural Hazards Information and Applications Center at the University of Colorado and held in Boulder. Participation is open to all public officials and academic researchers in the natural hazards area; notices and registration information are mailed to past participants as well as included in electronic and other newsletters. Funded by the National Science Foundation and several other federal agencies, the annual event began during the 1970s as an effort to link academic researchers and emergency management practitioners as "clients" for their research. Representatives from an array of local, state, and federal agencies share their policy and management concerns with academics who present summaries of their latest research projects. In addition to the workshop's formal objective, the three-day event serves other important purposes as well. Researchers and program managers from research funding agencies negotiate new projects and exchange ideas about future ones. Researchers make contacts with disaster professionals who can provide access to important data. And people establish and reestablish personal relationships that buttress the network of earthquake risk promoters. For the newcomer, attendance at the workshop is often jokingly but significantly described as a rite of passage for full-fledged membership in the disaster establishment.

In sum, the structure of the earthquake hazards movement is that of a loose-linked network or coalition of individuals representing different academic disciplines, governmental entities, and professional associations. The movement exists in and through frequent and overlapping joint activities funded primarily by federal agencies. The more important the activity (by a variety of criteria including the opportunity for international travel), the more likely that the most prestigious members of the earthquake hazard movement will be involved. International projects in particular such as the U.S. National Committee for the International Decade for Natural Disaster Reduction involve the elite among the nation's earthquake and disaster experts. Like many coalitions, leadership tends to be informal with no formal authority structure or chain of command. Administrators of earthquake programs within mission agencies such as FEMA and the Geological Survey and in research funding agencies such as Geological Survey and the National Science Foundation tend to set the direction for the movement in the short-run. Long-term objectives are set officially by policymakers (e.g., the president, members of the president's cabinet, sponsors of major legislation in Congress), but in most cases major policy directives are shaped by the products of the movement's joint activities. Thus, the unofficial "headquarters" of the earthquake hazard movement is Washington, D.C.

RESOURCES

Washington is the center because it is the hub through which resources flow to the rest of the movement. Compared to other collective efforts to promote change, the earthquake hazard movement has few traditional forms of resources. It has hardly any public visibility, apart from the negative visibility that sometimes plagues agencies like FEMA and the Small Business Administration after disasters. It has no long-term public support and very little political support.[1] Federal agencies at the core of the network such as FEMA have limited legal authority under the constitutionally created arrangement of shared governance (May and Williams 1986:4–10).

The earthquake hazard movement does have two important resources. One is its institutional base. The other is the esteem of its most visible members. By institutional base, I am referring to the housing of earthquake-related activities within a variety of public and nonprofit organizations. The seismological laboratories at various universities, the planning activities aligned with regional governments, the policy advocacy of a handful of commissions and advisory panels, the testing and technology transfer carried out by various nonprofit institutes, and the planning and mitigation programs at various levels of government provide full-time employment as well as public platforms for earthquake safety advocates. Although these activities are subject to the rise and fall of winds in the public budgeting process, they are established components of their host organizations not subjected to the ups and downs of public fund-raising and volunteer recruitment campaigns.

The other principal resource is esteem, especially that enjoyed by the earth scientists so frequently at the forefront of public risk-defining activities. Although participants in the earthquake hazards movement have a fairly wide array of analytical, technical, and administrative skills, it is the ability to explain about earthquakes—what causes them and when the next one can be expected—to which people outside the movement seem most responsive. Esteem is based on several things. Partly it reflects the cultural authority of the physical sciences in the United States. It also is a function of organizational prestige in that some of the most visible earth scientists have academic appointments at highly regarded universities such as the University of California at Berkeley, Stanford University, the California Institute of Technology, the Massachusetts Institute of Technology, and Columbia University. It is also partly a function of the fact that many of these earth scientists are respected scholars within their own disciplines. The importance of esteem to the earthquake hazards movement is one reason that anything threatening to diminish it is a potential source of trouble for the movement, a point discussed shortly.

The institutional base and personal esteem have drawbacks as well as benefits. Having a separate line in the budget of various public agencies provides some continuity for the people and programs involved in earthquake risk promotion, but there are legal limits on how these budgets can be spent. For example, support for research is permissible under some budgets, but the use of research funds to finance the reelection campaign of a legislator who has supported the cause of earthquake hazard reduction in the past is not. Esteem is a relationship between those with certain attributes and those impressed by those attributes, not an object that individuals possess. Job titles, organizational affiliations, and career accomplishments impress some people but not others, and they may be more persuasive under certain circumstances than others. The advantages and disadvantages of these two resources explain a good deal about the strategy and tactics of the earthquake hazard movement.

STRATEGY AND TACTICS

Resources do not allocate themselves. They must be put to use by those who control them. How they are used is as important for the success of claims-making as the quantity and type of resource. All social movements must make choices about how to use resources. Discussions of these choices usually fall under the heading of strategy and tactics.

Limited by its resource base, that is, the organizational resources provided by its institutional support and the intellectual authority of its technical experts, the earthquake hazard movement's strategy has been to promote voluntary change in its designated targets. Its primary tactics have been to provide resources, mostly money, which targeted groups can spend to undertake their own earthquake-related programs and to support the production of technical information that targeted groups will feel compelled to utilize.[2] Target groups vary according to which segment of the earthquake hazard movement one is considering. FEMA's primary targets are state and local governments. Local governments' targets have been households and, to a lesser extent, commercial property owners and businesses.

The first of the movement's two strategies—providing financial resources—resembles an attempt to buy change. Groups targeted by state and local governments seem responsive to hazard reduction programs—but only when the "feds" pay for them. Thus, federal earthquake and disaster legislation has often included appropriations for grants to state and local governments to pay for planning, training, and other preparedness and mitigation programs. A 1991–1992 report to Congress describes these tactics:

> FEMA is challenged with *encouraging* nationwide recognition of the earthquake hazard and *stimulating* state and local governments to commit to achieving goals and objectives of NEHRP [the National Earthquake Haz-

ard Reduction Program]. To meet this challenge, FEMA, through its state earthquake program, provides financial and technical assistance to state and local governments and multi-state organizations. (National Earthquake Hazard Reduction Program 1992:47, emphasis added)

Training in the craft of emergency management is provided by FEMA at its Emergency Management Institute (EMI) in Emmitsburg, Maryland, and at field training centers around the country. At the EMI, both resident faculty and outside experts teach courses in the art of dealing with disasters to invited local and state officials. The federal government also has entered into partnerships with multijurisdictional preparedness projects in the Northeast, Midwest, and West and in northern and southern California, providing partial financial support for regional earthquake awareness, planning, and mitigation efforts.

The second federal strategy has been to sponsor the production of new scientific and technical information that can be used by governments and others (e.g., developers, engineers, and building contractors). The Geological Survey conducts region-specific studies of earthquake potential, intending the results of these studies to meet "user needs":

If policymakers and decisionmakers in every community located in or near one or more of these seismic source zones could have basic answers to these questions [why, how, and how often do earthquakes occur?], they could plan, adopt, and implement realistic and cost-effective prevention, mitigation, and preparedness measures. [National Earthquake Hazard Reduction Program 1992:20)

Engineering and design standards are disseminated by various federal agencies and federally funded nonprofit organizations. These include the National Institute of Standards and Technology, the Applied Technology Council, the Building Seismic Safety Council, and the three major building code writing organizations, the International Congress of Building Officials, Building Officials and Code Administrators, and the Southern Building Code Congress International. Use of the information disseminated in this way is optional. The assumption underlying this tactic seems to be that once they become aware of the threat in their area and of the means for addressing it, target groups will do the right thing, that is, what the funding and technology-transferring agencies would like them to do. (Awareness, however, does not seem to translate into change; May (1991a:276) concludes that this process "is as much one of 'needing users' of information as it is of understanding 'user needs.'"]

A recently adopted federal tactic is to promote earthquake and hazard awareness under the auspices of professional associations. One such effort involved the International City Management Association, the National Association of Schools of Public Affairs and Administration, and the American Society for Public Administration. The idea was to incorporate awareness of hazards, including the earthquake hazard, and skills for managing them into the curricula of professional graduate programs like those in public administration. This collaborative effort resulted in a workshop at the Emergency Management Institute for faculty members from university programs in public administration and a special edition of the official journal of the American Society for Public Administration on emergency management issues (Petak 1985). Since the mid-1980s, earthquake and hazard awareness activities have been carried out with such professional organizations and associations as the Council of State Governments, the American Planning Association, and the American Institute of Architects. This tactic appears to be an attempt to use existing organizational structures to reach and to influence many potential targets more efficiently than on a member-by-member basis.

The second resource utilized in promoting awareness and action on behalf of the risk of earthquakes is the cultural authority of the movement's most esteemed experts. At the federal level, these experts are used to lay the foundation for funding requests and policy proposals. Reports containing recommendations by the "nation's leading minds" can be cited during budget negotiations within the executive branch and in debate over appropriations in Congress. This tactic involves an implicit form of moral suasion. By identifying the dimensions of the threat and the existence of the means to reduce it, the necessity of doing something is presumed to be self-evident. Only an "unenlightened" policymaker acting "irrationally" could ignore the "facts" of the case and fail to act "appropriately."

At the state and local levels, the same strategy and similar tactics are used. One difference from the federal level is that local governments have comparatively fewer resources with which to "buy" the voluntary compliance of targeted groups. With virtually no money to underwrite threat-related actions by others, local earthquake risk promoters are forced to rely almost exclusively on moral suasion. They will accept almost any opportunity to speak to groups assembled for luncheons, conferences, annual meetings, and so forth. Existing group structures provide a mechanism for "spreading the word" to group members. Presentations typically involve two types of speakers. The first type is the esteemed scientist or technical expert from a prestigious organization such as a leading research university or government agency (e.g., the Geological Survey or the Division of Mines and Geology in California). This speaker describes the nature of the threat, typically using a slide presentation featuring graphics of seismic fault systems and photographs of damage from a recent earthquake. The second type of speaker is usually a bureaucrat whose job involves disaster preparedness. This is the person who describes what members of the audience should do to prepare themselves, their families, and their workplaces for the catastrophic earthquake.[3] Brochures and handouts are often provided not only for the audience but also for other group members not in attendance. Again, the tactic assumes that reason will prevail: having been reminded of the threat and having heard about the preferred solutions, the only rational thing for a member of the audience to do is to implement what is recommended.

Another tactic used to promote individual change by local segments of the earthquake hazard movement is to capitalize on the occurrence of an earthquake. Earthquakes, both moderate ones nearby and large-scale ones abroad, represent a "teachable moment" (Stallings 1986) that can be used strategically. They are times when the topic of earthquakes is in the news and presumably on people's minds. They can become public education opportunities where people are reminded of what the future holds and what they can do to prepare for it. The esteem of earth scientists comes in handy. News reporters seek out "earthquake experts" to explain what has happened and, after that becomes "old news," what is in store. Some of these scientists have become celebrities in news markets like southern California. Dr. Kate Hutton and Dr. Lucile Jones of the California Institute of Technology, for example, are recognized from their many television news appearances by their

> fans who point and wave at them on the street as if they were Goldie Hawn . . . both seismologists added that on the whole they relish their time in the limelight. "It really seems to be a lot of help," said Jones. ". . . I go on television because I hope the information I can provide is useful for the community." (Weinstein 1992)

With limited resources, the earthquake hazard movement pursues a strategy of eliciting voluntary change through government-funded programs and the cultural authority of its most esteemed members. Limiting the movement's choice of strategy and tactics is the nature of its opponents, both visible and invisible.

VISIBLE AND INVISIBLE OPPONENTS

All social movements have opponents. For some movements, the opposition is a social elite that uses the coercive powers of the state to intimidate or suppress movement organizations. The early history of the civil rights movement in the South is an example. Other movements generate countermovements, that is, organized grass-roots opposition (often with elite financial support) whose goal is to prevent the movement from achieving its objectives. For example, when either the prolife movement or the prochoice movement steps up its efforts, the other one seems to be rejuvenated. In contrast, it is not uncommon for movements to experience periods in their careers when overt opposition seems to disappear. Joshua Gamson (1989, 1991) describes this situation and its consequences for the history of one local chapter of the gay rights movement.

The earthquake hazard movement has two types of opponents. A few are visible, but the majority are invisible. Visible opponents are easier to identify, of course. These include building property owners who challenge proposed changes in local building codes. They also include insurance industry representatives who become troubled by proposed public policies that they believe pose financial risks for their industry. Politicians who vote against earthquake safety legislation or earthquake safety appropriations could also be counted as visible opponents. However, such overt, publicly visible opposition is relatively infrequent. Most of the time opposition is invisible.

An invisible opponent is a potential opponent. It is a category of people whom movement leaders believe would be mobilized in opposition to some form of movement activity. Whether or not such beliefs are well-founded is irrelevant. For example, when a plan to ask a city council for more money for an earthquake-related program is abandoned because planners believe that council would never approve such a proposal, the city council is more an invisible than visible opponent of this segment of the movement. Numerically, the earthquake hazard movement has more invisible than visible opponents. (This is probably true for all social movements.)

The largest segment of invisible opponents is those whom movement participants label the "apathetic." These are ordinary citizens who dismiss the risk of earthquakes in the crush of what they consider to be more pressing concerns like making a living, raising children, and enjoying their leisure time. The apathetic do not overtly oppose what the earthquake hazard movement is trying to do, but they are unresponsive to calls for changing behavior in the face of risk. The extremists among the apathetic are what movement participants sometimes refer to as the "irrational." This term seems to be reserved for those who live in areas labeled extremely risky but who do nothing to prepare for the possibility of damaging earthquakes. From the federal perspective, home owners who "choose to be reckless" by not buying earthquake insurance are included among the irrational (e.g., U.S. Senate 1971:326). Other important invisible opponents from the federal perspective are local governments with no "self-control" that permit development on scientifically designated hazardous land (e.g., U.S. Senate 1971:323).

Three dilemmas face the earthquake hazard movement in dealing with its invisible opponents. First, it is difficult to engage an enemy that will not fight. Without an attack, there can be no counterattack. It is difficult to debate someone who is not interested in discussing the issue. There is no point in mounting a campaign to counter "misinformation" from the opposition with "facts" when there is no opposition—and no misinformation. There is no clear-cut enemy to blame for any setbacks or failures (Gamson 1991; see also Edelman 1988:30–31).

Second, some invisible opponents appear to have superior resources and are best kept potential opponents rather than aroused into overt opposition. At the local level, taxpayers mobilized into an antitaxation movement can be a formidable foe as they have shown in the past in several states. Voters who become angered over the prospect of more government and more regulation can pose a serious threat (they elect the politicians who control the funding for so much of the movement's activities). The private sector should not be alarmed by proposals that appear to be barriers to making a profit. Representatives of tourist-dependent industries can become touchy if too much is made of the potential for disaster in a particular locale. An invisible opponent can be real trouble when mobilized into active opposition (see examples from Los Angeles and St. Louis in Chapter 4).

The third and most important dilemma posed by invisible opponents is that most are also the very people whose cooperation is essential if the movement is to succeed in promoting voluntary change in the face of risk. Many potential enemies are simultaneously potentially valuable supporters. Local officials, for example, may behave "irresponsibly" in the eyes of federal bureaucrats by not adopting recommended land use controls and building codes, but the Constitution gives local government exclusive control of these public-policy instruments. Therefore, federal officials need cooperation from local government in order to achieve many of the goals of earthquake hazard reduction. The public at large may be an invisible opponent because of its general "apathy" and its failure to take the earthquake threat more seriously, but it is this same public at large whose cooperation is needed in preparing for earthquakes. Voters may be potential sources of opposition if they sense that higher taxes and more government are on the way, but they are also the only people who can provide political support for earthquake safety policies.

In short, the earthquake hazard movement could treat bystanders either as potential supporters or as potential opponents. With its limited resource base, head-to-head skirmishes with opponents are usually

by earthquake predictions made by outsiders. The challengers are not people who contend that there is *no* risk of earthquakes or even that the risk is exaggerated. They are people who offer an image of risk containing *greater* certainty than the official view.

Most frequent are earthquake predictions by psychics and seers. These are typically announced in lurid headlines in the weekly tabloids sold at supermarket checkout stands (for examples, see Turner et al. 1986:50–51). Because the predictor is a mystic or psychic, because the prediction technique involves reading astrological signs, and because the prediction is published in a tabloid, earth scientists usually feel no need for rebuttal. Occasionally, predictions of earthquakes by people outside the scientific establishment receive widespread attention and achieve a fair amount of legitimacy. The predictors seem to use scientific theories and methods. On such occasions earth scientists have engaged in a delicate form of boundary work[4] to separate official from unofficial definitions of risk, to maintain their ownership of the earthquake threat, and to preserve the resources of the earthquake hazard movement. Two examples illustrate the process of dealing with rivals.

Iben Browning was a seventy-year-old climatologist, former World War II test pilot, and consultant to businesses and investment firms. Speaking to a state agricultural conference organized by the governor of Missouri in 1989, he "projected" (he preferred this word rather than *predicted*) that a major earthquake would occur along the New Madrid fault (located in the Mississippi and Ohio River valleys) on December 3, 1990. Two things made his prediction attention-grabbing: the nation's strongest earthquakes occurred on this fault system in the winter of 1811–1812; and Browning reportedly had correctly predicted the Loma Prieta earthquake that struck the San Francisco Bay area in October 1989. The credibility of the 1990 projection was enhanced by Browning's age and scholarly demeanor, by the simplicity of his technique and the specificity of his prediction, by the official setting in which he made his projection, by the enthusiastic endorsement of a Ph.D. geologist who directed the Center for Earthquake Studies at Southeast Missouri State University, and, inadvertently, by extensive preparations undertaken by several state and local disaster preparedness agencies as a result of his forecast.

Browning based his projection on the effects of gravitational attraction of the sun and the moon on the earth's crust. He concluded that the alignment of sun, moon, and earth on December 3, 1990, would create a peak in the level of gravitational force. The resulting strain would be transmitted to the weakest places in the earth's crust (i.e., its fault system), triggering not only earthquakes but also volcanic eruptions. Browning's projection seemed supported by the fact that establishment scientists themselves had published papers reporting tests of this gravitational-attraction hypothesis.[5] No earthquake occurred on December 3, but New Madrid, Missouri—famous for its nineteenth-century earthquakes—was jumping in other respects as dozens of newspaper reporters and broadcasters milled about town.[6]

Henry Minturn was another grandfatherly looking person. On a Los Angeles television news broadcast in November 1976, he predicted that two earthquakes would occur within one month. He said the first would strike the Solomon Islands in the Pacific Ocean on December 7. The other would hit "somewhere in southern California" (his description) on December 22. He declined to predict the magnitude of the two quakes except to say that they would be about equal in intensity (Stallings 1977). His predictions attracted attention in part due to his apparently successful prediction of a small (Richter magnitude 3.9) earthquake that had occurred on the morning of the broadcast. They were given added credibility by their coverage on network television by the NBC-TV science reporter. Minturn was treated with a good deal of respect during his numerous appearances on local radio and television news broadcasts in Los Angeles over the next two weeks. He was continually referred to as "Dr. Minturn," and his dossier was said to include evidence of several previous successful predictions.

Minturn, like Browning, based his predictions on the effects of gravity on weaknesses in the earth's crust. He called his technique "multi-global earthquake forecasting" (Henry C. Minturn, personal communication, September 10, 1979) and said it involved interpretation of the interaction of four sets of forces:

1. The earth is a rotating malbalanced sphere seeking equilibrium.
2. The variations in gravimetric attraction of the moon during its cyclic orbiting.
3. The movement of heavy air masses and other atmospheric disturbances.
4. Shifting plate tectonics. (Minturn 1976:1)

Evidence for his past successes consisted primarily of two types of documents: Photocopies of clippings from a small-town newspaper, the *Pueblo (Colorado) Star-Journal*, in which his predictions were reported; and copies of several "To Whom It May Concern" letters such as the one from a television network news director who stated: "This is to confirm that Henry Minturn predicted an earthquake would occur in California on or about April 10, 1976." Attached to these letters were newspaper clippings (in the case of the news director's letter, a wire service report of a Richter magnitude 4.7 earthquake thirty miles north of Los Angeles on April 8, 1976). As on December 3, 1990, in New Madrid, December 20, 1976, in Los Angeles passed without major earthquake activity although there were two earthquakes, one of magnitude 5.1 and the other magnitude 6.3, in the Pacific Ocean 210 miles off Vancouver Island.

Predictions by outsiders like Browning and Minturn present a tricky challenge to the nation's earthquake hazard movement. Could outsiders—self-taught ones at that—"scoop" mainstream scientists? Could they know something that the revered, bespectacled academic and government scientists do not know?

The stakes are high in meeting the challenge of such rival predictions. Esteem is a liquid asset. Scientific esteem is especially vulnerable because of the public ambivalence about science (see Turner et al. 1986:253–75). Considerable damage could be done to the reputation of the earth sciences if an outsider, without the research funding provided by large government agencies, were able to accomplish something that scientists repeatedly contended was several years—and several millions of dollars—away. Loss of esteem would have negative consequences for the earthquake hazard movement. It would lessen the impact of scientific knowledge as a tool for increasing earthquake awareness and changing behavior. Furthermore, if earth scientists were shown up by an outsider, it might make Congress skeptical of what return it was getting on all of its R&D appropriations. It might even make it more difficult for federal agencies to justify their annual budget requests for earthquake-related programs.

Maintaining ownership of the earthquake threat, including the intellectual authority to describe the nature of that threat, is tricky business. Much of the confrontation has to take place in public since a majority of the people who "need to be set straight" about future earthquakes receive science news only through the general-audience media. This means that libel laws and the threat of litigation serve as constraints on the would-be defenders of science. Another tricky aspect is that earth scientists themselves expect major earthquakes on the faults in question, though they disagree with their rivals about the likelihood of occurrence on a specific date (such as December 20, 1976, or December 3, 1990). Therefore, mainstream scientists cannot counteract rival images of risk by stating flatly that *no* earthquake will occur on a given date. Third, establishment scientists face a paradox in using formally constituted earthquake prediction evaluation panels[7] to discredit outsider predictions. Many scientists fear that the act of convening such a panel would in itself confer legitimacy on outsider predictions, regardless of what the scientific verdict ultimately turned out to be. Finally, earthquake safety advocates inside and outside government crave periods of heightened receptivity to earthquake news for their strategic importance, as noted earlier. They value them as opportunities to get out their message about preparedness to an audience more receptive than usual. Thus, earth scientists may find that some of their comrades-in-arms in the earth-quake hazard movement are more enthusiastic about outsider predictions than they are (see Shipman, Fowler, and Shain 1993:385–88).

Putting down the challenge of outsider predictions can be aided by investigative reporters and science writers. Earth scientists can make oblique statements in public while giving reporters ammunition off the record to "go after" the rival predictor. For example, in the case of the Minturn prediction, scientists were quoted on the record as saying that reliable earthquake prediction was years away and that of course there was always the probability of a serious earthquake in southern California—not exactly devastatingly negative comments. In the case of Browning's prediction, earth scientists countered with their own estimate of the earthquake probability in the central United States soon after Browning's December 1989 speech. (Apparently, newspapers treated Browning more kindly than they had Minturn two decades earlier; see Dearing and Kazmierczak 1993.) Using recurrence patterns rather than cycles of gravitational attraction, the Geological Survey estimated that the probability of a Richter magnitude 6.5 earthquake in the New Madrid fault zone by the year 2005 to be between 16 and 63 percent. Presumably, people could use this information to figure out the probability for a single date like December 3.

Discrediting outsider predictions by earth scientists and their journalistic surrogates had three dimensions in these two cases. One was the debunking of outside predictors' scientific credentials. This was accomplished by identifying outsiders' lack of standard academic training and appropriate work experience. Browning's academic degrees were in mathematics and biology, not geophysics; he described himself as a self-taught volcanologist. He was a climatologist who published a newsletter for stock market investors and was a consultant to business, including the brokerage firm of PaineWebber. His chief academic supporter at Southeast Missouri State University was described by the *St. Louis Post-Dispatch* as someone who had been denied tenure at the University of North Carolina in the 1970s after his endorsement in that state of an earthquake prediction by a psychic (Hubbell 1991:82). Minturn claimed to have a doctorate in geophysics and a master's degree in geology, but he refused to answer questions about where and when he received these degrees. His resume lists nothing before his military service in 1940 and has no educational entries after the war. Friends of Minturn interviewed by reporters from the *Los Angeles Times* were surprised by his claims of advanced degrees and described his prior jobs in the oil exploration industry as those of a technician (Alexander 1976). His recent employment history included jobs as a night watchman and a mail sorter. How effective this denial of standard academic credentials was in the eyes of nonacademics is questionable. Turner and his colleagues (1986:49) argue that Minturn had a more compelling public image after his refusal to discuss his academic qualifications because he seemed to be a self-made person who, single-handedly and inexpensively, was doing what the scientific establishment had been unable to do.

The second weapon used against these outside predictors was to undermine the scientific status of the technique upon which their predictions were based. Establishment scientists once again provided reporters with the ammunition. For example, Minturn described his technique as one based on gravitational forces exerted by the moon on the plates making up the earth's outer layer. Seismologists from both the California Institute of Technology and the Geological Survey supplied reporters from the *Los Angeles Times* with assessments of the published research on this hypothesis. They described in particular one statistical analysis by an academic scientist that failed to show any relationship between the location of the moon and seismic activity in southern California. Replications using data for other parts of the earth also were described as unsuccessful. In the words of the *Times*: "[E]xtensive studies—done with digital computers—have failed to show any correlations" (Alexander 1976). The panel reviewing Browning's prediction for the New Madrid fault actually reanalyzed his data and described his technique as "no better than guessing" (Hubbell 1991:82).

The third method for putting down these outsider challenges involved denying the predictors' track record of previous successes. Even if the outsiders lacked the standard credentials and even if the techniques used were not corroborated by a body of research published in scientific journals, these predictors still might be on to something. Whether a prediction is successful or not depends on the criteria for judging success. Here establishment scientists had the upper hand because they created the accepted benchmarks against which all predictions are measured:

> An earthquake prediction must specify the expected magnitude range, the geographical area within which it will occur, and the time interval within which it will happen with *sufficient precision* so that the ultimate success or failure of the prediction can readily be judged. (Panel on Earthquake Prediction 1976:7, emphasis added)

Three components of this scientific definition of prediction are magnitude, location, and time. The principal weapon used against these outsider predictions was the undefined term "sufficient precision." For example, imprecise location was one of the points made in undermining Minturn's claims to previous successful predictions. He argued that his November 29, 1976, prediction for an earthquake "south of Mexico" was satisfied by an earthquake that day on the Peru-Chile border. A California Institute of Technology earth scientist snorted, "[I]t was 2,400 miles off. To me, that's simply ludicrous!" (Alexander 1976). This scientist added that if the December 20 prediction were equally as accurate, then the earthquake could occur anywhere between Alaska and Guatemala.

Magnitude was a second criterion with which these outsider predictions were challenged. Because low-magnitude earthquakes are a daily occurrence in seismically active areas like California, predicting an earthquake without specifying its magnitude guarantees success (i.e., one can never be wrong). Minturn's refusal to specify the magnitude of the earthquake he expected in the Solomon Islands, for example, prompted a Geological Survey scientist to tell a reporter that Minturn had "about a 99.9% chance of being right" since there were on average three magnitude 3.7 and one magnitude 4.7 earthquakes each day in that region (Alexander 1976).

The reaction of earth scientists and others within the earthquake hazard movement to outsider predictions contrasts with their reaction to unsuccessful predictions made by insiders. Generally speaking, as long as one "plays by the rules," prediction failures are treated as merely part of the learning process that occurs when doing normal science. The fact that the "discovery" of the so-called Palmdale Bulge (see Turner et al. 1986:27–60) was not followed by a catastrophic southern California earthquake did not produce public character assassinations and discounting of credentials. The recent failure of the Parkfield (California) earthquake prediction experiment (Mileti and Fitzpatrick 1993) seems to have been treated as the sort of outcome that is typical of scientific fields in which there is much unexplained variance and small sample sizes. Criticism within the earth sciences of efforts to predict earthquakes is treated as professional disagreement. Charles Richter of the California Institute of Technology, for example, was outspoken in his belief that attempts to develop earthquake prediction were misguided (e.g., Richter 1964:6–7). While many insiders remarked privately about his eccentricities (he apparently was a lifelong nudist, for example), no one publicly challenged his scientific credentials. Only insider scientists James Whitcomb (California Institute of Technology) and Brian Brady (U.S. Bureau of Mines) seem to have run afoul of their earth science colleagues. Whitcomb's problems with his peers apparently were the result of what they perceived as his failure to play by the rules. He announced his "earthquake prediction hypothesis test" to the news media before submitting his findings for peer review by referees of a reputable scientific journal. Brady's prediction, which provoked bad feelings between the U.S. and Peruvian governments, was controversial in part because of the long-standing interorganizational tension between two federal agencies, the Bureau of Mines and the Geological Survey (see Olson, Podesta, and Nigg 1989:9–25).

The contrast in reaction by earth scientists in particular and earthquake experts in general to insider versus outsider predictions of earthquakes suggests that more than petty jealousy is involved. All social movements must manage their resource base. In the case of the earthquake hazard movement, both governmental appropriations and professional esteem are usually enhanced following an earthquake disaster. On the other hand, both are at risk when outsiders appear to have produced results that have eluded the experts. Outsider predictions of earthquakes not only threaten the resource base of the movement. They also have the capability of turning potential supporters into actual opponents. If the earthquake hazard movement is unable to distance itself from an outsider prediction and that prediction fails (as they usually do), then the fear is that subsequent "real" warnings, forecasts, and predictions will be dismissed by the public at large as another false alarm and that the experts are merely "crying wolf" once again. Put in the language of contemporary advertising, image may not be everything to the earthquake hazard movement, but it is very important. The image that the experts know what they are talking about and therefore their recommendations should be acted upon is fundamental for success.

CONCLUSION

It is time to assess this treatment of claims-making on behalf of the earthquake threat as if it were a social movement. Social movements are collective efforts to change something. Their success or failure depends on how they are organized, the resources at their disposal, the strategy and tactics they choose, and the influence of their supporters and opponents. Is it appropriate to compare those who contribute to the cause of reducing the risk of earthquakes with such seemingly different efforts as securing women's right to have abortions, eliminating the performance of abortions, advancing the cause of gay rights, and the like? Is it fair to treat the earthquake establishment as a social movement despite the fact that most, or perhaps all, of those who can be identified as its members would not characterize what they and their colleagues do in this way?

Obviously, I think that it is both appropriate and fair to do so. The process of constructing a social problem—in this case, promoting risk—is conceptually indistinguishable from the activities of social movements. Mauss made this same argument many years ago:

> No social condition, however deplorable or intolerable it may seem to social scientists or social critics, is inherently problematic. It is made problematic by the

entrepreneurship of various interest groups, which succeed in winning over important segments of public opinion to the support of a social movement aimed at changing that condition. Since, therefore, a social problem is dependent on a social movement for its very existence and is, practically speaking, coterminous with it, we might say that a *social problem is simply a kind of social movement.* . . . [T]he present author takes the position that *social movements generate social problems.* (Mauss 1975:xvi–xvii, emphasis in the original)

Claims-making is about raising levels of consciousness and promoting change. Groups of people carry out these activities, and the characteristics of those groups both facilitate and constrain what they are able to accomplish.

The earthquake establishment seems poorly equipped to function as a social movement. Its structure is only loosely integrated with several fault lines along which disagreement and conflict frequently erupt (for example, when budgets are being negotiated). There is no formal authority structure, no chain of command, and only informal leadership. The movement's power relative to that of its potential opponents is meager. Though it can claim a good deal of cultural authority, thanks to the esteem of its scientific participants and contributors, it has at best only pockets of support among elites and no sustained support within the public at large. A majority of its potential opponents are also the primary targets of its consciousness-raising and change promotion activities. Thus its strategy is limited to winning voluntary cooperation, and its tactics are constrained to such consensus-based tools as reason, rationality, and moral suasion.

In other words, the earthquake establishment is organizationally limited vis-à-vis other social movements. It is capable of engaging in some forms of claims-making activities but not those likely to "win over important segments of public opinion," in Mauss's words. Its structure and resources, along with its ideology and the values of its members, constrain its ability to promote the putative condition of future earthquakes into a fully constructed social problem.

NOTES

1. Both usually increase in the aftermath of damaging earthquakes (e.g., Meltsner 1978), but neither remains high for very long and their impact on change is decidedly mixed (May and Williams 1986:2–4).

2. The best description of strategy and tactics in the earthquake hazard movement, including an assessment of their effects, is presented by May (1991a), although he does not explicitly treat earthquake hazard reduction as a social movement.

3. For an analog of these presentations, one could substitute a PBS science-oriented program such as the "NOVA" episode "Earthquake!" for the technical presentation and the KCET (Los Angeles) program "Surviving the Big One" for the preparedness presentation.

4. I am borrowing the term "boundary work" from Gieryn (1983). His analysis focuses on struggles between biological science and creationism.

5. Overall, the results show no systematic relationship between variations in planetary alignment and earthquakes.

6. For a journalistic account by an area resident, see Hubbell (1991).

7. Such as the Geological Survey's National Earthquake Prediction Evaluation Council (NEPEC) or California's Earthquake Prediction Evaluation Council (CEPEC).

7

Explaining the Career of the Earthquake Threat

The United Nations has proclaimed the 1990s the International Decade for Natural Disaster Reduction. The 1970s, however, was the decade of the earthquake threat. The paradigmatic revolution in the earth sciences had ended with the triumph of plate tectonics. Earth scientists by and large were excited about prospects for predicting the time and location of moderate-sized earthquakes within more narrow limits than ever before. Cultural exchanges between the United States and the Peoples' Republic of China as well as between the United States and the former Soviet Union appeared to offer prospects for advances in the earth sciences. Social scientists were being recruited into the earthquake establishment to help plan for the arrival of predictions and warnings as routine as the daily weather forecast. Workshops bringing together members of the academic community and government officials for the purpose of making research more useful were becoming regular occurrences. And the Earthquake Hazards Reduction Act would finally be passed by Congress and signed into law by a newly elected president. If the decade of the 1970s was not the zenith of claims-making activities on behalf of the earthquake threat, it was clearly its Golden Era.

A rough idea of the takeoff in the career of the earthquake threat in the early 1970s is provided by the data in Table 7.1. The data are counts of all documents produced by Congress dealing with earthquakes and the earthquake threat (e.g., hearings transcripts, reports, and proclamations) from 1891 through 1990. The data clearly show an explosion of activity after 1970. After a slow decade to end the nineteenth century, the first decade of the twentieth century, driven by the 1906 earthquake and resulting fire in San Francisco, saw a rise in the number of congressional documents related to earthquakes. The decade of the 1930s was the second most active period before 1970, though documented activity was only two-thirds that of 1901–1910. Interestingly, despite the Great Alaska earthquake of 1964, the decade of the 1960s was only a moderate one in terms of the production of congressional documents. Since 1970

Table 7.1.   Congressional Documents Related to Earthquakes
and the Earthquake Threat, 1891–1990

Years*	Frequency	Major earthquakes
1891–1901	8	
1901–1911	27	San Francisco
1911–1921	3	
1921–1931	10	Santa Barbara
1931–1941	18	Long Beach, Managua
1941–1951	7	
1951–1960	2	Kern County (CA)
1961–1970	12	Alaska, Santa Rosa (CA)
1971–1980	99	San Fernando/Sylmar
1981–1990	119	Loma Prieta

*Frequencies based upon documents associated with specific sessions of the Congress; hence, many years overlap. Sources: *CIS U.S. Serial Set Index,* Subject Index, A–K (Washington, DC: Congressional Information Service, 1975); *CIS Five-Year Cumulative Index, 1970–1974,* Subject Index, A–L (Washington, DC: Congressional Information Service, 1975); *CIS Four-Year Cumulative Index, 1975–1978,* Subject Index, A–L (Washington, DC: Congressional Information Service, 1979); *CIS Four-Year Cumulative Index, 1979–1982,* Subject Index, A–L (Washington, DC: Congressional Information Service, 1983); *CIS Congressional Masterfile, 1983–1993* (Washington, DC: Congressional Information Service, 1993).

there has been an average of 104 documents produced per decade, a rate of roughly 10 documents per year.

What was behind this surge in activity? Why was there such an increase in earthquake-related activity? What have been some of the consequences of these activities that are evident now at the halfway point in the International Decade for Natural Disaster Reduction? Questions about consequences are part of the assessment of whether or not the earthquake threat is a social problem; they will be deferred until the next chapter. In this chapter I will try to account for the career of the earthquake threat over the past three decades. Specifically, I am interested in understanding why an earthquake hazards movement came together during this period rather than in some other decade of the twentieth century. In other words, I am interested in explaining the career of earthquake risk promotion.[1]

EXPLANATION NO. 1:
THE "WAKE-UP CALL" HYPOTHESIS

For many people, including many sociologists and social scientists, the explanation for increased activity on behalf of the earthquake threat in the past three decades is simple. Nature gave us a "wake-up call" in the form of the Alaska earthquake in 1964 and followed up with a reminder not long afterwards in Los Angeles. With these two events, occurring as they did less than a decade apart, the threat became "self-evident." It "obviously" had to be addressed.

There have been disastrous earthquakes throughout the twentieth century. Why was the risk of earthquakes any more evident in the late 1960s and early 1970s than in 1906? Why was the need to do something more obvious than in 1923, or in 1933, or in any year in which a serious earthquake disaster occurred? Policy and other changes took place after the San Francisco and Long Beach earthquakes, of course. However, at the national level there had never been anything to compare with the scale and frequency of activity in the years leading up to the passage of the Earthquake Hazards Reduction Act of 1977 and the institutionalization of the National Earthquake Hazards Reduction Program.

The wake-up call hypothesis begs the question. Whether something is a warning alarm or just an irritating noise depends on what people believe they are hearing. Nature may send wake-up calls in the form of earthquakes, but whether or not that is the message attributed to them depends on other factors.

EXPLANATION NO. 2:
THE ADVANCES-IN-SCIENCE HYPOTHESIS

A second possibility is that until recently we were not ready to respond to the warnings that nature seemed to be sending us. The state of scientific understanding of earthquakes earlier in this century was insufficiently advanced for government to act. With advances in the earth sciences that were occurring in the 1960s and 1970s, the time had finally come to "do something" about the threat. Growing knowledge about the causes, characteristics, and consequences of earthquakes allowed policymakers and policy implementers to incorporate the latest developments to advance the cause of earthquake safety.

Close examination suggests that the advances-in-science hypothesis also does not fit the circumstances surrounding promotion of the earthquake threat. For one thing, it exaggerates the overall influence of science on public policymaking in general (see Lindblom and Woodhouse 1993:13–22). In the case of the earthquake threat in particular, most observers conclude that information produced by earth scientists is more often ignored than used, especially by local and state governments (e.g., May and Birkland 1993; May 1991a). Examples are numerous. Most local governments in areas defined as high risk outside California do not have earthquake safety design features in their local building codes. The State of South Carolina, whose major city, Charleston, is in a scientifically designated high-risk earthquake zone, does not even have building codes (Mittler 1993). Even in California, seismic safety provisions in local building codes apply to the construction of new structures but seldom to existing buildings. And governments at all levels—federal, state, and local—typically exempt their own buildings from the earthquake-resistant code requirements that they enforce on private-property owners. Such exemptions include not only government office buildings but also classrooms, laboratories, libraries, and parking structures on college campuses. (The federal government recently acknowledged its own complicity in these matters; Executive Order 12699, issued by President Bush in January 1990, requires that new buildings owned, leased, or regulated by the federal government incorporate seismic safety standards appropriate for their location. And the collapse of a newly constructed parking structure on the campus of California State University–Northridge brought public attention to another "double standard" at the state level.)

The advances-in-science hypothesis also exaggerates the level of understanding of the earthquake threat beyond what scientists themselves acknowledge. While earth scientists believe that all major fault systems in the United States have been identified, new earthquakes usually reveal the existence of active faults that were previously unknown. Research on the precursors of earthquakes (changes in physical and chemical properties of the earth that may precede a major earthquake) has to date failed to establish any as an unequivocal sign that an earthquake is imminent. And recent studies suggesting that the difference between large-scale and minor earthquakes is determined by conditions so far below the earth's surface that they cannot be studied led earth scientists interviewed by a newspaper reporter to suggest "that reliable quake prediction may prove unachievable in the near future" (Reich 1992).

EXPLANATION NO. 3:
THE SOCIAL-CHANGE HYPOTHESIS

The advances-in-science hypothesis, although raising more questions about the career of the earthquake threat than it is able to answer, does imply a more satisfactory explanation. Not the state of science but the state of scientists is one element. Earth scientists admitted that their knowledge of earthquake processes was meager, but in the early 1970s most were excited about the future of their field. The rise and rapid acceptance of plate tectonic theory gave the earth sciences a sense of theoretical cohesion. Successes in predicting small and moderate-sized earthquakes, both in the United States and elsewhere, suggested an impending scientific breakthrough. In other words, it was not what scientists knew but what they believed they were about to know that made earthquake research such a growth industry in the mid-1970s.

Coincidentally, the federal government was in a position where the prospect of an impending scientific breakthrough was welcome news. Concerns were growing within the federal disaster relief establishment about the increasing annual costs of disasters. The tendency of Democratically controlled Congresses to continually expand the scope of disaster aid was about to encounter more fiscally conservative Republican administrations. Those administrations, by then in charge of executive-branch agencies, favored a form of federalism featuring greater responsibility at local and state levels and a lessening of federal involvement in local matters. They were also unhappy about the lack of local effort to minimize the consequences of disasters and the tendency of local officials to rely on Washington to pay for everything.

The convergence of these two trajectories, one in the sciences and the other in government, provides a better understanding of why the earthquake threat experienced such an increase in claims-making during this period. Neither trend was as simplistic as this brief overview makes it seem. The convergence of scientific and governmental interests was rooted in a variety of antecedents dating back to the Great Depression, the Second World War, and the cold war that followed. I will describe a few of what seem to have been the most important of these antecedents.

ANTECEDENTS OF THE RISE
IN CLAIMS-MAKING ACTIVITY

Central to the promotion of the risk of earthquakes were changes in the federal government and in the relationship between government and the scientific community that occurred just prior to and during World War II. One of these changes was the growth in the size of the federal government (critics call it the growth of bureaucracy) in the administration of Franklin Roosevelt. First the New Deal programs for dealing with the Great Depression of the 1930s and then the expansion of the military and other agencies related to the war effort resulted not only in the increased size of the executive branch but also in the expansion of its role as an instrument for solving societal problems.

At the same time, the relationship between government and the sciences was changing. The role of scientists as advisers to the federal government greatly expanded during this period. So too did federal funding for research and development (R&D), especially for disciplines related to the development of hardware, including weapons, for the war effort. The cold war era continued the government's policies of giving priority to science and technical education. Maintaining superiority over the Soviets in missiles and nuclear weapons was one aspect. Another was competition for the exploration of space, accelerated in this country after the flight of Sputnik in 1957 and the resulting race during the 1960s to be the first nation to send people to the moon. Signaling the increasing importance of policy input from the engineering professions was the founding of the National Academy of Engineering in 1964 within the National Academy of Sciences–National Research Council complex.

The cold war had two direct effects on the career of the earthquake threat. One resulted from efforts to monitor underground testing of nuclear weapons by the Soviet Union. With the signing of international agreements calling for the cessation of testing above ground, the race to develop nuclear weapons literally went underground. Seismological methods were employed by U.S. scientists to detect the occurrence of Soviet detonations and to extrapolate from these data information about the strength of the devices detonated. While one could easily overestimate the importance of this program, known as Project Vela, it did assist in developing methods of data collection and analysis that spilled over into nonmilitary applications.

Another direct consequence of the cold war was the emergence of disaster research as a legitimate field of academic inquiry. Social-science research methods had been used extensively during World War II, most notably in studies of the effects of combat on American soldiers (Stouffer et al. 1949, 1950) and of Allied bombing on the morale of German and Japanese civilians (U.S. Strategic Bombing Survey 1947a, 1947b). Cold war defense planners worried about the effects of new types of weapons—biological, chemical, and nuclear—on civilian morale and social order. With no world wars to study, Defense Department officials turned to the academic community for analyses of civilian reactions to chemical and other so-called man-made disasters. These were the next best things to actual military attacks. In 1949, the National Opinion Research Center (NORC) of the University of Chicago was asked to carry out a study of a chemical incident in Donora, Pennsylvania. When NORC staff members visited the small town, they decided that too much time had elapsed for a survey of local households to yield any data on the kind of phenomena the military was interested in. As an alternative, NORC proposed the creation of a stand-by research team that could move to the site of future disasters quickly enough to conduct meaningful interviews with civilian survivors.

The NORC project ran for four years. With funding from the Defense Department, it conducted survey research at the site of eight disasters as well as a variety of other studies (Marks 1954; for a summary, see Fritz and Marks 1954). This relatively short-lived project had two important consequences. One was that it employed and trained a handful of research associates, most of whom were graduate students in the Department of Sociology at the University of Chicago, who developed a professional interest in research on disasters and related phenomena. After the NORC project ended, its assistant director moved to the National Academy of Sciences, where he administered a government-funded Disaster Research Group that conducted further social-science research on natural disasters. The second consequence was that the original NORC proposal broadened the focus of study from the military's initial narrow interest in a chemical incident to the entire range of natural and so-called technological disasters. Both were treated as analogs for the kind of stress situation envisioned following a nuclear or chemical attack. The broadened focus would eventually lead social scientists to study individual and organizational behavior in earthquake disasters. (The same NORC project veteran would later be responsible for involving still other social scientists in studies of the Alaska earthquake.)

The most important outcome of this government investment in social-science research on disasters as analogs of nuclear warfare was unintentional. Creating a research infrastructure to aid the cold war civil defense effort produced an interest in the study of natural disasters for their own sake. Much of this research focused on responses by local government organizations to disastrous events (Drabek 1986). Both the topic and the agencies involved in disaster preparedness and response were legitimated independent of the negative connotations of terms such as *civil defense* and *dual use*.[2] By the mid-1970s, the study of natural disasters and the threat of natural disasters, including earthquakes, had become a recognized field with reasonably consistent funding. These funds no longer came entirely from military, defense, or civil defense sources. They were provided by the federal government's conventional funding agency for basic and applied science, the National Science Foundation.[3]

Political events in the 1960s and early 1970s also influenced changes in the federal government and in the relationship between the government and scientists. These changes further affected the career of the earthquake threat. One was the inclusion within the inner circles of White House science advisers of a prominent earth scientist who was personally convinced of the prospects for predicting earthquakes. Frank Press, geophysicist at Massachusetts Institute of Technology at the time, served in Democratic administrations in the 1960s and 1970s; he was President Carter's chief science adviser when the National Earthquake Hazards Reduction Program (NEHRP) was created. Having an advocate for earthquake prediction so close to the Oval Office clearly made a difference in the priority given to the issue during this period and to the content of subsequent policy initiatives. The process of "capacity building" (McCarthy 1912; Mittler 1993:5–6) in regard to the earthquake hazard continues into the 1990s.

Republican administrations had distinctive impacts on the career of the earthquake threat during this period as well. One trend, mentioned previously, was the growing concern for the economic impact of disasters, especially of a future catastrophic urban earthquake. Economic impacts were never exclusively a theme of Republican administrations, however. The major revision of the enabling legislation for federal disaster relief took place during the Nixon administration, but its thrust continued under Jimmy Carter. Shifting greater responsibility onto state and local governments was a main tenet of Ronald Reagan's New Federalism, but Bill Clinton's administration continues to emphasize partnerships and mitigation (see Chapter 5).

Three other Republican-administration influences had their origins in the early 1970s. One was the philosophical difference between Democrats in Congress and Republicans in the executive branch over the role of the federal government in solving societal problems. Congressional Democrats, veterans of Lyndon Johnson's Great Society policy initiatives such as his War on Poverty, approached the threat of disasters with a belief that an expanded federal program of disaster aid was good policy. Republican administrations, on the other hand, favored reducing the size and scope of federal programs (candidate Ronald Reagan would attract much political support in the 1980 presidential campaign by promising to "get government off people's backs"). Republican political philosophy favored getting government out of the disaster relief business.

Second, by the middle of the 1970s the war in Vietnam had run its course. This had two consequences for the earthquake threat. With a divisive foreign military action removed from public-policy agendas, domestic issues began to dominate political discourse once again. As the costs of military involvement in Southeast Asia were being tabulated and the economic effects of the transition to peace beginning to be felt, the state of the economy became a major political issue. For the earthquake threat, this meant that the emphasis on cost reduction through mitigation would continue to be a major emphasis.

Third, the shift in foreign policy toward the Soviet Union and the

Peoples' Republic of China under Richard Nixon and his secretary of state, Henry Kissinger, also affected the career of the earthquake threat. Scientists in the Soviet Union appeared to have successfully predicted earthquakes in the early 1970s. China was touting a successful short-term prediction and subsequent evacuation of the city of Haicheng in 1975 that apparently had saved several thousand lives. With the negotiation of scientific exchanges as one of the first outcomes of the new policy of *détente* among the cold war foes, the opportunity was seemingly at hand for earth scientists to put the finishing touches on an earthquake prediction capability. One of the first exchanges saw a team of U.S. earth scientists visit China in 1974 (American Earthquake Study Delegation 1975). Two years later, a second delegation of scientists and a sociologist (the social sciences having emerged by this time as an element of the earthquake establishment) visited China to study the Haicheng prediction (Haicheng Earthquake Study Delegation 1977; Turner 1978, 1993: 455–58). The international direction that earthquake risk promotion had taken was underscored by an International Symposium on Earthquake Prediction held at the Paris headquarters of the United Nations Education and Scientific Organization (UNESCO) at the end of the decade. The arrival of earthquake prediction on the international agenda gave increased legitimacy to promotion of the earthquake threat in the United States.

In short, earthquakes happen. How scientists and governments react to them is a function of their histories as well as their interests at the time. The partnership between the earth sciences, engineering, and the social sciences on the one hand and government on the other that led to the emergence of an earthquake hazards movement grew out of social changes converging in the 1970s. The decade was the Golden Era of earthquake risk promotion. Are there any theories in the social sciences that seem consistent with the career of the earthquake threat?

SOCIAL-SCIENCE THEORY AND THE CAREER OF THE EARTHQUAKE THREAT

Most of the claims-making effort on behalf of the earthquake threat has been undertaken by government officials and by earth scientists employed by the government (e.g., at the Geological Survey) or at universities where their research is supported by government grants and contracts. Most of the programs and activities promoting the risk of earthquakes, furthermore, have been carried out with funds provided by the federal government. How well do existing social-science theories developed to explain the activities of government, especially the national government, explain this largely government-sponsored effort? I will limit this examination to major groups of theories without discussing the similarities and differences among individual contributors to these theoretical traditions. I will also not worry about subgroups within each theoretical tradition, such as differences between strong and weak forms of theories (e.g., Shover, Clelland, and Lynxwiler 1986:3–9; Hooks 1993).

Theories attempting to explain government activity may be divided into two broad categories: society-centered theories and state-centered theories. Society-centered theories share the point of view that the forces that determine governmental activity reside *outside* government. They differ on where these forces are located in the social structure. Some see government policy as driven by an elite composed of business leaders who control the major corporations and businesses (e.g., Useem 1984). Others agree that the direction of government is set by an elite, but they identify the elite as a privileged class of the very wealthy whose power base is not directly tied to any specific corporation (e.g., Domhoff 1983, 1990). Still other society-centered theorists argue that government policy is driven by a broad plurality of the people rather than by a small, narrowly interested elite (e.g., Dahl 1982). State-centered theories, in contrast, see government agencies as active players in policymaking rather than as passive instruments controlled by either an elite or by interest groups. The administrative apparatus of the state—that is, its public bureaucracy—is seen as sufficiently autonomous and powerful to set directions for its own programs (e.g., Weber 1978, esp. pp. 990-994; Skocpol 1979, esp. pp. 24-33; Block 1981).

The description of the career of the earthquake threat in the United States presented in this and in previous chapters suggests little that fits either the elite or the grass-roots variant of society-centered theory. Pluralist theories would have predicted a consensus among differing interest groups about the earthquake threat, arrived at through a process of public debate and discussion, that would be translated by elected officials into public programs and activities. The "will of the public" would be expressed as government policy. Regardless of the general merits of pluralistic interest group theory, in the specific case of the earthquake threat there is no evidence that the rise of activity in the 1960s and 1970s was produced by an expression of public interest. There was no national debate about the seriousness of the earthquake threat. Grass-roots groups were not springing up around the country to call attention to another newly discovered threat. Politicians were not sensing a growing restlessness among voters about government foot-dragging on the earthquake question. May's (1991b:194–97) characterization of "policies without publics" accurately expresses the type of policymaking and politics in this domain.

Applicability of elite theories is somewhat trickier to evaluate. Elites often prefer to remain in the background, using their direct access to policymakers to exert influence without attracting public attention. There is always the possibility that more was going on behind closed doors in the 1970s than nonelites—including researchers—were aware of. Based upon information that is publicly available, however, there is no evidence to support the hypothesis that the rise in earthquake-related activity was driven by the interests of the business elite. The "captains of industry" were not making public speeches about the risk of earthquakes. Think tanks were not turning out white papers and reports on the issue. Later on, in the 1980s, one industry did turn its attention to the issue: the insurance industry. Insurance companies had two concerns. One was their exposure to claims in the event of a catastrophic earthquake. The National Committee on Property Insurance estimated that the industry's exposure could be as high as $52.4 billion for the worst-case earthquake on the Newport-Inglewood Fault, which runs through the Los Angeles metropolitan area (The Earthquake Project 1989). The second industry concern was that Congress might pass mandatory earthquake insurance legislation without taking the interests of the insurance industry into account. The property and casualty insurance industry in the 1980s formed the Earthquake Project in an effort to prevent Congress from doing any harm to its industry in the name of earthquake hazard reduction. Overall, though, the corporate elite has been silent on the earthquake issue.

There is also no evidence that the upper class has been concerned about the earthquake threat. Perhaps the superrich who live in designated seismically active areas have abundant resources making the risk of earthquakes even less salient for them than for the public at large. They live in single-family homes, the safest form of housing. Most have homes in more than one location. They have sufficient wealth to hire engineers and consultants to design and retrofit the property they inhabit as well as to purchase whatever level of insurance seems warranted. Also they have the know-how and the political clout to "work the system" should disaster strike. This includes not only the ability to take advantage of tax laws but also to get the best out of available public and private services. Whatever the case, the upper class seems not to have had any interest in government earthquake policies and programs in the 1960s and 1970s.

Only two visible but infrequent roles of grass-roots groups and elites are evident in the career of the earthquake threat. One is the opposition sometimes engendered among elements of the corporate world when policy proposals are afloat that are deemed too costly or detrimental to business interests. The organized campaign of the Apartment Association of Los Angeles County aimed at defeating the Los Angeles hazard-ous building abatement ordinance in 1976 is one example. The other visible role is pseudosupport for earthquake risk promotion that occurs when groups adopt seismic safety as a means to achieve other ends such as preventing the licensing of a nuclear reactor or stopping development of a tract of land. Opposition by elements of the business community is clearly contrary to the hypothesis that business interests prompted attention to the earthquake threat. The support of antinuclear and slow-growth movement organizations for earthquake safety has been too spo-radic and short-lived to confirm a pluralistic interest group explanation.

The career of the earthquake threat does make sense in terms of state-centered theories. The basic tenet of these theories is that state managers— especially top appointed officials—act independently in the larger interests of the capitalistic economy and the state. The state has its own interest in maintaining and enhancing the functioning of the econ-omy. It has sufficient autonomy to be more than an instrument of a ruling class or a corporate elite. Often, the state takes action that elites find contrary to their immediate and more narrow concerns. State-centered theorists argue that action of this sort is undertaken in the long-term interests of the political economy as a whole.

I think that these state-centered theories provide the only explanation for the career of the earthquake threat. In a single sentence, the largely government-sponsored effort to promote the risk of earthquakes and natural hazards in general is explained by an autonomous state whose managers are acting to ensure the stability of a capitalist democracy. Stated this simplistically, the hypothesis may seem overblown. Neither the Big One nor increasing annual losses are likely to destroy the Ameri-can economy or cause the collapse of the government. A comparison with the Peoples' Republic of China is instructive. In China, the state's heavy emphasis on earthquake prediction can only be explained by its interest in regime stability. Given the type of construction in which most of its population lives and works, death tolls in even moderate-intensity earthquakes can be enormous. The 1976 Tangshan earthquake, for ex-ample, probably killed at least six hundred thousand people. A govern-ment that cannot otherwise reduce the risk to its population could only rely on short-term earthquake warnings to prevent erosion of its hold on political power.

The case of the United States is less extreme but, I would argue, is also about regime stability. In this country state managers fear that the eco-nomic effects of the catastrophic earthquake—symbolized by the Big One—could weaken the nation's less than robust economy and, as a result, its role as the world's only remaining superpower. Despite an expanded definition of risk, the focus remains on California because of that state's influence on the national economy:

The economic linkages between California and the rest of the nation and the world are so important that any interference in their functioning would have immediate and visible impact. The immediate destruction following an earthquake would cause the shutdown of economic activities with a cascade effect on other activities. People would be forced out of work; payments would be affected, with further economic ripples beyond the immediate damaged area. Some major industries, including aerospace and electronics, would be most affected by the earthquake. . . . [O]ne of the economic relationships disrupted during a post-earthquake period would never recover, and California suppliers might be replaced by suppliers from other regions or foreign countries. . . . Because the U.S. financial system is so interdependent, losses to financial institutions in California would have effects throughout the nation. . . . [U]nder present [i.e., 1990] circumstances, the insurance industry would suffer major losses. . . . This impact would affect the availability of health, life and property insurance, with further impacts on the daily well-being of all Americans. (Palm et al. 1990:9–10)

The section from which this passage is quoted was titled "California Earthquakes as a National Problem" (p. 7). The authors are describing a national *economic* threat. Damaging California's economy damages the nation's economy. One California congressman estimates that the Big One could reduce the U.S. gross domestic product (GDP) by as much as 5 percent (quoted in Palm et al. 1990:7–8). Long-term consequences by some estimates could persist for half a decade (Science and Technology Program 1991). Damaging the nation's economy also damages the nation's political and economic position in the new world order.

The explanation for state-sponsored activity on behalf of the earthquake threat is similar to that for social-welfare policies in the United States. State-centered theories explain welfare policies as safety valves for economic and labor unrest when economic conditions take a downturn (Quadagno 1984). They are a form of insurance policy to reduce the possibility of threats to political stability. The level of funding for the nation's welfare programs is only as great as is necessary to prevent social disorder. This seemingly cynical explanation does not mean that the people implementing these policies at the street level are uncaring or insensitive. State-centered theories are not about the motives of individuals. They are about the interests of the managers who control the administrative apparatus of the state.

There is another, less cynical-sounding interpretation of the same pattern. In an era when people in the United States are questioning the efficiency and effectiveness of government, especially of the federal government, and where term limitation movements have considerable support from voters who would like to "throw the bums [i.e., politicians] out," we may have stumbled upon an example of responsible government actually looking out for the well-being of its citizens. However, closer inspection of the empirical evidence does not support a public-safety interpretation of increased government attention to the earth-quake threat. Earthquake safety advocates, who care sincerely about such matters, have never been content with Congress's dedication to dealing with this risk. Two weeks after a small earthquake killed fifty-eight in Los Angeles, a Geological Survey scientist challenged a special subcommittee of the House to "get with it on reducing the hazards of earthquakes" (U.S. House of Representatives 1971b:260). An engineer complained to another House committee investigating damage and deaths at a Veterans Administration Hospital in the same earthquake about a lack of federal support for even basic data gathering:

> For 30 years I have been active in the Structural Engineers Association, and every year, except for a few when we got discouraged, we have asked our Congressmen, our legislators, officials in Washington, for more money for the Coast and Geodetic Survey to get strong motion records. (U.S. House of Representatives 1971a:145)

Nearly two decades later identical statements were still being heard. During testimony on reauthorization of the federal earthquake hazard program, an earthquake safety advocate from California agreed with a member of the House who described the earthquake effort as "outra-geously underfunded":

> The national government really isn't carrying its own [weight]. We are in a rowboat and one side is pulling harder than the other. I'm afraid in this case, it is California that is pulling much harder than the Federal Govern-ment is in earthquake safety in California. (U.S. House of Representatives 1987:353)

Congress is not the only branch of government to disappoint those trying to do something about the risk of earthquakes. One senator ac-cused a previous occupant of the White House of scuttling an earlier earthquake bill while expressing hope for support from a new admini-stration:

> My bill, S. 126 is nearly identical to S. 1174 which passed the Senate unanimously in the last Congress and which might have been enacted if we had the support of the previous administration. (U.S. Senate 1977:52)

Agencies within the executive branch also have been criticized for ac-tions detrimental to the earthquake hazards reduction effort. A promi-nent earth scientist, testifying on the makeup of the nation's earthquake research program, commented:

I think it is clear, though, that much of the project's research has to be carried out by the governmental agencies themselves—this, of course, being agencies such as the U.S. Geological Survey and NOAA [the National Oceanic and Atmospheric Administration]. And I know it is my own wish that these two agencies could get together and somehow form an integrated program in the area. I think, quite frankly, that we have suffered in this country from competition between these two agencies; and I think it has gone beyond the point of competition I think there is a definite need for some reorganization in the area of earth science. (U.S. Senate 1971:568)

Government, of course, is one word referring to more than just the federal government. Critics charge that many state governments have ignored the threat of earthquakes to the detriment of their citizens' safety. Even in California, the one state that has done the most about earthquakes according to conventional wisdom, government has been indicted for foot-dragging that leaves millions exposed to risk. In other words, evidence does not support the interpretation that public-safety concerns drive state managers in their efforts to reduce the risks of earthquakes. This does not mean that earthquake safety advocates are not really concerned about safety. Nor does it mean that improved safety is not one of the consequences, albeit an indirect one, of earthquake safety policies. Improving the safety of structures means less economic disruption as well as less loss of life.

I am proposing an explanation for the career of the earthquake threat that parallels that often used to explain social-welfare policies. State managers, especially top appointed federal officials, are acting on behalf of the American political economy as a whole in funding programs of earthquake and hazard reduction in general. Neither the public at large nor economic elites have demanded such programs. Earthquake risk reduction as a state-sponsored activity is necessary to protect the country from the threat of an economic downturn brought on by a catastrophic earthquake in a sluggish economy. But the cost of this protection cannot be so high that the cure is worse than the disease. Protection always must be purchased at an acceptable cost.

CONCLUSION

If this explanation is correct—if earthquake risk promotion is a state-sponsored hedge against the negative economic impact of a catastrophic (especially California) earthquake—then what are the prospects for the future of claims-making on behalf of the earthquake threat? The prospects for elite support for earthquake hazard reduction seem unlikely.

Pseudosupport is likely to increase, especially within local groups trying to slow growth and curb development. Any increase in pseudosupport, however, is unlikely to have much effect on the career of the earthquake threat because of its ephemeral nature. On the other hand, continued state manager support seems certain. In the long run, the cost of doing nothing, both politically and economically, would be too great. However, continued support is only likely if the costs of earthquake hazard reduction remain low. The street-level bureaucrats who believe in the cause of earthquake safety will always be constrained by superiors who seem to want to strike a balance between safety and current economic well-being. Infrequent moderate-sized earthquakes may produce temporary increases in support, but the principle of acceptable cost—known publicly by the technical-sounding term acceptable risk—will ensure that the amount of resources devoted to the threat will not approach that of other policy issues such as crime and health care.

What about changes within the public at large? What are the prospects for increased support for earthquake hazard reduction at the grass-roots level? The kind of change that would be required has been expressed by several writers working in vastly different traditions. For the German sociologist Niklas Luhmann (1993), the "danger" of earthquakes would need to be translated into the "risk" of earthquakes. This means for him that a potentially harmful future outcome would have to come to be seen as coupled with today's decisions. For the anthropologist Mary Douglas (Douglas and Wildavsky 1982; Douglas 1966), earthquakes would need somehow to be culturally transformed into a secular manifestation of evil. For the political scientist Peter May (1991a, 1991b), it would mean transforming a public risk into a private risk, that is, seeing the threat as a personal one so that incentives for addressing it are increased. For political scientist Deborah Stone (1988:147–65, 1989), it would mean public acceptance of a "causal story" in which the destruction of future earthquakes is linked to purposeful human action.

What would make such changes come about? I have already discounted the role of earthquake disasters. Their effects are too short-lived and tend to produce claims-making over restitution gone wrong rather than future harm. The logic of Douglas and Wildavsky's argument (1982) suggests that broad cultural change would alter the selection of risks to worry about. Luhmann's general approach (e.g., 1982) suggests that a change in the way the risk of earthquakes is treated will eventually come about due to increasing differentiation as modern societies attempt to reduce the complexity of their environments.

My explanation is somewhat different. I suggest that change in the way the public at large views the earthquake threat could be initiated by claims-makers within the earthquake establishment. Whether they are likely to do so or not and what might be done if they were to try is discussed at the end of the next chapter. Before returning to this question, I address two other questions that have to do with the earthquake threat as a social problem: What kind of social problem is the risk of earthquakes? What kind of social problem is it likely to become in the near future?

NOTES

1.   By career, I mean the longer periods of increases and decreases in claims-making activities that take place over years and sometimes decades rather than the short-term cycles of interest and inattention that surround earthquake disasters.

2.   *Dual use* was a civil defense term coined during the period to justify the use of funds, earmarked for nuclear-attack preparedness, for programs and research on natural disasters. Technically this could be construed as a misappropriation of federal dollars unless their use had an attack-related purpose (see Perry 1982).

3.   Contracts with other federal agencies like FEMA and the Geological Survey have also provided funding for social-science and policy-focused earthquake research.

8

The Earthquake Threat and
Social-Problems Theory

At the beginning of this book, I asked a basic question about the risk of earthquakes in the United States. With the possibility of negative consequences from a future catastrophic earthquake seemingly as great as those from street crimes, epidemics, and other publicly recognized risks of the day, why has the earthquake threat attracted so little public attention and concern? The strategy that I followed throughout was to treat the existence of this threat, like any other, as an *accomplishment* rather than as given. That is, to exist in a socially and politically meaningful sense, risk must be promoted. Some risks apparently are more difficult to promote than others. I identified some of the people who have been promoting the risk of earthquakes, outlined the basic elements of the image of risk that they have offered, and described some of the settings in which they have operated. I also tried to evaluate the capacity of risk promoters to accomplish the tasks of elevating public awareness of the risk of earthquakes, changing people's behavior in regard to this risk, and increasing governmental efforts to address it.

These descriptions and examinations have been guided by the constructionist theory of social problems augmented by the resource mobilization theory of social movements. Constructionist theory locates the existence of problems in activity about putative conditions (or condition-categories) and in the response to that activity rather than in conditions themselves. Resource mobilization theory concentrates on the means by which people attempt to press complaints rather than on the causes of those complaints. Neither theory assumes that social problems and public issues are self-evident. What remains to be done in this final chapter is to sum up this evaluation of the earthquake threat from the perspective of these theories, especially constructionist theory, and afterward to evaluate constructionist theory in light of this examination of the earthquake threat.

My hypothesis all along has been that the risk of earthquakes has not been in the past and is not at this time a fully accomplished social problem as the term "social problems" is used in constructionist theory. I have tried to understand why it is not by treating the earthquake threat as a negative case, like the control group in a laboratory experiment. The contrast between the general features of successfully accomplished problems and the features of this threat, judged against the yardstick of social-problems theory, should identify some of the reasons for the difference. If the earthquake threat differs from social problems, then the source of that difference must reside in activity or the consequences of activity on its behalf.

In this chapter I will do three things. First, I will reexamine the defining properties of social problems expressed either explicitly or implicitly in constructionist theory and compare them with the materials presented in the preceding chapters. My reexamination will highlight what is different about the earthquake threat. Then I will turn to the question of *why* it is different. My answer will be that, while there has been much activity on behalf of the threat, both the nature and the consequences of that activity differ from those described in social-problems theory. This section will also identify some of the ways in which social-problems theory fails to anticipate important features of this threat. Third, I will address prospects for the future. Given recent developments in the career of the threat such as its retypification, what are its prospects for achieving social-problems status?

IS THE EARTHQUAKE THREAT A SOCIAL PROBLEM?

This question essentially asks, What kind of phenomenon is the earthquake threat in the United States at the end of the twentieth century? In deciding how best to classify it, we are also deciding with what other phenomena it should be compared. I have chosen to equate the risk of earthquakes with other phenomena identified as social problems by the constructionist theory of social problems. This theory is most fully spelled out in the works of Spector and Kitsuse (1973, [1977] 1987), Mauss (1975), and Ibarra and Kitsuse (1993; for an overview, see Schneider 1985 and Best 1993). I chose to equate the earthquake threat with social problems to emphasize that risks do not just happen; people make them happen. I also hoped to extend constructionist theory by seeing if it is equally capable of explaining what seems like the failure of a problem to emerge as it is in explaining the emergence of full-blown problems. Obviously, a single case (i.e., an N of 1) is not sufficient to reject or not reject any hypothesis. However, by accumulating numerous cases such as this one, the basic propositions of a theory can be revised, augmented, or abandoned as necessary.

The place to begin is with the defining features of social problems identified in constructionist theory. The existence of claims-making activity is the most fundamental property. What exactly is claims-making, and have earthquake safety advocates really been engaged in it?

Claims-Making

Constructionist theorists define claims-making as activity through which groups are *"making assertions of grievances and claims to organizations, agencies, and institutions about some putative conditions"* (Spector and Kitsuse 1973:146, emphasis in the original; see also Spector and Kitsuse [1977] 1987:73–96). Problems differ from nonproblems according to whether claims-making activity is present or absent (also Blumer 1971). The term *claim* is defined as "a demand that one party makes upon another" (Spector and Kitsuse [1977] 1987:83). In general, claims are *statements about conditions* including the causes of those conditions, what should be done about them, and justifications for doing something. Synonyms include grievances, complaints, and expressions of dissatisfaction.

Statements about the earthquake threat seem to qualify as claims in the broad if not in the narrow sense. While neither grievances nor demands, they are expressions of dissatisfaction with the current level of risk associated with a particular natural hazard. The activity that earthquake risk promoters have engaged in also seems consistent with the meaning of claims-making activity. They have used the media to promote earthquake awareness and change behavior, contributed to government reports defining this risk and identifying ways to reduce it, and worked to increase government's commitment to addressing the risk. Each of these is a conventional form of claims-making activity.

One potential difference from conventional claims-making is apparent in the definition. The term *claims-maker* is usually applied to members of groups other than government agencies or official institutions. Claims-makers typically are located *outside* formal structures of authority and therefore must bring their claims *to* organizations, agencies, and institutions. Organizations, agencies, and institutions then respond (or do not respond) to these demands. Spector and Kitsuse imply that both claims-making and responding are necessary for the existence of a social problem.

It is clear from material presented in earlier chapters that a majority of earthquake risk claims-makers are "insiders" rather than outsiders. They are technocrats and bureaucrats employed in government agencies. However, constructionist theory as developed in the work of both Spector and Kitsuse and Mauss (1975:96–98, for example) recognizes that government insiders are frequently claims-makers. Spector and Kitsuse ([1977] 1987:155) further acknowledge that their presentation of the theory emphasizes a "grass-roots view of social problems." They attempt to balance this view by citing three examples in which officials have engaged in claims-making with few or no demands from outside groups. They admit that, in instances where claims-makers and responders do not "play the roles stereotypically assigned to them" (p. 155), these terms "become vague and less useful as descriptive or analytic devices" (p. 156). This conclusion seems too harsh. In the case of the earthquake threat, it is relatively easy to distinguish action that advances the cause of earthquake safety from action in response to grievances from others (such as those dissatisfied with disaster relief efforts), even when both actions involve the same individuals or organizations.

Another potential difference between the case of earthquake risk promotion and social problems described in constructionist theory is that earthquake safety advocates, as government insiders, often press claims on other government insiders. Insider-to-insider claims-making (as opposed to the more conventional outsider-to-insider claims-making) is illustrated by agency officials pressing their superiors in the White House to launch a new earthquake safety program and by agency heads lobbying members of Congress to increase appropriations for ongoing earthquake-related programs. Constructionist theory does not reject insider-to-insider claims-making as a type of social-problems activity, however. It is the essence of Spector and Kitsuse's ([1977] 1987:97–129) exemplar involving a controversy within the American Psychiatric Association over the use and abuse of psychiatric diagnoses. Even in cases of insider-to-insider claims-making, the basic asymmetry in the relationship between claimants (as lower participants) and responders (as higher-ranking officials) is maintained. Claims-makers press claims because they themselves cannot simply act upon those claims. Someone else has the resources necessary for doing something to alter the putative condition.

In sum, the existence of claims-making activity justifies placing the earthquake threat in the category of phenomena labeled social problems. The fact that often both claims-makers and responders are insiders (for example, in the federal government) is also not inconsistent with constructionist theory. By its single most important defining property, the constructionist theory of social problems identifies the earthquake threat as at least one type of social problem.

Contentiousness

One correlate of social-problems activity appears so often, especially in the examples of social problems presented by Spector and Kitsuse, that it may well be a defining characteristic rather than a by-product of claims-making activity. This characteristic is controversy. The first sign of the emergence of a social problem seems to be the appearance of conflict. There are several examples of this in Spector and Kitsuse's monograph. One is their reexamination of earlier articles about trailer camps as social problems in both Detroit and California (Spector and Kitsuse [1977] 1987:130–34). In Detroit, trailer camps themselves became controversial, whereas in California they were but one aspect of a different controversial issue. Conflicts in California were about the arrival of migrants from Texas and Oklahoma referred to as "Okies." The social problem in California was the presence of the migrants themselves, not the trailer camps in which they often clustered. In this as in other examples, the appearance of conflict is not only the signal that a problem is emerging. The nature of that conflict also identifies the content of the problem itself (trailer camps in one case, migrants in the other).

Is controversy always an element of a social problem? Put differently, can something be a social problem without being controversial? It seems logically possible but empirically unlikely. Even if the issue itself is not contested (no one seems to be arguing for more crime, for example), it is unlikely that everyone will be happy with proposed solutions (e.g., gun control on the one hand versus increasing criminal penalties and building more prisons on the other). In addition, advocates for other problems may be critical of the high priority that a given problem seems to enjoy.

The case of the earthquake threat is unlike many other social problems analyzed in the literature, as the previous discussion of opponents and supporters showed (Chapter 6). Clearly the growth of policymaking in the 1970s did not emerge from either a local conflict or a nationwide controversy. Currently, most of what earthquake safety advocates do on a daily basis is not at all controversial. They seldom deliberately try to "stimulate controversy, and create a public or political issue" (Spector and Kitsuse [1977] 1987:142). If anything, they seem to go out of their way to avoid stirring up trouble for reasons outlined in Chapter 6.

When controversies involving the risk of earthquakes do arise, they have taken two different forms. One form involves complaints that disaster relief agencies are failing to properly serve the victims of some earthquake disaster. Here agencies whose members are claims-makers in other settings become targets of claims by others (e.g., disaster victims), and the content of the controversy defines its "problem" as the failure of existing programs rather than as the threat of some future hazard. The second form of controversy involves reactions to proposed earthquake safety measures such as conflict over the introduction of a mandatory retrofit ordinance in Los Angeles during the 1970s. Again, the problem is the proposed new requirement, claims-makers are the opponents of change such as the apartment managers association in Los Angeles, and responders are the original claims-makers who are being asked to withdraw or amend their proposal.

In short, even though claims-makers promoting the risk of future catastrophic earthquakes have seldom deliberately stirred up controversy to accomplish their objectives, the career of the earthquake threat is not without its share of controversies. As one might expect in the case of such a seemingly consensual issue, these have been controversies about solutions rather than about the desirability of future earthquakes. Furthermore, there is conflict in day-to-day earthquake risk promotion that seldom becomes visible in the news. Most pervasive is the conflict among levels of government over appropriate distribution of the potential costs of future earthquakes. Other conflicts exist between disciplines over the appropriate mix of research funding necessary to discover empirical "solutions" to the dilemmas of earthquakes. The chief difference between these and the conflicts usually associated with social problems is that they occur "backstage," out of public view. Perhaps the earthquake threat is different not because controversy is absent but because somehow it is the "wrong kind" of controversy.

Natural History versus the Career of the Earthquake Threat

In the Spector and Kitsuse natural-history model of social-problems activity, controversy is a key element in two stages. At the beginning of the career of a social problem (Stage 1), controversy erupts about a putative condition. The putative condition is the subject of claims-making. Later, after officials or authorities have responded to these initial claims in some manner (Stage 2), controversy again arises. However, at this point (Stage 3), controversy is about the failure of responding agencies to make good on what claims-makers thought was a pledge to do something about the condition. Failure to act is the basis for this controversy, not the original claims or grievances.

Examining the examples of controversy in the career of the earthquake threat leads to the observation that most are of the Stage 3 variety. That is, they are usually complaints about what government has or has not done about the earthquake threat. Many of these complaints are publicly expressed only in the aftermath of an earthquake disaster in the United

States. The larger question here is not about the presence or absence of controversy but about the natural history model itself.

The career of the earthquake threat, at least that portion of its history between 1964 and the end of 1992, does not exhibit the four stages comprising the natural history of social problems as described by Spector and Kitsuse ([1977] 1987:141–58, esp. 142). Claims-makers, both insiders and outsiders, have defined the earthquake threat as harmful and the current level of risk associated with it as undesirable, but, because of their access to the appropriate responding organizations, they have never had to "go public" with these assertions in order to be heard (Stage 1). Government agencies have accepted numerous reports (most of which they themselves have sponsored), thereby not only establishing the legitimacy of claims but in the process accepting responsibility for the threat (Stage 2). Claims-makers frequently complain about the lack of responsiveness and the slowness of government agencies (in many cases the very agencies in which claims-makers are employed) to take recommended steps (Stage 3). On the other hand, there is no evidence of the emergence of alternatives or counterinstitutions in response to disappointments over lack of action (Stage 4).[1]

One explanation for the difference between social-problems theory and the career of the earthquake threat could be that the latter is a case history rather than natural history (Spector and Kitsuse [1977] 1987:135–36). That is, what has been described in this book is the career of a single threat. The tasks of adding new cases, comparing them with one another, and identifying the elements common to all have not been attempted. What has been done is to describe a single history and then compare it with the general description of natural history presented by Spector and Kitsuse (1973, [1977] 1987). A single history is neither grounds for declaring that a model holds conclusively nor for declaring that it should be abandoned.

Rather than pose a series of challenges to the natural-history model based upon a single case (such as, is the trajectory always recursive— one-way—or can it be nonrecursive? Is the starting point always Stage 1, or can the process begin at other stages?), it seems more appropriate to ask a different question: Are there different natural histories for problems that do not have their origins in grass-roots claims-making? Spector and Kitsuse themselves ([1977] 1987:155–56) raise this question with their introduction of elite generated problems. The case described here has been described as neither elite-generated nor grass-roots generated. State manager–generated claims-making has its origins in the bureaus, agencies, and programs of government. In what ways are the careers of these issues similar to and different from those of grass-roots claims? of elite-sponsored claims? Identification of such issues and comparative analysis of their histories seems necessary before the applicability of Spector and Kitsuse's natural-history model is taken for granted.

Awareness of Making Claims

Must claims-makers themselves think of their activities as claims-making for those activities to count as part of the social-problems process? In other words, do earthquake safety advocates have to be aware that they are engaged in the promotion of risk, whether or not they use those same words to describe what they are doing? If they do not consider what they do as contributing to the creation of a social problem, does the problem creation process exist? Part of the answer to these questions is a matter of semantics, that is, the use of one term rather than another. More important than whether members of the earthquake establishment would use such terms as *claims-making* and *risk promotion*, or even whether they are aware of participating in something called the "earthquake establishment," is whether risk promoters are aware that they are attempting to increase awareness of the threat, induce changes in behavior in response to it, and use government policies and programs as a means for reducing risk.

Stated in these terms, it is clear that earthquake safety advocates are aware that they are promoting risk. Whether by scientists or federal officials, appearances before the public at large attempt to improve public well-being. For example, earth scientists appear in public largely in hopes that they can improve the general level of understanding of earthquake processes and dispel scientifically unfounded notions such as California disappearing into the ocean after a catastrophic earthquake. Government officials address public audiences in hopes of inducing individuals to undertake voluntary safety measures that will lessen the likelihood of injuries and damage—and the demand for services—in the event of an earthquake. I have no doubt that these same officials, when they negotiate increased budgets for the earthquake hazard programs that they manage, are sincere in seeking to increase public safety regardless of whatever hidden agendas (such as bureaucratic turf battles and individual career advancement) may also be involved.

Are these people also aware of contributing to the promotion of risk in their less publicly visible activities? That is, when serving on expert panels and commissions, reviewing research proposals, and attending meetings of groups advising earthquake-related programs, are they aware that they are contributing to risk promotion even though the public at large is not directly involved? Again, my impression is that the answer is clearly Yes. Whatever the personal, career, and organizational benefits of these activities, participants are aware that the principal official justification for the activity is earthquake hazard reduction in some form. That the public at large is one step removed does not mean that it is not the ultimate target of the activity. Indeed, the *majority* of claims-making activity on behalf of the earthquake threat takes place outside direct public view. Donald Cressey, a sociologist who participated in a presidential commission on organized crime—another public issue that at the time (i.e., the 1960s) had many of the same characteristics of the earthquake threat outlined here—describes his experience in a way that would easily be recognized by social scientists participating on earthquake hazard panels:

> [W]e joined the ranks of men who are paid to recognize organized crime as a social problem. These men, mostly police officers and prosecutors . . . when they plead for "education of the public," they are asking that a major social problem be created. (Cressey 1967:106; quoted in Spector and Kitsuse [1977] 1987:5)

Some caution is called for here, however. The question is not one of motivation, as in the causes of individual participation in earthquake hazard activity. I am concerned about the characterization of activity, as in *what* the participants are doing, not *why* they are doing it. It would be normal for participants to provide multiple descriptions rather than a single description of the reason for their actions. As long as "doing something to reduce the risk of earthquakes" is one of those descriptions, then they may be said to be aware of engaging in claims-making activity.

In sum, the elements of constructionist theory that identify a given phenomenon as a social problem rather than some other type of phenomenon do not rule out treating the earthquake threat in this way. At the same time, however, these defining elements do not account for the difference between the earthquake threat and other phenomena in this category, that is, other social problems. Claims-making activity, albeit by insiders for the most part, is present. So, too, is conflict, though it is publicly visible only intermittently. Although the career of the earthquake threat differs in some respects from the natural history of social problems described by Spector and Kitsuse, there is no reason why the history of any single problem should conform exactly to this model. And earthquake safety advocates and officials, by all visible indicators, are aware that their activities contribute to creation of a social problem even if they would not use this term to describe what they do or what they hope to achieve. If it is not activity, then it must be the *product* of that activity that sets the earthquake threat apart from other social problems.

WHY THE EARTHQUAKE THREAT IS DIFFERENT:
PROBLEMS ACTIVITY VERSUS
"SUCCESSFUL" PROBLEMS PROMOTION

Objectivist and constructionist theories of social problems[2] provide different ways for determining what is and what is not a social problem (cf. Mauss 1989:20–23). Objectivists cite statistical data on the existence of harmful conditions such as rates of behavior, incidence of victimization, or levels of contamination as evidence that problems exist (e.g., Kingdon 1984:95–99). However, my view is that statistics tell us about conditions and about the people who generate those statistics but not why or for whom a condition is a problem (Spector and Kitsuse [1977] 1987:23–30; Quarantelli 1989:23). Objectivist theories do not specify *who* gets to decide what conditions qualify as social problems or how such decisions are made (Spector and Kitsuse 1973:145).

Constructionist theory, especially the strict-constructionist variety, distinguishes problems from nonproblems by the presence or absence of certain types of activity with regard to putative conditions. Specifically, social problems exist when groups are asserting grievances and making claims. Claims-making, however, is not an end in itself; one purpose (there is probably always more than one) is to achieve results. Spector and Kitsuse portray this activity as a process with several twists and turns. Different social problems may be at different stages in their careers (Spector and Kitsuse 1973; also [1977] 1987:141–58). For example, one problem may have failed to progress beyond an initial stage in which groups are attempting "to assert the existence of some condition, define it as harmful, . . . publicize the assertions and stimulate controversy and to create a public or political issue" (Spector and Kitsuse 1973:147). Such a problem has been called an unconstructed social problem (Troyer and Markle 1984; Ball and Lilly 1984; also Best and Horiuchi 1985). On the other hand, another problem may have moved through the four stages that Spector and Kitsuse see as the typical natural history of "real" or fully constructed social problems. The earthquake threat seems to fit neither of these two descriptions, based on materials examined here.

There is one further ingredient in distinguishing among different social problems. Spector and Kitsuse's natural-history model makes progress from one stage to another problematic rather than automatic, thus forcing analysts to pay attention to factors that make some claims-making efforts more successful than others. A crucial difference among various claims-making efforts is success in getting an official response from a government agency or other influential institution (Spector and Kitsuse 1973:151–52), that is, in advancing the career of a problem from

State 1 to Stage 2. Having attained official recognition, a social problem has "arrived." Here, Spector and Kitsuse seem to change the definition of a social problem by including not only activity but also the *outcome* of that activity. For example, they note that some claims "do not *lead to* the creation of social problems" while others culminate "in *the establishment of* a social problem" (1973:149, emphasis added). The final sentence of their 1973 article is more explicit: "The so-called 'crime problem' as a social problem . . . is *generated* and sustained by the activities of complaining groups and institutional responses" (p. 158, emphasis added).[3] In other words, social problems are both processes *and* products. Claims-making activity is necessary but not sufficient for full problem construction. Fully constructed social problems are *the result of* successful claims-making.

The issue of successful versus unsuccessful claims-making is central to the question of why the risk of earthquakes is different from other types of social problems. The fact that claims-making on behalf of the earthquake threat exists means that, by the most basic element in its definition, the threat is some form of social problem. However, the difference between the earthquake threat and fully constructed social problems is more than a difference in careers or individual histories. The history of the earthquake threat includes the most important activity in Stage 2 of the Spector-Kitsuse model: recognition by government agency or other influential institution. Indeed, such recognition activities seem to have comprised much of the first phase of the threat's history. There is also some evidence of disaffection among claims-makers—especially those in the scientific and academic communities—with the official response to the threat (Stage 3).

The principal difference between the earthquake threat and fully constructed social problems may be found by examining Stage 1 of the Spector-Kitsuse model. Claims-making on behalf of the risk of earthquakes has never succeeded in stimulating controversy or creating a public issue. Claims-making activity exists, but the consequences of this activity differ from that addressing other putative conditions. Though legitimated by government (the federal government has had an earthquake hazards policy since 1977 and a natural disaster policy since 1950), the risk of earthquakes and other natural disasters has never attracted sustained popular attention or support (Meltsner 1978; May 1985:6–9). It is constructed around "policies without publics" (May 1991b:190–97). In other words, the promotion of the risk of earthquakes has failed to generate a base of support at the grass-roots level within the public at large.

The best general description is to label the earthquake threat a *partially constructed social problem*. Like organized crime in the 1960s and white-collar crime in the 1980s, it remains visible to insiders but nearly invisible to those outside the earthquake establishment. The materials examined here reveal the reason why. The image of risk that both primary and secondary claims-makers (Best 1990:87–89) have created is one in which the earthquake threat is an act of nature that may or may not occur in the future. Insiders use the phrase "low probability, high risk" to say the same thing. That is, members of the public at large are assumed to perceive that the potential consequences of a major earthquake could be enormous but also to perceive that the chances they personally will become victims are remote. May (1991a, 1991b) characterizes these as "public" risks as distinct from the more personal and more immediate private risks. More colloquially, the future is a long way off, the event may or may not occur, and even if it does there is nothing anyone can do about it anyway.

Claims-makers have promoted the earthquake threat as a putative condition that does not yet exist. Promoters of fully constructed social problems in contrast define intolerable conditions as existing in the present. Child abusers, drinking drivers, carriers of the AIDS virus, abortionists as well as those who would prevent abortions, polluted air, lead in paints, etc., are "out there as we speak." In contrast, the destruction that will follow a future catastrophic earthquake has yet to occur. Strain may be building up in the earth right now, and buildings that will collapse already exist, but the harmful conditions that claims-makers warn about are part of the future, not the present. Without linking the present and the future, claims-makers have made it more difficult for the public at large to attach harm to existing conditions and activities.[4]

Claims-makers also stress impersonal forces, both natural and social, in images that they create of the earthquake threat. One reason for this, as we have seen, is that the human beings whom claims-makers could identify as "causing" unsatisfactory conditions are people whose cooperation is essential if these conditions are to be changed. For example, the public at large may be a major cause of these unsatisfactory conditions through its general "apathy" and its failure to take the possibility of a future catastrophic earthquake seriously, but it is this same public at large whose voluntary assistance is also needed to anchor hot-water heaters and secure houses to their foundations. Whatever the reasons, images of impersonal forces maintain the impression that the threat is uncontrollable, that "nothing can be done." The belief that something can be done about an "obnoxious aspect of life" (Spector and Kitsuse [1977] 1987:128) is a prerequisite for social-problem construction (Spector and Kitsuse [1977] 1987:84).

THE FUTURE OF THE EARTHQUAKE THREAT

I am arguing that the earthquake threat is currently only a partially constructed social problem. I base my contention not on the absence of claims-making activity but rather on the products of that activity. Claims-makers have not created a public issue about earthquakes that can compete in the already-crowded social-problems marketplace with issues like child abuse, drinking drivers, and street crime. They have not been forced to create public controversy in order to provoke official recognition and action because they enjoy access to governmental institutions that outsiders do not. Such access has costs as well as benefits for the efforts of claims-makers. By not "taking to the streets," as one might say, risk promoters have failed to assemble a constituency of grass-roots support.

What is remarkable about the earthquake threat is how much public policymaking and how many government programs there have been in spite of the lack of concern within the public at large. Furthermore, the existence of an ongoing federal program, the National Earthquake Hazards Reduction Program, guarantees a permanent spot on the legislative agenda through reauthorization and appropriations activities, if nothing else. This may be a good reason for "staying the course." Given the current composition of the earthquake hazards movement, drastic changes in strategy seem out of the question. Changes in the nature of claims and in the claims-making process could occur if new claims-makers entered the picture. However, new and different claims-makers would undoubtedly construct the issue differently, with positive as well as negative consequences.[5]

Constructionist theory suggests the type of program that would be necessary to alter the career of the earthquake threat in a way that would increase its chances of eventually becoming a fully constructed social problem. Most importantly, a fundamental retypification would be necessary. A new rhetorical idiom (Ibarra and Kitsuse 1993:35–42) would be required. New ways of thinking about the earthquake threat would need to be created and promoted. Current categories of understanding make it difficult for the public at large to think of the threat in different ways. Gusfield (1981), writing about another public-policy issue, pinpoints this difficulty:

> Precisely because the categories of understanding and meaning provide so powerful a constraint to what we experience and how we think about that experience, they prevent awareness of alternative ways of conceiving events and processes. Because they lead us to "see" the accustomed forms as the

only reality, they minimize and obscure the possible conflicts and the
volitionary decisions that have helped construct "reality." (Gusfield 1981:28)

If our images of earthquakes include only the forces of nature, then it is
hard to see how human actions contribute to risk. It is also hard to see
how anything can be done about them. If the most important questions
about earthquakes are scientific questions, then it is hard to see them
instead as political questions.

Anecdotal evidence suggests that changing the imagery of putative
conditions can have important consequences for claims-making activity.
John Kingdon's (1984:117–19) interviews with federal officials showed
that a "change of categories" often moved a problem up the policy
agenda. Deborah Prothrow-Stith, of the Harvard Medical School, began
teaching and writing about violence as a public health problem rather
than strictly a law enforcement issue in the late 1970s (Cavander 1992).
There are signs currently that the typification of violence as a health
issue is gaining acceptance among insiders dealing with the problems of
crime. As this typification grows, the range of "solutions" for dealing
with problems of violent crime may change. As far as the career of the
earthquake threat is concerned, the only circumstances under which
actions on its behalf might change dramatically would come as a result
of an equivalent shift in definition and the use of alternative vernacular
resources (Ibarra and Kitsuse 1993). We have seen that an alternative
way of viewing the threat, as a potential catastrophic economic disaster,
is already emerging. Beyond a continuation of this retypification, what
other forms of redefinition would alter the career of this threat?

One change that should have major consequences would be to personalize the earthquake threat. Currently, claims about the risks of
earthquake are ambiguous as to who is responsible for damage and
injuries should disaster strike. Since no individual or type of individual
(e.g., slum lords) is singled out beforehand for placing others at risk,
disaster victims have little choice but to explain their misfortune as luck,
fate, or God's will. Personalizing the threat would be the equivalent of
"naming names." People responsible for failing to take measures to
reduce risk would be linked to the likelihood of future harm. Personalizing the threat would shift the "causal story" about earthquakes from one
with an unintended cause to one whose cause is inadvertent (Stone
1989, 1988:147–65). Naming names would also begin to alter the image
that everyone is equally likely to become a victim in a future earthquake.
Personalizing responsibility for consequences would also outline the
structure of risk, that is, the fact that it is not equally shared. In other
words, personalizing risk would also personalize victimization. As human agents begin to replace nature, fate, and the luck-of-the-draw as

explanations for why some people die in earthquakes and others do not, the belief that "nothing can be done" becomes harder to sustain. Furthermore, identifying people responsible for exposing other people to risk makes it harder to "blame the victim" for exposure to harm (as in, "Those are the chances you take [i.e., the risks you voluntarily accept] when you live in a rickety old apartment building like that"). The number of possible villains here is great, including greedy developers, venture capitalists, corrupt politicians, and even egghead scientists.

A second change that could alter the career of the risk of earthquakes would be to politicize the threat. Currently claims about the threat are steadfastly apolitical. They do not urge people to vote against politicians who do not support hazard reduction legislation. They do not urge registered voters to write to members of Congress to support earthquake safety legislation, even though business routinely lobbies Congress to protect its interests when they seem threatened by earthquake proposals. They do not urge passage of bond measures that would generate funds for retrofitting public schools and college classroom buildings such as California Propositions 1A, 1B, and 1C in the 1994 primary elections. Claims-makers are even silent on buying earthquake insurance. They do not encourage legal action against developers or realtors who fail to inform prospective home buyers about seismic risks, as required by law in California.

The message of claims-makers to the public at large is decidedly voluntaristic. It is a middle-class, family-oriented message that probably misses both the poor and the wealthy. Its current intent is to reduce the potential demand for emergency services by shifting responsibility from government to individual citizens. It directs attention away from the structure of risk. There are no penalties for noncompliance.

Earthquake preparedness programs for businesses are a good example. Whether in the public or private sector, these programs focus on employee safety and include drills such as taking cover under office furniture and exercises such as building evacuations led by designated company safety officers. They do not mention pressuring local officials to incorporate seismic provisions in building codes or to control construction in designated hazardous areas. They do not urge employees to vote against politicians who do not support strong seismic safety measures. Employers are not likely to encourage their employees to engage in activity that could drive up the cost of doing business. Employees would not welcome more government regulation, which might result in layoffs or encourage the employer to move to another state with less stringent seismic requirements.

Claims that politicize the threat would emphasize what can be done through the normal political process. Identifying political candidates and urging their election or reelection (or rejection), urging citizens to write their legislators in support of pending earthquake legislation, hiring lobbyists to do the same thing, and sponsoring and supporting ballot initiatives and referenda are all conventional forms of political expression. None are the equivalent of overturning police cars, looting liquor stores, or setting fire to public buildings. Yet none have been associated with efforts to reduce the risk of earthquakes.

A third obvious change that could alter the career of the earthquake threat would be to "presentize" the threat. That is, claims could emphasize that risk resides in existing conditions, not future ones. Claimsmakers could argue that everyday decisions, not future ones, determine who is exposed to harm and to what extent. Currently, images of risk emphasize future events. Fixation with earthquake prediction—knowing when and where the Big One will strike and what it will be like—perpetuate this future orientation. Locating risk in the present would further undermine the presumption that nothing can be done. Like cigarette smoking, "bad eating habits," lack of exercise, and prolonged exposure to asbestos, presentizing the risk of earthquakes could increase the likelihood that people will connect action in the present with possible future costs and benefits.

Regardless of whether such changes should be made (a question dealt with in the Postscript), it is unlikely that they will take place. The nature of the claims-makers who comprise the earthquake establishment is the principal reason. Government officials are constrained, legally and temperamentally, from behaving in overtly political fashion. Scientists tend to be better at running their laboratories than at manning the barricades, so to speak. Earthquake safety advocates seem to maintain a polite distance from more activist outsiders. Earthquake risk promoters tend not to be confrontational people. They are unlikely, for example, to enthusiastically join no-growth groups in order to prevent development of scientifically designated hazardous land. This would not only mean taking sides in a controversy, it would also risk being labeled an opponent of affordable housing or as being in favor of government restriction on the right of business to make a profit.

Nevertheless, change will—indeed, has—come to the promotion of the risk of earthquakes. The retypification of risk as an economic threat with its increasing emphasis on mitigation will continue to bring human beings and human agency into the definition of risk. Specific human choices and their implications for increasing or decreasing risk and hence costs present a competing image of risk that may eventually overshadow the long-dominant image of uncontrollable natural forces. As public policies emerge such as those tying mitigation to the availability of federally subsidized earthquake insurance for home owners, forms of personalization and presentization will also occur. The nature and dynamics of the earth may remain as they presumably have been for thousands of years, but the earthquake threat as a social construction continues to evolve.

NOTES

1.   Many people have moved out of California, citing the earthquake threat as one reason for leaving, and employees of earthquake-related programs have left their jobs, sometimes expressing frustration that nothing significant is being done to reduce risk. However, neither of these constitutes the creation of parallel mechanisms or arrangements that Spector and Kitsuse's Stage 4 envisions.

2.   I am ignoring for the moment differences between strict constructionists such as Spector and Kitsuse (1973, [1977] 1987; see also Ibarra and Kitsuse 1993) and contextual constructionists such as Best (1989, 1993).

3.   In the sentence preceding this one in their 1973 article, Spector and Kitsuse even imply that social problems have *quantitative* as well as qualitative defining characteristics. Evidence that crime is a social problem comes from the fact that "there are *many* individuals and groups complaining" about crime and "the *myriad* agencies that are mandated to do something about these complaints" (Spector and Kitsuse 1973:158, emphasis added).

4.   In contrast, claims-makers concerned with other agents—cigarettes, dioxin, asbestos, etc.—have been successful in creating putative conditions out of harms whose specific effects will not be known with certainty until a future date. The unwillingness of many people to stay in a hotel or to work in a building without smoke detectors and automatic sprinklers and the willingness of most people to do both in structures considered seismically unsound further illustrates the lack of success on the part of earthquake risk promoters in linking low-probability, high-risk future consequences with present conditions.

5.   A recent example of such a shift was the recasting of the condition of the nation's bridges and highways from a safety issue (Stallings 1990a) to an economic one in anticipation of former President Bush's bid for reelection in 1992.

Postscript

Two matters that have come up but have not been dealt with in the preceding chapters remain to be discussed. One, which can be dispensed with fairly quickly, is the relationship between the materials examined in this book and the Northridge, California, earthquake of January 17, 1994. The other matter is the relationship among social problems, partially constructed or otherwise, the analysis of social problems, and the social-problems analyst. Among other issues, the question of whether or not the researcher has a "hidden agenda" frequently is raised. I conclude with some personal thoughts about the earthquake threat and my examination of it.

UPDATE: THE NORTHRIDGE, CALIFORNIA, EARTHQUAKE

The first draft of this book was completed at the end of December 1993. Less than three weeks later, the latest earthquake disaster to strike the United States occurred in Los Angeles and neighboring cities. The timing of these two events posed a dilemma: How could anyone write a book about earthquakes and the earthquake threat in the United States without including the most recent—and most dramatic—example? That is by and large what I have done. Let me explain why.

The primary reason that I have elected not to incorporate the Northridge earthquake disaster in the present examination is that it is too early to do so. While a few hearings have been held, the published transcripts from them are not yet available (as of the end of May 1994). Several pieces of legislation have been introduced at federal, state, and local levels, but their ultimate fate has not been decided. Some preliminary research reports have been issued on geophysical aspects of the earthquake, but the bulk of engineering and social science research is just getting under way. Lawsuits have been filed against apartment owners and builders, but court dates have not been set. Investigations continue into fraudulent claims for disaster aid and charges have been filed against a few individuals, but the criminal cases have not gone to trial.

A second reason that I have elected not to systematically introduce what is known about how this most recent disaster is likely to influence the definition of the risk of earthquakes is that so far it has produced very little that is new or different. The same themes that characterized the earthquakes in the 1960s, 1970s, and 1980s are visible once again. For example, "We were lucky"—the earthquake occurred at 4:30 A.M. and was not nearly as intense as the Big One will be; scientists expect a more severe earthquake in the future but cannot yet predict precisely when; earthquake insurance is still a nettlesome public-policy issue; mitigation must be accelerated to ease the strain on the federal budget. At this writing (late May 1994), there are a few elements that may one day extend or expand the image of risk: steel frame high-rise buildings do not seem to have been as immune to earthquake damage as had been assumed; a major "weak link" in the building code process is the field inspection; and the mind-set of most disaster relief agencies, for so long grounded in images of and experience with disasters in homogeneous small towns and suburbs, may come to recognize the implications of heterogeneity and diversity for urban disasters. This is speculation; some of these may disappear without a trace, and others may emerge over time.

It is not true that I have completely ignored the experience of the January 1994 earthquake. I have used examples, based mostly on newspaper accounts, to illustrate aspects of the earthquake threat that were visible during the study period, from 1964 through 1992. I have made no major revisions because this experience so far has not dictated any. It will be at least another four or five years before we begin to see what mark—if any—this earthquake disaster has left on the definition of risk.

SHOULD THE EARTHQUAKE THREAT BE A FULLY CONSTRUCTED SOCIAL PROBLEM?

A lingering question usually follows an examination such as the one presented here. People often want to know where the author *really* stands on the issues involved, what she or he *really* thinks about the situation. Whose side is the author on, anyway? On the side of those who are both personally and professionally committed to saving lives, reducing damage, and minimizing losses due to earthquakes? It is hard to see how anyone would not endorse such activities, or at least the values that they reflect. But does not the refusal to consider the scientific "facts" about earthquakes and their destructiveness and the focusing instead on "claims" about "putative" conditions and on the people making those claims deny the issue credibility? Have we not, however unintentionally, trivialized the earthquake threat as well as the people who work so hard to see that it is abated?

There are two ways to answer these questions, each of which is really a form of the single question, What *should* we be doing about the earthquake treat? One answer is based on the discipline of sociology and the theories of social problems that its participants have developed over the years. The other is based on the values and beliefs of sociologists as individual human beings.[1]

There are two groups of theories of social problems in the field of sociology. Objectivist theories (there are several varieties) are the older of the two theoretical traditions. Constructionist theory is the "new kid on the block," though its antecedents reach back several decades. While objectivist theories give contradictory answers to the question of how we should treat the risk of earthquakes, the answer provided by constructionist theory—at least by a strict reading of it—is unequivocal.

Objectivist theories give contradictory answers to the question of what should be done about the earthquake threat because their adherents use different yardsticks to measure the extent of harm associated with it. Most objectivists accept the descriptions of risk provided by earth scientists and earthquake safety advocates.[2] This means that sociologists "inevitably put themselves in the position of borrowing findings from other disciplines whose reliability and validity they cannot evaluate" (Spector and Kitsuse [1977] 1987:77). For objectivists, however, these descriptions are sufficient to lead to the conclusion that the earthquake threat and other natural hazards are in fact social problems even if the public at large does not recognize them as such. Drabek's (1989) paper on disasters as nonroutine social problems is the most explicit of these recent statements (see also Short 1989).

A strict reading of constructionist theory provides an unequivocal answer to the question of what should be the status of the earthquake threat: Whatever the people promoting it are able to accomplish. In other words, constructionist theory is neutral with respect to the fate of this issue; "on the side," in the words of Gusfield (1984). This means that constructionist theory sides with neither claims-makers nor with their opponents:

> A constructivist approach, however, drives a wedge between elites in the know—the cognoscenti—and the practical people who attempt to achieve programmatic and personal victories. . . . It takes the affective starch—the driving sense of mission—out of social problems by viewing them as matters of partisan or professional *choice* rather than conclusions forced upon us by the *nature* of things. . . . The gap here, between cognoscenti and populace, is the gap between the skeptic and the believer. What the practitioner and the partisan see as true phenomena, the cognoscenti see

as public relations, political choice, social movement, or some other form
which reduces its value as a basis for partisanship or occupational authority. (Gusfield 1984:45, emphasis in the original)

Constructionist theory views claims-making as a topic for investigation
not a process requiring partisan support (or opposition).

There is a second way to approach the question of what we should
make of the risk of earthquakes. This is what we as individual human
beings should make of the threat. Analysts of social problems are as
entitled as anyone else to have beliefs about what we should or should
not do about earthquakes. As individuals, some may support efforts to
raise the level of public awareness about the threat and government
action to reduce it. A few may become personally involved in claims-
making activity as committed partisans. Whatever their personal beliefs
or partisan commitments, these are matters that are not decided by a
theory of social problems.

As with any area where both personal and professional conduct are
involved, there is inevitable spillover between the two. One's personal
values and beliefs make certain disciplines and selected theories in them
attractive. One's discipline and theoretical stance undoubtedly influence
personal values and outlooks. Joel Best underscores the impossibility of
keeping the two separate in the dedication of his constructionist examination of threats to children, including the threat of abduction by
strangers. After dedicating his book to his two young sons, he concludes
with the inscription "whose father worries anyway" (Best 1990:v). The
trick is not to do the impossible (i.e., to completely eliminate personal
values), but rather to recognize the difference between the two spheres
of activity. (For a different point of view, see Mauss 1989.) The difference
for me parallels May's (1991a, 1991b) distinction between public and
private risks. At home and at work, the earthquake threat for me is very
much a private risk. Our family has followed the advice of safety experts
for the most part; we have stored bottled water, taken special precau-
tions with the china and other breakables, moved beds out from under
bedroom windows and taken down anything heavy from the walls
above them, purchased earthquake insurance (when it was still available), stored a complete change of cloths at work, placed emergency
supplies in the trunk of the car, etc.

As a public risk, however, the earthquake threat generates mixed
feelings. I personally applaud the efforts of earthquake safety advocates.
I hope they succeed in making my future and the future of those I care
about safer. However, I also have concerns about other forms of risk
such as that posed by the air that I breath, the modes of transportation
that I utilize, and the diseases to which I am exposed. I have no way of

knowing how to prioritize these risks in terms of their seriousness or importance apart from what I am doing at any given time (gasping on polluted air on a hot summer day, waiting for a bus at a bus stop at night, etc.). Furthermore, I recognize that other people have concerns about things that threaten them that are very different from my concerns. I have no way to decide, apart from personal self-interest, whether my concerns are more important than theirs. And there is the even more troubling recognition that I am probably being exposed to things now that will shorten my life-span but about which I will be unaware until I hear some future news report or read about some new government study.

It may seem cynical or fatalistic, but my general response to the question of whether the earthquake threat should become a fully constructed social problem and the answer derived from constructionist theory are the same: the marketplace will decide. Events that I can do little about will determine how the threat fares in competition with other issues. This answer seems to provide little to hold on to. What is the point of this kind of examination? What, then, is the value of this kind of theory? The answer to both questions is, I think, the same:

> Its social value lies in widening our understandings of self and others and in revealing the many alternatives from which to make choices and interpret events. (Gusfield 1984:48)

NOTES

1. Unfortunately, these two categories are not mutually exclusive. The values of individual sociologists have frequently been smuggled in to fill in the gaps in theories of social problems (Spector and Kitsuse [1977] 1987:23–58; Woolgar and Pawluch 1985; Best 1993).

2. Some recent work in the sociology of science is relevant here. Stephen Cole (1992) examines the question of whether findings in the natural sciences are exclusively products of social interaction, as social constructionists contend, or whether scientific knowledge is constrained by nature itself, as nearly everyone else assumes. He concludes that, while social variables may explain the content of knowledge on the frontiers of research, findings accepted into the core of knowledge in scientific fields reflect objective reality. Similarly, Rosa (1993) attempts to reconcile social constructionism with what he calls "grounded realism" in studies of risk. He, too, argues that there are types of risk where knowledge is characterized by both high repeatability and high ostensibility that can only reflect the objective reality of nature.

Appendix

Discussions of methods typically accompany reports of positive research. Investigators describe research designs, sampling procedures, variables, and analytic procedures, usually in cryptic fashion because from a few code words such as "cross-sectional design," "secondary data," and "OLS regression," readers know instantly what was done. In qualitative research, it is conventional to describe in some detail various components of the fieldwork that have a bearing on the conclusions reached such as the general approach used (e.g., participant observation), the setting in which observation took place, how entree into the setting was managed, and the role that researchers adopted in the field.

It is more difficult to write a discussion of methods for the present study since a variety of analyses were performed to construct what is basically a theoretical argument and to see where it led. However, there are points at which choices among alternatives were made. These need to be described in more detail than has been done in the text, because these choices could have affected some of the conclusions I reached. The things I have in mind do not fall neatly into the usual assortment of topics either in quantitative or qualitative research. I will comment on four of them: the choice of a level of analysis; the unit of analysis; "sampling" considerations, that is, choices in the type of risk to consider, the public arenas or settings to investigate, and the materials from those settings to examine; and my personal involvement with some of the events, people, and documents described in the book.

LEVEL OF ANALYSIS

Perhaps the most important decision affecting this examination of promoting the risk of earthquakes was the choice of an appropriate level of analysis. I contend that a sociological theory of social problems is a theory about *societal* (as in "societywide") problems. It deals with the public issues that are attended to by the institutions of society as a whole. Of course, one can easily and properly speak of "regional" social problems or "local" social problems, and at the other extreme of "international" social problems. In fact, a virtue of the constructionist theory developed over the years by Kitsuse and his collaborators (Spector and Kitsuse 1973, [1977] 1987; Ibarra and Kitsuse 1993) is its empirical flexibility. Problems processes at any level of social organization, including within occupations and professions, are theoretically accessible.

The choice of a societal level of analysis had immediate consequences. Most importantly it meant concentrating on national rather than state, regional, local, or even sublocal arenas. Both the nature and the outcomes of claims-making are different in each of these. I tried to take this into account by introducing some of the differences that exist as one moves about the country. For example, California in particular and the West Coast in general have been sites for more sustained and more systematic claims-making activity than have other regions of the country. Claims-making in the East, the Midwest, and, to a lesser extent, in the South Atlantic region is more recent. I noted especially the consequences of such differences for the public policymaking process.

The choice of a societal level of analysis raises another question about the outcome of this examination. Would my conclusions have been different if I had chosen to examine the promotion of *natural hazards* in general rather than the earthquake hazard in particular? One might argue that if the threat of hurricanes, which seem to be a "problem" along the Atlantic and Gulf Coasts, were combined with the threat of tornadoes, which seem to affect the Midwest, Mideast, and South, were combined with the threat of snows and blizzards, etc., that one could find evidence at the societal level for the existence of something more than merely a partially constructed social problem. Or, one might argue that the earthquake threat is unique among hazards and that a more "representative" hazard such as the flood threat (which seems to be a concern in nearly every state) would have produced different results.

It is only speculation since such analyses have not been attempted, but I believe that the conclusions reached from either an all-hazards examination or from the examination of another specific hazard would have been the same as those presented here. I can think of only a few scattered examples of activity that might be labeled claims-making and responding on behalf of a putative condition characterized as a "natural hazards in general" problem. There is also no readily apparent sign that natural hazards as a whole are more highly situated on the national agenda than are individual hazards such as the earthquake threat. Whether another type of hazard would have been more representative than the risk of earthquakes is a similar question. A case could be made that the flood hazard in particular has a longer history, a more voluminous public-policy record, and perhaps even a larger, more geographically dispersed "constituency" than the earthquake threat. However, I believe that the descriptions and analyses in this book parallel those of the flood threat (i.e., an act of nature rather than a product of human decision-making; an issue that recedes from public attention faster than does the level of flood water; an issue with neither grass-roots nor elite support; one with relatively weak advocates inside government; etc.; see, for example, Burby and French 1981; May 1985). Of course, this is exactly why research reports end with a recommendation about future work that remains to be done: until such analyses are undertaken, my conclusions are only speculations.

UNIT OF ANALYSIS

Throughout this examination, I have tried to deal consistently with claims-making as a group or collective phenomenon. I believe this to be consistent with social-problems theory, consistent even with the constructionist variant of this theory. Individual characteristics such as professional esteem or management skills have been treated as collective resources that vary across claims-making and opposing groups. Historical circumstances and social-structural arrangements such as class structures or policy domains are the context in which groups operate. Two important consequences follow from the choice of this unit of analysis. One has to do with methodological dimensions most commonly recognized as "sampling" and "measurement" decisions. The other is a theoretical issue that has been associated with social-problems theory for at least the last twenty years.

By focusing on groups rather than individuals in the study of risk promotion, the analyst immediately confronts the issues of relativism and reification. While "putative conditions" may exist as subjective reality for *individuals* (that is, the reality of those conditions *as* conditions is in their personal view or outlook), the conceptual status of putative conditions at the *group* level is more ambiguous. Presumably, groups do not "perceive" their environment in the way individuals perceive the world around them. Furthermore, no two individuals (presumably) perceive the world, including putative conditions such as future risks, in exactly the same way. Yet, I have treated risk just as social-problems theory treats claims about other types of putative conditions—as a collective phenomenon. Does this not change the status of risk from a subjective to an objective phenomenon? Or am I inventing something that does not exist by talking about risk as though it were a characteristic of groups?

I prefer to steer clear of the theoretical, philosophical, and meth-

odological issues involved here. Some aspects of these issues have received renewed attention in recent years in discussions about the relationship between microlevel data and macrolevel theories (see the
chapters in Alexander, Giesen, Munch, and Smelser 1987). While side-
stepping these issues here, I do have two reactions to them. First, I
personally am comfortable with the assumption that groups are the
appropriate unit of analysis for studying risk, social problems, public
issues, or whatever despite the dangers of reification. Sociologists and
others after all have been engaged in this type of inquiry for centuries.
Whether or not it is merely shorthand, we do routinely speak of groups
"acting" (promoting risk, making claims, etc.). Second, it strikes me that
this distinction between the individual level and the group or collective
level underlies the theoretical infighting between strict and contextual
constructionists (see the various papers in Holstein and Miller 1993) as
well as charges of "ontological gerrymandering" (Woolgar and Pawluch
1985) in social problems theory. The theoretical underpinnings of constructionist theory seem inconsistent with most of the empirical work
that constructionists do. These theoretical roots lie in individual-level
symbolic interactionist social psychology traceable to the work of George
Herbert Mead and Herbert Blumer in particular (Mead [1934] 1962;
Blumer 1969). Yet most empirical work that uses constructionist theory
does not deal with data on the subjective states of individuals but with
the actions and products of groups. The difference between these two
units of analysis makes it inevitable that critics will note the departure
from the assumption of relativism and raise the charge of reification.

SAMPLING

Strictly speaking, sampling is not an accurate label for the topics in
this section. Sampling conventionally refers to identifying all the elements of some population or universe through a sampling frame (Babbie
1989:170–71) and then selecting a subset of elements from that universe
from which data will be collected. The goal of the selection process is
always to produce a sample that is *representative* of the universe so that
empirical patterns identified through the sample data may be inferred to
hold for the universe as well. Typically, chance is used to guide the
selection process since either the information necessary to hand pick a
representative sample is lacking or the universe is sufficiently complex
to make this hazardous, or both. I use the term *sampling* here to emphasize that choices were made (things to examine were selected and other
things ignored) that should be considered in assessing the generaliz-

ability of the findings and conclusions presented. I will discuss three types of selection briefly: selecting the earthquake threat as the focus of study; selecting the public arenas or settings in which images of the earthquake threat were to be studied; and selecting the documents to use as sources of "data" on those images.

The Choice of a Single Hazard

Focusing on a single type of risk such as the earthquake threat may seem of limited theoretical use. However that may be, the alternatives are anything but ideal. An examination of all natural hazards (i.e., the universe) seems more sound but would be extremely difficult for both methodological and theoretical reasons. Methodologically, the amount of time and effort required to examine the individual histories of a dozen or more distinct threats would be enormous even if it were possible. It may not even be possible, because it is far from clear what the universe of hazards consists of. One could draw up a list by convention, of course. The three-volume report to Congress by the Office of Emergency Preparedness (1972) explicitly examines ten types of natural disasters. The assessment of research needs directed by White and Haas (1975) identifies twelve natural hazards whose study merits federal research support. The U.S. National Committee for the Decade for Natural Disaster Reduction (1991) is vague about how many different types of natural disasters there are, but explicitly presents loss data on eight (p. 8) and uses photographs of at least that many more. Researchers have recently been rethinking whether the risks of natural hazards are sufficiently unique to be studied separately from other types of risk (see Kreps 1989). There is currently little consensus on a definition of the term *hazard* and the types of phenomena it encompasses. Even if there were, sampling— especially probability sampling—makes no sense given the relatively small size of this universe, however it is defined.

My choice of a single threat was a matter of expedience. I saw this effort at the outset as a pilot study or trial run. If a constructionist theory of social problems could meaningfully deal with one type of natural hazard, then it could be applied to others. Choosing the earthquake threat was a matter of convenience. My past involvement in various activities related to this hazard (see below) was more extensive than that related to other types of hazards. Having lived in southern California for two decades also meant that materials about this threat had come into my possession, inadvertently for the most part. So the earthquake threat represented a little bit of a head start over other topics. Subsequent work will show how generalizable the findings presented here are.

The Choice of Public Arenas

I know of no "sampling frame" for identifying the universe of public arenas or settings in which risk promotion or claims-making activity takes place. Hilgartner and Bosk (1988), who present the most systematic discussion of the term *public arena* and its importance for social problems research, offer an extensive list of examples (pp. 58-59) but not one that is exhaustive. Similarly, Ibarra and Kitsuse (1993:53–56) identify three of the most important types of settings in which claims-making occurs—the media (including several subtypes), the legal-political, and the academic—but they too make no effort to identify all types. It is difficult therefore to know if one has been systematic or selective in an examination of a variety of public arenas.

I tried to do two things in selecting arenas. Given my assumption that social problems are societal problems, I first wanted to make sure that I chose settings that were *national* in character, the kind of things that come to mind when someone speaks about how things are playing on the "national stage." This meant including not only branches of the federal (i.e., national) government such as the White House, executive-branch departments, and Congress but also the national news media. In so far as images of the risk of earthquakes exist in the entertainment media (movies, television specials, etc.), these too had to be products available to a nationwide rather than local audience. While the federal government leaves a fairly large paper trail for researchers to follow, other arenas do not. News reports in particular are problematic because the types of media available are so numerous (specialized cable television channels, local FM radio stations that in the aggregate provide a few seconds of news between rock music recordings to an audience larger than the combined readership of the so-called "prestige press," "talk radio" programs, newsletters sent to dues-paying members of voluntary associations, local television news available anywhere via home satellite dishes, etc.) and because their news products are so perishable.

I followed a shortcut used by other researchers who study the national electronic news media over time. Although in previous research (Stallings 1989, 1990b) I had found newspaper indexes very useful, especially the several indexes of local newspapers compiled by University Microfilms, I concentrated on the glimpses of earthquake news available in the *Television News Index and Abstracts*. Television network news is important strategically for promoting risk. Claims-makers appearing on network television are usually aware that, whatever the size of the viewing audience, they have reached in a few seconds more people than they could through any other medium. Moreover, stories are likely to diffuse outward from the networks to other news organizations that have fewer resources. In short, while television network news is neither typical nor exhaustive of all news available to a nationwide audience, it is an arena that deserves to be included in analyses such as this. That news in other arenas is less accessible is an unfortunate practical circumstance.

The second thing I tried to do in selecting settings for examining claims and claims-making was to represent some of the variance across different types of arenas. This was necessary not only to round out the picture, so to speak, but also to show the (variable) effects of arenas on the claims-making process. For practical reasons, I decided to present the diversity of risk promotion across the several geographic regions of the country only in general terms. To go into more detail would have presented a difficult challenge given limited resources. I was more interested in examining differences among local, state, and federal levels of policymaking. Subsequent analyses might well examine how different regional histories influence the social-problem status of the earthquake threat at the regional level.

The Choice of Documents

The choice of documents to examine is mostly a decision about which government reports, transcripts, and publications give an accurate picture of risk promotion. Again, there is neither a clear definition of what the universe of such documents might be nor a useful sampling frame. I have tried to select a purposive sample of documents that have been influential in how the earthquake threat is defined. Influence is less a function of such objective features of a document as who prepared it, which agency published it, etc. (although these properties of course can be relevant); it has to with the way a document is subsequently used by claims-makers. Sometimes the influence of a document is evident in other documents as when witnesses at a congressional hearing refer to a previous report or when a document is cited extensively in the report of a subsequent committee of experts. More often, I have relied on my recollection of events, in particular what people over the years have said, both professionally and privately, explicitly and implicitly, about various documents and what their existence meant to the promotion of risk.

The main check on the subjectivity and bias that this type of selection may introduce is the considerable overlap of both content and participants apparent in the documents available. This overlap, however, holds primarily within levels of government and for relatively short periods of time. It does not hold across different levels (i.e., local, state, and federal), nor does it hold for more than a decade. In other words, transcripts of congressional hearings in the 1970s contain roughly the same image of the earthquake threat and feature many of the same participants (with the exceptions explicitly noted in the Chapters 3 and 4, for example). This is not necessarily the case for a hearing held in the early 1970s and one held in the late 1980s, for example. In short, the redundancy contained in the results of content analyses gives me some confidence that I have not skewed my description of claims, claims-makers, or claims-making by my choice of documents.

THE ROLE OF THE AUTHOR

The first thing to know about my involvement in the subject examined here is that my participation in the earthquake establishment has been intermittent and mostly peripheral. It seems as though I have always been turning away from the subject of earthquakes and natural hazards, only to be drawn back for "just one more" interesting project. Usually the reason for returning to the area was the realization that I could explore quite usefully in it some new intellectual development that I had experienced. Although a résumé might give the appearance of a continuing interest, my interest is better described as discontinuous rather than sustained. There are clearly disadvantages to being somewhat marginal to the day-to-day activities of a world that one attempts to study, but there is a major advantage as well. The advantage is the ability to maintain a certain amount of detachment while remaining reasonably well-informed about new developments.

The second thing worth noting is that my exposure to people and events connected with the earthquake threat is skewed by my graduate degrees and research experience. As a sociologist, I have had greater exposure to those aspects of claims-making that social scientists are most often invited to participate in. This usually has involved something to do with public policy or public management. I have been relatively farther removed from the activities of earth scientists and engineers, though many forms of public service activity have meant collaboration with both. Some examples will illustrate what I mean.

In the mid-1970s—at the height of activity triggered by the expected arrival of routine earthquake predictions—I was a member of an interdisciplinary committee of the National Academy of Sciences, which produced a report on the topic of probable socioeconomic effects of earthquake predictions and the policy-focused research that would be needed to address them. Anyone who has ever been involved with one of the academy's committees in the days when Charles Fritz was at the National Research Council knows that this meant that I was on the receiving end of every report (published or unpublished), newspaper clipping, and journal article on the subject. Membership on this committee later brought me into contact with the late Henry Minturn, author of a famous earthquake prediction for southern California, who, perhaps needing to "tell his side of the story," gave me some fascinating documents. Membership also led to other public service activities including speeches and seminars as some sort of "expert" on the policy implications of earthquakes. Actually, as is true for most researchers, I learned more from other panelists and audience members than they did from me.

For a while, I was an alternate on the Policy Advisory Board of the Southern California Earthquake Preparedness Project (SCEPP). This jointly funded federal-state planning partnership brought me into contact with earth scientists, engineers, state and local earthquake safety and preparedness officials, and representatives of major "lifeline" utilities. Service on advisory panels of National Science Foundation research projects is another setting in which I came into contact with researchers and practitioners with a variety of disciplinary and professional backgrounds. I used to attend fairly regularly the annual workshop in Boulder, Colorado, that brings together practitioners and members of the research community (see Chapter 6), though I have not been there in recent years. There have also been a number of retreats, workshops, and seminars where I have been able to listen to and talk with some of the leading members of the earthquake establishment.

These kinds of experiences, together with my writing and research in the area of natural hazards, have put me on mailing and distribution lists for government reports, unpublished documents of all kinds, and research reports plus announcements of other publications of interest. They have connected me with many of the "bureaucrats" who do the day-to-day work of earthquake risk promotion and who are always great sources of advice and information. Finally, they have given me access to the researchers in this field who follow policy and other events much more closely than I do and who always know what is going on.

In sum, *participant observation* is not an accurate term to describe my relationship as a researcher with the earthquake threat claims-making process, but then neither is the term *nonparticipant observation*. Perhaps *intermittent participant observation* is the most accurate description.

References

Abney, F. Glenn, and Larry B. Hill. 1966. "Natural Disasters as a Political Variable: The Effect of a Hurricane on an Urban Election." *American Political Science Review* 60:974–81.

Alesch, Daniel J., and William J. Petak. 1986. *The Politics and Economics of Earthquake Hazard Mitigation: Unreinforced Masonry Buildings in Southern California.* Boulder: Institute of Behavioral Science, University of Colorado.

Alexander, George. 1976. "Quake Predictor Generating Tremors." *Los Angeles Times*, December 5.

Alexander, Jeffrey C., Bernhard Giesen, Richard Munch, and Neil J. Smelser (eds.). 1987. *The Micro-Macro Link.* Berkeley: University of California Press.

Algermissen, S. T. 1970. *Seismic Risk Studies in the United States.* Washington, DC: U.S. Coast and Geodetic Survey, Department of Commerce.

American Earthquake Study Delegation. 1975. "Earthquake Research in China." *EOS* 56:838–81.

American Public Opinion Index 1990. 1991. Volume 1, A–L. Tallahassee, FL: Opinion Research Service.

Anderson, William A. 1969. *Local Civil Defense in Natural Disasters: From Office to Organization.* Newark, DE: Disaster Research Center.

Austin, Teresa. 1989. "RTD Annoyed by Studio Tour 'Quake.'" *Downtown News*, April 24.

Ayre, Robert S. 1975. *Earthquake and Tsunami Hazards in the United States: A Research Assessment.* Boulder: Institute of Behavioral Science, University of Colorado.

Babbie, Earl. 1989. *The Practice of Social Research*, 5th ed. Belmont, CA: Wadsworth.

Ball, Richard A., and J. Robert Lilly. 1984. "When Is a 'Problem' Not a Problem?: Deflection Activities in a Clandestine Motel." Pp. 114–39 in *Studies in the Sociology of Social Problems*, edited by Joseph W. Schneider and John I. Kitsuse. Norwood, NJ: Ablex.

Best, Joel. 1989. "Afterword: Extending the Constructionist Perspective: A Conclusion—And an Introduction." Pp. 243–53 in *Images of Issues: Typifying Contemporary Social Problems*, edited by Joel Best. Hawthorne, NY: Aldine de Gruyter.

Best, Joel. 1990. *Threatened Children: Rhetoric and Concern about Child-Victims.* Chicago: University of Chicago Press.

Best, Joel. 1993. "But Seriously Folks: The Limitations of the Strict Constructionist Interpretation of Social Problems." Pp. 129–47 in *Reconsidering Social Constructionism: Debates in Social Problems Theory*, edited by James A. Holstein and Gale Miller. Hawthorne, NY: Aldine de Gruyter.

Best, Joel, and Gerald T. Horiuchi. 1985. "The Razor Blade in the Apple: The Social Construction of Urban Legends." *Social Problems* 32:488–99.

Block, Fred. 1981. "Beyond Relative Autonomy: State Managers as Historical Subjects." *New Political Science* 2:33–49.

Blumer, Herbert. 1969. *Symbolic Interactionism: Perspective and Method*. Englewood Cliffs, NJ: Prentice-Hall.

Blumer, Herbert. 1971. "Social Problems as Collective Behavior." *Social Problems* 18:298–306.

Bolin, Robert. 1982. *Long-Term Family Recovery from Disaster*. Boulder: Institute of Behavioral Science, University of Colorado.

Bolin, Robert, and Patricia Bolton. 1986. *Race, Religion, and Ethnicity in Disaster Recovery*. Boulder: Institute of Behavioral Science, University of Colorado.

Bolt, Bruce A. 1978. *Earthquakes: A Primer*. San Francisco: W. H. Freeman.

Bolton, Patricia A., Edward B. Liebow, and Jon Olson. 1993. "Community Context and Uncertainty Following a Damaging Earthquake: Low-Income Latinos in Los Angeles, California." *Environmental Professional* 15:240–47.

Buckle, Ian G. 1993. "Improving Lifeline Systems." Pp. 39–63 in *Improving Earthquake Mitigation: Report to Congress*, edited by Office of Earthquakes and Natural Hazards. Washington, DC: Federal Emergency Management Agency.

Building Technology, Inc. 1990. *Financial Incentives for Seismic Rehabilitation of Hazardous Buildings—An Agenda for Action*, Volume 1. Washington, DC: Federal Emergency Management Agency.

Burby, Raymond J., and Steven P. French. 1981. "Coping with Floods: The Land Use Management Paradox." *Journal of the American Planning Association* 47:289–300.

Cavander, Sasha. 1992. "Doctor Seeks to Cure Violence by Battling It Like Any Disease." *Los Angeles Times*, June 24.

Clarke, Lee. 1992. "Power, Risk, and Work." *Contemporary Sociology* 21:704–6.

Cohen, Michael, James March, and Johan Olsen. 1972. "A Garbage Can Model of Organizational Choice." *Administrative Science Quarterly* 17:1–25.

Cole, Stephen. 1992. *Making Science: Between Nature and Society*. Cambridge, MA: Harvard University Press.

Colvin, Richard Lee, and Larry Gordon. 1994. "L.A. Plans Cash Infusion to Revive Quake Ghost Towns." *Los Angeles Times*, May 3.

Comerio, Mary C., John D. Landis, and Yodan Rofe. 1994. *Post-Disaster Residential Rebuilding*. Working Paper 608, Institute of Urban and Regional Development, University of California, Berkeley.

Committee on Disasters and the Mass Media. 1980. *Disasters and the Mass Media*. Washington, DC: Commission on Sociotechnical Systems.

Committee on the Alaska Earthquake. 1968–1973. *The Great Alaska Earthquake of 1964*, 8 volumes. Washington, DC: Division of Earth Sciences, National Research Council—National Academy of Sciences.

Committee on the Alaska Earthquake. 1970. *The Great Alaska Earthquake of 1964:*

Human Ecology. Washington, DC: Division of Earth Sciences, National Research Council—National Academy of Sciences.

Comptroller General of the United States. 1980. *Federal Disaster Assistance: What Should the Policy Be?* Washington, DC: U. S. General Accounting Office.

Constable, Angela. 1993. "How Individuals and Organizations Perceive Risk in Association with Earthquakes and Toxic/Hazardous Waste." Unpublished paper, Department of Sociology, University of Southern California, Los Angeles.

Cook, James A. 1975. "Earthquake Prediction: An Ominous 'Public Service' That Could Give the Economy the Shakes." Memorandum, August 28, California Business Properties Association, Hawthorne.

Cressey, Donald R. 1967. "Methodological Problems in the Study of Organized Crime as a Social Problem." *Annals of the American Academy of Political and Social Science* 374:101–22.

Dacy, Douglas C., and Howard Kunreuther. 1969. *The Economics of Natural Disasters: Implications for Federal Policy*. New York: Free Press.

Dahl, Robert A. 1982. *Dilemmas of Pluralist Democracy*. New Haven, CT: Yale University Press.

Dearing, James W., and Jeff Kazmierczak. 1993. "Making Iconoclasts Credible: The Iben Browning Earthquake Prediction." *International Journal of Mass Emergencies and Disasters* 11:391–403.

Domhoff, G. William. 1983. *Who Rules America Now?: A View for the '80s*. New York: Simon and Schuster.

Domhoff, G. William. 1990. *The Power Elite and the State*. Hawthorne, NY: Aldine de Gruyter.

Douglas, Mary. 1966. *Purity and Danger: An Analysis of Concepts of Pollution and Taboo*. New York: Praeger.

Douglas, Mary, and Aaron Wildavsky. 1982. *Risk and Culture: An Essay on the Selection of Technological and Environmental Dangers*. Berkeley: University of California Press.

Drabek, Thomas E. 1986. *Human System Response to Disaster: An Inventory of Sociological Findings*. New York: Springer-Verlag.

Drabek, Thomas E. 1989. "Disasters as Nonroutine Social Problems." *International Journal of Mass Emergencies and Disasters* 7:253–64.

Drabek, Thomas E., and William H. Key. 1984. *Conquering Disaster: Family Recovery and Long-Term Consequences*. New York: Irvington.

Drabek, Thomas E., Alvin H. Mushkatel, and Thomas S. Kilijanek. 1983. *Earthquake Mitigation Policy: The Experience of Two States*. Boulder: Institute of Behavioral Science, University of Colorado.

Draper, Elaine. 1991. *Risky Business: Genetic Testing and Exclusionary Practices in the Hazardous Workplace*. New York: Cambridge University Press.

Dunne, Rachel Gulliver. 1978. *Consensus Report of the Task Force on Earthquake Prediction*. Los Angeles: City of Los Angeles.

Dynes, Russell R. 1978. "Review of 'Everything in Its Path.'" *Social Forces* 57:721–22.

Edelman, Murray. 1988. *Constructing the Political Spectacle*. Chicago: University of Chicago Press.

Erikson, Kai T. 1976. *Everything in Its Path: Destruction of Community in the Buffalo Creek Flood*. New York: Simon and Schuster.

Feldman, Paul. 1992. "Fear of Unknown is Rattling." *Los Angeles Times*, July 27.

Federal Emergency Management Agency. 1980. *An Assessment of the Consequences and Preparations for a Catastrophic California Earthquake: Findings and Actions Taken*. Washington, DC: Federal Emergency Management Agency.

Foundation for Public Affairs. 1992. *Public Interest Profiles, 1992–1993*. Washington, DC: Congressional Quarterly, Inc.

Frederick, Calvin J. 1977. "Current Thinking About Crisis or Psychological Intervention in United States Disasters." *Mass Emergencies* 2:43–50.

Fried, John J. 1973. *Life Along the San Andreas Fault*. New York: Saturday Review Press.

Fritz, Charles E. 1961. "Disaster." Pp. 651–94 in *Contemporary Social Problems: An Introduction to the Sociology of Deviant Behavior and Social Disorganization*, edited by Robert K. Merton and Robert A. Nisbet. New York: Harcourt, Brace, and World.

Fritz, Charles E., and Eli S. Marks. 1954. "The NORC Studies of Human Behavior in Disaster." *Journal of Social Issues* 10:26–41.

Fumento, Michael. 1990. *The Myth of Heterosexual AIDS*. New York: Basic Books.

Gallop, George, Jr. 1992. *The Gallup Poll: Public Opinion 1991*. Wilmington, DE: Scholarly Resources Inc.

Gamson, Joshua. 1989. "Silence, Death, and the Invisible Enemy: AIDS Activism and Social Movement 'Newness.'" *Social Problems* 36:351–67.

Gamson, Joshua. 1991. "Silence, Death, and the Invisible Enemy: AIDS Activism and Social Movement 'Newness.'" Pp. 35–57 in *Ethnography Unbound: Power and Resistance in the Modern Metropolis*, edited by Michael Burawoy and others. Berkeley: University of California Press.

Gamson, William A., and Andre Modigliani. 1989. "Media Discourse and Public Opinion on Nuclear Power: A Constructionist Approach." *American Journal of Sociology* 95:1–37.

Gans, Herbert J. 1979. *Deciding What's News: A Study of the CBS Evening News, NBC Nightly News, Newsweek, and Time*. New York: Random House.

Gentry, Curt. 1968. *The Last Days of the Late, Great State of California*. New York: G. P. Putnam's Sons.

Gieryn, Thomas F. 1983. "Boundary-Work and the Demarcation of Science from Non-Science: Strains and Interests in Professional Ideologies of Scientists." *American Sociological Review* 48:781–95.

Goltz, James. 1984. "Are the News Media Responsible for the Disaster Myths?: A Content Analysis of Emergency Response Imagery." *International Journal of Mass Emergencies and Disasters* 2:345–68.

Gusfield, Joseph R. 1976. "The Literary Rhetoric of Science: Comedy and Pathos in Drinking Driving Research." *American Sociological Review* 41:16–34.

Gusfield, Joseph R. 1981. *The Culture of Public Problems: Drinking-Driving and the Symbolic Order*. Chicago: University of Chicago Press.

Gusfield, Joseph R. 1984. "On the Side: Practical Action and Social Constructivism in Social Problems Theory." Pp. 31–51 in *Studies in the Sociology of Social Problems*, edited by Joseph W. Schneider and John I. Kitsuse. Norwood, NJ: Ablex.

Haas, J. Eugene, and Dennis S. Mileti. 1976. *Social Effects of Earthquake Prediction.* Boulder: Institute of Behavioral Science, University of Colorado.

Haicheng Earthquake Study Delegation. 1977. "Prediction of the Haicheng Earthquake." *EOS* 58:236–72.

Heclo, Hugh. 1978. "Issue Networks and the Executive Establishment." Pp. 87–124 in *The New American Political System*, edited by Anthony King. Washington, DC: American Enterprise Institute.

Hewitt, Kenneth. 1983. *Interpretations of Calamity from the Viewpoint of Human Ecology.* Winchester, MA: Allen and Unwin.

Hilgartner, Stephen. 1992. "The Social Construction of Risk Objects: Or, How to Pry Open Networks of Risk." Pp. 39–53 in *Organizations, Uncertainties, and Risk*, edited by James F. Short, Jr., and Lee Clarke. Boulder, CO: Westview.

Hilgartner, Stephen, and Charles L. Bosk. 1988. "The Rise and Fall of Social Problems: A Public Arenas Model." *American Journal of Sociology* 94:53–78.

Hill, Stuart. 1992. *Democratic Values and Technological Choices.* Stanford, CA: Stanford University Press.

Hirshleifer, Jack. 1966. *Disaster and Recovery: The Black Death in Western Europe.* Santa Monica, CA: Rand Corporation.

Holstein, James A., and Gale Miller (eds.). 1993. *Reconsidering Social Constructionism: Debates in Social Problems Theory.* Hawthorne, NY: Aldine de Gruyter.

Hooks, Gregory. 1993. "The Weakness of String Theories: The U.S. State's Dominance of the World War II Investment Process." *American Sociological Review* 58:37–53.

Hubbell, Sue. 1991. "Earthquake Fever." *New Yorker* (February 11):75–84.

Iacopi, Robert. 1964. *Earthquake Country.* San Francisco: Lane Book Company.

Ibarra, Peter R., and John I. Kitsuse. 1993. "Vernacular Constituents of Moral Discourse: An Interactionist Proposal for the Study of Social Problems." Pp. 5–58 in *Reconsidering Social Constructionism: Debates in Social Problems Theory*, edited by James A. Holstein and Gale Miller. Hawthorne, NY: Aldine de Gruyter.

Joint Technical Committee on Earthquake Protection. 1933. *Earthquake Hazard and Earthquake Protection.* Los Angeles: Los Angeles Chamber of Commerce.

Kahneman, Daniel, Paul Slovic, and Amos Tversky. 1982. *Judgement under Uncertainty: Heuristics and Biases.* London: Cambridge University Press.

Kingdon, John W. 1984. *Agendas, Alternatives, and Public Policies.* Boston: Little, Brown.

Klapp, Orrin E. 1954. "Heroes, Villains and Fools as Agents of Social Control." *American Sociological Review* 19:54–62.

Kreps, Gary A. 1989. "Future Directions in Disaster Research: The Role of Taxonomy." *International Journal of Mass Emergencies and Disasters* 7:215–41.

Kuhn, Thomas. 1962. *The Structure of Scientific Revolutions.* Chicago: University of Chicago Press.

Kuhn, Thomas. 1970. *The Structure of Scientific Revolutions*, 2nd ed. Chicago: University of Chicago Press.

Kunreuther, Howard, and Elissandra S. Fiore. 1966. *The Alaska Earthquake: A Case Study in the Economics of Disaster.* Washington, DC: Institute for Defense Analysis.

Layton, Edwin T., Jr. 1986. *The Revolt of the Engineers: Social Responsibility and the American Engineering Profession*. Baltimore, MD: Johns Hopkins University Press.

Lindblom, Charles E., and Edward J. Woodhouse. 1993. *The Policy-Making Process*, 3rd ed. Englewood Cliffs, NJ: Prentice-Hall.

Logan, John R., and Harvey L. Molotch. 1987. *Urban Fortunes: The Political Economy of Place*. Berkeley: University of California Press.

Los Angeles County Earthquake Commission. 1971. *Report of the Los Angeles County Earthquake Commission: San Fernando Earthquake February 9, 1971*. Los Angeles: County of Los Angeles.

Luhmann, Niklas. 1982. *The Differentiation of Society*. New York: Columbia University Press.

Luhmann, Niklas. 1993. *Risk: A Sociological Theory*. Hawthorne, NY: Aldine de Gruyter.

Mader, George C., and Martha Blair Tyler. 1993. "Land Use and Planning." Pp. 93–105 in *Improving Earthquake Mitigation: Report to Congress*, edited by Office of Earthquakes and Natural Hazards. Washington, DC: Federal Emergency Management Agency.

March, James G., and Johan P. Olsen. 1976. *Ambiguity and Choice in Organization*. Bergen, Norway: Universitetsforlaget.

Marks, Eli S. 1954. *Human Reactions in Disaster Situations*. Chicago: National Opinion Research Center, University of Chicago.

Marske, Charles E. 1986. "A Community of Fate: The Political-Economics of Risk in College Athletic Travel." *Journal of Sport and Social Issues* 10:6–26.

Mauss, Armand L. 1975. *Social Problems as Social Movements*. Philadelphia: J. B. Lippincott.

Mauss, Armand L. 1989. "Beyond the Illusion of Social Problems Theory." *Perspectives on Social Problems* 1:19–39.

May, Peter J. 1985. *Recovering From Catastrophes: Federal Disaster Relief Policy and Politics*. Westport, CT: Greenwood.

May, Peter J. 1991a. "Addressing Public Risks: Federal Earthquake Policy Design." *Journal of Policy Analysis and Management* 10:263–85.

May, Peter J. 1991b. "Reconsidering Policy Design: Policies and Publics." *Journal of Public Policy* 11:187–206.

May, Peter J. 1992. "Policy Learning and Failure." *Journal of Public Policy* 12:331–54.

May, Peter J., and Thomas J. Birkland. 1993. "Earthquake Risk Reduction: An Examination of Local Regulatory Efforts." Paper presented at the Annual Meeting of the American Political Science Association. Washington, D.C., September.

May, Peter J., and Walter Williams. 1986. *Disaster Policy Implementation: Managing Programs under Shared Governance*. New York: Plenum.

McAdam, Doug, John D. McCarthy, and Mayer N. Zald. 1988. "Social Movements." Pp. 695–737 in *The Handbook of Sociology*, edited by Neil J. Smelser. Newbury Park, CA: Sage.

McCarthy, Charles. 1912. *The Wisconsin Idea*. New York: Macmillan.

McCarthy, John D., and Mayer N. Zald. 1973. *The Trend of Social Movements in*

America: Professionalization and Resource Mobilization. Morristown, NJ: General Learning Press.

Mead, George Herbert. [1934] 1962. *Mind, Self, and Society: From the Standpoint of a Social Behaviorist*. Chicago: University of Chicago Press.

Meltsner, Arnold J. 1978. "Public Support for Seismic Safety: Where Is It in California?" *Mass Emergencies* 3:167–84.

Merton, Robert K., and Robert A. Nisbet (eds.). 1961. *Contemporary Social Problems: An Introduction to the Sociology of Deviant Behavior and Social Disorganization*. New York: Harcourt, Brace, and World.

Merton, Robert K., and Robert A. Nisbet. 1966. *Contemporary Social Problems*, 2nd ed. New York, Harcourt, Brace and World.

Merton, Robert K., and Robert A. Nisbet. 1971. *Contemporary Social Problems*, 3rd ed. New York, Harcourt, Brace and World.

Merton, Robert K., and Robert A. Nisbet. 1976. *Contemporary Social Problems*, 4th ed. New York, Harcourt, Brace and World.

Meyer, Josh. 1993. "Viewing Autopsies Draws Fire." *Los Angeles Times*, January 24.

Mileti, Dennis S. 1976. *Natural Hazard Warning Systems in the United States: A Research Assessment*. Boulder: Institute of Behavioral Science, University of Colorado.

Mileti, Dennis S., Thomas E. Drabek, and J. Eugene Haas. 1975. *Human Systems in Extreme Environments: A Sociological Perspective*. Boulder: Institute of Behavioral Science, University of Colorado.

Mileti, Dennis S., and Colleen Fitzpatrick. 1993. *The Great Earthquake Experiment: Risk Communication and Public Action*. Boulder, CO: Westview.

Mill, John Stuart. [1843] 1919. *System of Logic*, Book III. London: Longmans, Green, and Company.

Miller, Alan C. 1994. "U.S. Officials Dissect Quake Response." *Los Angeles Times*, April 26.

Mills, C. Wright. 1961. *The Sociological Imagination*. New York: Grove.

Minturn, Henry C. 1976. "Proposal for the Refinement of a Working Technique That Has Successfully Forecast Multi-Global Earthquakes." Unpublished manuscript, Hawthorne, CA.

Mittler, Elliott. 1989. *Natural Hazard Policy Setting: Identifying Supporters and Opponents of Nonstructural Hazard Mitigation*. Boulder: Institute of Behavioral Science, University of Colorado.

Mittler, Elliott. 1991. "State Earthquake Insurance." Pp. 153–80 in *California Policy Choices*, Volume 7, edited by John J. Kirlin and Donald R. Winkler. Sacramento: Sacramento Public Affairs Center, School of Public Administration, University of Southern California.

Mittler, Elliott. 1992. *A Fiscal Responsibility Analysis of a National Earthquake Insurance Program*. Boston: The Earthquake Project of the National Committee on Property Insurance.

Mittler, Elliott. 1993. *The Public Policy Response to Hurricane Hugo in South Carolina*. Working paper #84, Institute of Behavioral Science, University of Colorado, Boulder.

Molotch, Harvey, and Marilyn Lester. 1974. "News as Purposive Behavior: On the Strategic Use of Routine Events, Accidents, and Scandals." *American Sociological Review* 39:101–12.

Moore, Wilbert Estill. 1958. *Tornadoes over Texas: A Study of Waco and San Angelo in Disaster*. Austin: University of Texas Press.

Mulligan, Thomas S. 1992. "Millions Due Quake Fund Rebates." *Los Angeles Times*, November 21.

Mulligan, Thomas S. 1993. "Risky Business: Riots, Earthquakes, Hurricanes and Floods Have Weakened the Insurance Industry and Narrowed Policyholders' Options." *Los Angeles Times*, February 21.

Nader, Ralph. [1965] 1972. *Unsafe at Any Speed: The Designed-In Dangers of the American Automobile*. New York: Grossman.

Nakamura, Robert T., and Frank Smallwood. 1980. *The Politics of Policy Implementation*. New York: St. Martin's.

National Earthquake Hazard Reduction Program. 1992. *Building for the Future*. Washington, DC: Federal Emergency Management Agency.

Nazario, Sonia. 1994. "Two Neighborhoods, Two Destinies." *Los Angeles Times*, May 2.

Nichols, Lawrence T. 1990. "Discovering Hutton: Expression Gaming and Congressional Definitions of Deviance." *Studies in Symbolic Interaction* 11:309–37.

Nichols, Lawrence T. 1991. " 'Whistleblower' or 'Renegade': Definitional Contests in an Official Inquiry." *Symbolic Interaction* 14:395–414.

Nigg, Joanne M. and Kathleen J. Tierney. 1990. "Explaining Differential Outcomes in the Small Business Disaster Loan Application Process." Paper presented at the 12th World Congress of Sociology, July 9–13. Madrid.

Nixon, Richard M. 1974. "Annual Message to the Congress on the State of the Union, January 20, 1972." Pp. 41–74 in *Public Papers of the President of the United States: Richard Nixon*. Washington, DC: U.S. Government Printing Office.

Norton, Frank R. B., and J. Eugene Haas. 1970. "The Native Villages." Pp. 357–401 in *The Great Alaska Earthquake of 1964: Human Ecology*, edited by Committee on the Alaska Earthquake. Washington, DC: Division of Earth Sciences, National Research Council—National Academy of Sciences.

Office of Earthquakes and Natural Hazards. 1993. *Improving Earthquake Mitigation: Report to Congress*. Washington, DC: Federal Emergency Management Agency.

Office of Emergency Preparedness. 1972. *Report to Congress: Disaster Preparedness*. Washington, DC: U.S. Government Printing Office.

Olson, Richard Stuart. 1985. "The Political Economy of Life-Safety: The City of Los Angeles and Hazardous-Structure Abatement." *Policy Studies Review* May:670–79.

Olson, Richard Stuart, and Robert A. Olson. 1993. " 'The Rubble's Standing Up' in Oroville: The Politics of Building Safety." *International Journal of Mass Emergencies and Disasters* 11:163–88.

Olson, Richard Stuart, Bruno Podesta, and Joanne Nigg. 1989. *The Politics of Earthquake Prediction*. Princeton, NJ: Princeton University Press.

Palm, Risa I., Michael E. Hodgson, R. Denise Blanchard, and Donald I. Lyons.

1990. *Earthquake Insurance in California: Environmental Policy and Individual Decision Making*. Boulder, CO: Westview Press.

Panel on Earthquake Prediction. 1976. *Predicting Earthquakes: A Scientific and Technical Evaluation—With Implications for Society*. Washington, DC: National Academy of Sciences.

Panel on the Public Policy Implications of Earthquake Prediction. 1975. *Earthquake Prediction and Public Policy*. Washington, DC: National Academy of Sciences.

Pearson, R. G., and M. G. Joost. 1983. *Egress Behavior Response of Handicapped and Elderly Subjects to Simulated Residential Fire Situations*. Washington, DC: Department of Health and Human Services and Center for Fire Research, National Bureau of Standards.

Pereira, Joseph. 1989. "When East's Quake Comes, Will Boston Be Back in the Bay?" *Wall Street Journal*, July 11.

Perry, Ronald W. 1982. *The Social Psychology of Civil Defense*. Lexington, MA: Lexington Books.

Perry, Ronald W., Marjorie Greene, and Alvin Mushkatel. 1983. *American Minority Citizens in Disaster*. Seattle: Battelle Human Affairs Research Centers.

Perry, Ronald W., Michael K. Lindell, and Majorie R. Greene. 1980. *Evacuation Decision Making and Emergency Planning*. Seattle: Battelle Human Affairs Research Centers.

Petak, William J. (ed.). 1985. "Emergency Management: A Challenge for Public Administration." *Public Administration Review* 45 (special issue).

Quadagno, Jill. 1984. "Welfare Capitalism and the Social Security Act of 1935." *American Sociological Review* 49:632–47.

Quarantelli, E. L. 1975. *The Role of Local Civil Defense in Disaster Planning*. Newark, DE: Disaster Research Center.

Quarantelli, E. L. 1989. "Conceptualizing Disasters From a Sociological Perspective." *International Journal of Mass Emergencies and Disasters* 7:243–51.

Quarantelli, E. L., and Russell R. Dynes. 1972. "When Disaster Strikes: (It Isn't Much Like What You've Heard and Read About)." *Psychology Today* 5:66–71.

Reich, Kenneth. 1992. "Quake Theories Get Rattled by Scientists." *Los Angeles Times*, June 28.

Reich, Kenneth. 1993. "4.5 Million to Receive Refunds on State Quake Insurance." *Los Angeles Times*, May 12.

Reinarman, Craig. 1988. "The Social Construction of an Alcohol Problem: The Case of Mothers Against Drunk Drivers and Social Control in the 1980s." *Theory and Society* 17:91–120.

Richter, Charles F. 1964. *Our Earthquake Risk—Facts and Non-Facts*. Sacramento: California Disaster Office.

Risen, James. 1993. "Damage to Crops May Cost Farmers $1 Billion, Espy Says." *Los Angeles Times*, July 12.

Rogers, Everett M. 1988. *1988 Symposium on Science Communication: Environmental and Health Research*. Annenberg School of Communications, University of Southern California.

Rosa, Eugene A. 1993. "Mirrors and Lenses: Toward Theoretical Method in the Study of the Nature-Culture Dialectic." Paper presented at Conference International, "Les Fonctions Socialies de le Nature," Chantilly, France, March.

Ross, Robert, and Graham L. Staines. 1972. "The Politics of Analyzing Social Problems." *Social Problems* 20:18–40.

Rossi, Peter H., James D. Wright, and Eleanor Weber-Burdin. 1982. *Natural Hazards and Public Choice: The State and Local Politics of Hazard Mitigation.* New York: Academic.

Rubin, Claire B., and Roy Popkin. 1991. *Disaster Recovery After Hurricane Hugo in South Carolina.* Working paper #84, Institute of Behavioral Science, University of Colorado, Boulder.

Salholz, Eloise. 1989. "Recovery by the Bay: Counting the Blessings, Tallying the Losses." *Newsweek,* November 6.

Sandman, Peter M., David B. Sachsman, Michael R. Greenberg, and Michael Gochfeld. 1987. *Environmental Risk and the Press.* New Brunswick, NJ: Transaction.

Scanlon, Joseph, Suzanne Alldred, Al Farrell, and Angela Prawzick. 1985. "Coping with the Media in Disasters: Some Predictable Problems." *Public Administration Review* 45:123–33.

SCEPP. No date. "The Southern California Earthquake Preparedness Project." Los Angeles: The Southern California Earthquake Preparedness Project.

Schneider, Anne, and Helen Ingram. 1993. "Social Construction of Target Populations: Implications for Politics and Policy." *American Political Science Review* 87:334–47.

Schneider, Joseph W. 1985. "Social Problems Theory: The Constructionist View." *Annual Review of Sociology* 11:209–29.

Science and Technology Program. 1991. *Managing the Economic Consequences of Catastrophic Earthquakes.* Washington, DC: Center for Strategic and International Studies.

Scott, Wilbur J. 1993. *The Politics of Readjustment: Vietnam Veterans Since the War.* Hawthorne, NY: Aldine de Gruyter.

Shipman, Marlin, Gil Fowler, and Russ Shain. 1993. "Whose Fault Was It?: An Analysis of Newspaper Coverage of Iben Browning's New Madrid Fault Earthquake Prediction." *International Journal of Mass Emergencies and Disasters* 11:379–89.

Short, James F., Jr. 1989. "On Defining, Describing and Explaining Elephants (and Reactions to Them): Hazards, Disasters, and Risk Analysis." *International Journal of Mass Emergencies and Disasters* 7:397–418.

Shover, Neal, Donald A. Clelland, and John Lynxwiler. 1986. *Enforcement or Negotiation: Constructing a Regulatory Bureaucracy.* Albany: State University of New York Press.

Skocpol, Theda. 1979. *States and Social Revolutions: A Comparative Analysis of France, Russia, and China.* New York: Cambridge University Press.

Spector, Malcolm, and John I. Kitsuse. 1973. "Social Problems: A Re-formulation." *Social Problems* 21:145–59.

Spector, Malcolm, and John I. Kitsuse. [1977] 1987. *Constructing Social Problems.* Hawthorne, NY: Aldine de Gruyter.

Stallings, Robert A. 1977. "Collective Behavior and the Prediction of an Earthquake: Preliminary Considerations." Paper presented at the Annual Meeting of the Pacific Sociological Association, Sacramento, California, April.

Stallings, Robert A. 1986. "Reaching the Ethnic Minorities: Earthquake Public Education in the Aftermath of Foreign Disasters." *Earthquake Spectra* 2:695–702.

Stallings, Robert A. 1988. "Conflict in Natural Disasters: A Codification of Consensus and Conflict Theories." *Social Science Quarterly* 69:569–86.

Stallings, Robert A. 1989. "Newspaper Coverage of Dramatic Events and the Reconstruction of Risk: A Collective Behavior Approach." Paper presented at the Annual Meetings of the American Sociological Association, San Francisco, August.

Stallings, Robert A. 1990a. "Media Discourse and the Social Construction of Risk." *Social Problems* 37:501–16.

Stallings, Robert A. 1990b. "Media Discourse and the Reconstruction of Risk: U. S. Newspaper Coverage of Major Airline Disasters." Paper presented at the Twelfth World Congress of Sociology, Madrid, July.

Stallings, Robert A., and William Freeling. 1977. "Corrections Policies for Natural Disasters." Paper presented at the Annual Meetings of the American Sociological Association, Chicago, August.

Stallings, Robert A., and E. L. Quarantelli. 1985. "Emergent Citizen Groups and Emergency Management." *Public Administration Review* 45:93–100.

State [of California] Earthquake Investigation Commission. 1908–1910. *The California Earthquake of April 18, 1906*, 2 volumes. Washington, DC: Carnegie Institution of Washington.

Steinbrugge, Karl V. 1968. *Earthquake Hazard in the San Francisco Bay Area: A Continuing Problem in Public Policy*. Berkeley: Institute of Governmental Studies, University of California.

Steinbrugge, Karl V., Eugene E. Schader, Harry C. Bigglestone, and Carl A. Weers. 1971. *San Fernando Earthquake February 9, 1971*. San Francisco: Pacific Fire Rating Bureau.

Stewart, John. 1990. *Drifting Continents and Colliding Paradigms: Perspectives on the Geoscience Revolution*. Bloomington: Indiana University Press.

Stone, Deborah A. 1988. *Policy Paradox and Political Reason*. Glenview, Ill.: Scott, Foresman.

Stone, Deborah A. 1989. "Causal Stories and the Formation of Policy Agendas." *Political Science Quarterly* 104:281–300.

Stouffer, Samuel A., et al. 1949, 1950. *The American Soldier: Studies in Social Psychology in World War II*, Volumes I–IV. Princeton, NJ: Princeton University Press.

Swidler, Ann. 1986. "Culture in Action: Symbols and Strategies." *American Sociological Review* 51:273–86.

Taylor, Verta A. 1977. "Good News About Disaster." *Psychology Today* (October): 93, 94, 124, 126.

Taylor, Verta A., with G. Alexander Ross and E. L. Quarantelli. 1976. *Delivery of Mental Health Services in Disasters: The Xenia Tornado and Some Implications*. Columbus: Disaster Research Center, The Ohio State University.

The Earthquake Project. 1989. *Catastrophic Earthquakes: The Need to Insure against Economic Disaster*. Boston: National Committee on Property Insurance.

Thomas, Gordon, and Max Morgan Witts. 1971. *The San Francisco Earthquake.* New York: Stein and Day.

Tierney, Kathleen J. 1985. *Report on the Coalinga Earthquake of May 2, 1983.* Sacramento: Seismic Safety Commission, State of California.

Tierney, Kathleen J., William J. Petak, and Harlan Hahn. 1988. *Disabled Persons and Earthquake Hazards.* Boulder: Institute of Behavioral Science, University of Colorado.

Toulmin, Stephen Edelston. 1958. *The Uses of Argument.* Cambridge: Cambridge University Press.

Troyer, Ronald J., and Gerald E. Markle. 1983. *Cigarettes: The Battle over Smoking.* New Brunswick, NJ: Rutgers University Press.

Troyer, Ronald J., and Gerald E. Markle. 1984. "Coffee Drinking: An Emerging Social Problem?" *Social Problems* 31:403–16.

Tuchman, Gaye. 1978. *Making News: A Study in the Construction of Reality.* New York: Free Press.

Turner, Ralph H. 1978. "Earthquake Prediction Volunteers: What Can the United States Learn from China?" *Mass Emergencies* 3:143–160.

Turner, Ralph H. 1993. "Reflections on the Past and Future of Social Research on Earthquake Warnings." *International Journal of Mass Emergencies and Disasters* 11:453–68.

Turner, Ralph H., Joanne M. Nigg, and Denise Heller Paz. 1986. *Waiting for Disaster: Earthquake Watch in California.* Berkeley: University of California Press.

U.S. Department of Justice. 1991. *Sourcebook of Criminal Justice Statistics—1990.* Washington, DC: U.S. Government Printing Office.

U.S. House of Representatives. 1971a. *Earthquake Disaster at the Veterans' Administration Hospital, San Fernando, CA, on February 9, 1971.* Hearings before a Special Subcommittee, Committee on Veterans' Affairs. 92nd Cong., 1st sess. 18 February.

U.S. House of Representatives. 1971b. *California Earthquake Disaster.* Hearing held before a Special Subcommittee on Economic Development Programs, Committee on Public Works and Transportation. 92nd Cong., 1st sess. 24 February.

U.S. House of Representatives. 1976. *Earthquake.* Hearings held by the Subcommittee on Science, Research, and Technology, Committee on Science, Space, and Technology. 94th Cong., 2nd sess. 22–24 June.

U.S. House of Representatives. 1977. *Earthquake Hazards Reduction.* Hearings held by the Subcommittee on Science, Research, and Technology, Committee on Science, Space, and Technology. 95th Cong., 1st sess. 20 April.

U.S. House of Representatives. 1983. *Emergency Preparedness and the Licensing Process for Commercial Nuclear Reactors.* Part II. Hearings held by the Subcommittee on Oversight and Investigations, Committee on Interior and Insular Affairs. 98th Cong., 1st sess. 18 April.

U.S. House of Representatives. 1986a. *Mexico Earthquake: Scientific and Engineering Implications.* Hearings held by the Subcommittee on Science, Research, and Technology, Committee on Science, Space, and Technology. 99th Cong., 1st sess. 5 November.

U.S. House of Representatives. 1986b. *Perry Nuclear Powerplant*. Hearings held by the Subcommittee on Energy and the Environment, Committee on Interior and Insular Affairs. 99th Cong., 2nd sess. 8 April.

U.S. House of Representatives. 1987. *Earthquake Reauthorization for Fiscal Year 1988*. Hearings held by the Subcommittee on Science, Research, and Technology, Committee on Science, Space, and Technology. 100th Cong., 1st sess. 10 March.

U.S. House of Representatives. 1988a. *Whittier Narrows, California, Earthquake: Lessons Learned*. Hearings held by the Subcommittee on Science, Research, and Technology, Committee on Science, Space, and Technology. 100th Cong., 1st sess. 10 November 1987.

U.S. House of Representatives. 1988b. *Relationship Between Offshore Oil Drilling and the Proposed Pacific Palisades Onshore Drilling Project*. Hearings held by the Subcommittee on General Oversight and Investigations, Committee on Interior and Insular Affairs. 100th Cong., 2nd sess. 24 October.

U.S. House of Representatives. 1989. *Soviet Armenian Earthquake Disaster: Could a Similar Disaster Happen in the U.S?* Hearings held by the Subcommittee on Science, Research, and Technology, Committee on Science, Space, and Technology. 101st Cong., 1st sess. 15 March 1989.

U.S. House of Representatives. 1990. *Housing Needs in Earthquake Disaster Areas*. Hearings held by the Subcommittee on Housing and Community Development Ad Hoc Panel on Housing Assistance in Earthquake Disaster Areas, Committee on Banking, Finance, and Urban Affairs. 101st Cong., 2nd sess. 11–12 April 1990.

U.S. House of Representatives. 1991. *Earthquake Hazard Mitigation and Earthquake Insurance*. Hearings held by the Subcommittee on Policy Research and Insurance, Committee on Banking, Finance, and Urban Affairs. 101st Cong., 2nd sess. 11–12 September 1990.

U.S. National Committee for the Decade for Natural Disaster Reduction. 1991. *A Safer Future: Reducing the Impacts of Natural Disasters*. Washington, DC: National Research Council.

U.S. Senate. 1964a. *Alaska Earthquake Insurance*. Hearings held by the Committee on Interior and Insular Affairs. 88th Cong., 2nd sess., 14–15 April, 5 May.

U.S. Senate. 1964b. *Alaska Reconstruction*. Hearings held by the Committee on Interior and Insular Affairs. 88th Cong., 2nd sess., 3 June.

U.S. Senate. 1964c. *Disaster Road Program*. Hearings held by the Subcommittee on Public Roads, Committee on Public Works. 88th Cong., 2nd sess., 8 July.

U.S. Senate. 1970. *Santa Barbara Oil Pollution*. Hearings held by the Committee on Interior and Insular Affairs. 91st Cong., 2nd sess. 13–14 March.

U.S. Senate. 1971. *Government Response to the California Earthquake Disaster of February 1971*. Hearings held by the Committee on Public Works. 92nd Cong., 1st sess. 10–12 June.

U.S. Senate. 1973–1974. *To Investigate the Adequacy and Effectiveness of Federal Disaster Relief Legislation*. Parts 1–6. Hearings held by the Subcommittee on Disaster Relief, Committee on Public Works. 93rd Cong, 1st and 2nd sess. 4 March, 30–31 March, 11–12 May, 1–2 June, 11–13 Sept 1973; 6 March 1974.

U.S. Senate. 1977. *Earthquake Hazards Reduction Act*. Hearings held by the Subcommittee on Science, Technology, and Space, Committee on Commerce, Science, and Transportation. 95th Cong., 1st sess. 19 April.

U.S. Senate. 1986. *Earthquake in Mexico.* Hearings held by the Subcommittee on Science, Technology, and Space, Committee on Commerce, Science, and Transportation. 99th Cong., 1st sess. 3 October 1985.

U.S. Senate. 1990. *To Consider Current Federal Disaster Relief Efforts.* Hearings held by the Subcommittee on Water Resources, Transportation, and Infrastructure, Committee on the Environment and Public Works. 101st Cong., 1st sess. 23 October 1989.

U.S. Strategic Bombing Survey. 1947a. *The Effects of Strategic Bombing on German Morale,* Volumes I and II. Washington, DC: U.S. Government Printing Office.

U.S. Strategic Bombing Survey. 1947b. *The Effects of Strategic Bombing on Japanese Morale.* Washington, DC: U.S. Government Printing Office.

Useem, Michael. 1984. *The Inner Circle: Large Corporations and the Rise of Business Political Activity in the U.S. and U.K.* New York: Oxford University Press.

Walters, Lynne Masel, Lee Wilkins, and Tim Walters (eds). 1989. *Bad Tidings: Communication and Catastrophe.* Hillsdale, NJ: Lawrence Erlbaum Associates.

Warren, Jenifer. 1992. "Southlanders See a Link Between A-Tests, Quakes." *Los Angeles Times,* July 2.

Weber, Max. 1978. *Economy and Society,* Volume 2, edited by Guenther Roth and Claus Wittich. Berkeley: University of California Press.

Wegener, Alfred. 1924. *The Origin of Continents and Oceans.* London: Methuen.

Weinstein, Steve. 1992. "Shaking up Stereotypes: Caltech 'Earthquake Ladies' Give Science a Human Face." *Los Angeles Times,* July 4.

Wenger, Dennis E., James D. Dykes, Thomas D. Sebok, and Joan Neff. 1975. "It's a Matter of Myths: An Empirical Examination of Individual Insight into Disaster Response." *Mass Emergencies* 1:33–46.

White, Gilbert F., and J. Eugene Haas. 1975. *Assessment of Research on Natural Hazards.* Cambridge, MA: MIT Press.

Wilkins, Lee. 1987. *Shared Vulnerability: The Media and American Perceptions of the Bhopal Disaster.* Westport, CT: Greenwood.

Witt, James L. 1993. "Foundations for the Future." *Natural Hazards Observer* 17:1–3.

Wolensky, Robert P. 1983. "Power Structure and Group Mobilization Following Disaster: A Case Study." *Social Science Quarterly* 64:96–110.

Woolgar, Steve, and Dorothy Pawluch. 1985. "Ontological Gerrymandering: The Anatomy of Social Problems Explanations." *Social Problems* 32:214–27.

Working Group on California Earthquake Probabilities. 1990. *Probabilities of Large Earthquakes in the San Francisco Bay Region, California.* Washington, DC: United States Geological Survey Circular 1053.

Wright, James D., and Peter H. Rossi. 1981. "The Politics of Natural Disaster: State and Local Elites." Pp. 45–67 in *Social Science and Natural Hazards,* edited by James D. Wright and Peter H. Rossi. Cambridge, MA: Abt.

Zald, Mayer N., and John D. McCarthy. 1977. "Resource Mobilization and Social Movements: A Partial Theory." *American Journal of Sociology* 82:1212–41.

Index